Frayed
The Disputes Unraveling Religious Zionists

Toby

Yair Ettinger

FRAYED

THE DISPUTES UNRAVELING RELIGIOUS ZIONISTS

TRANSLATED FROM THE HEBREW BY
Eylon Levy
and
Mitch Ginsburg

FOREWORD BY
Yehuda Mirsky

The Toby Press

Frayed
The Disputes Unraveling Religious Zionists

First English Edition, 2023

The Toby Press LLC
POB 8531, New Milford, CT 06776–8531, USA
& POB 4044, Jerusalem 9104001, Israel
www.tobypress.com

ISBN 978-1-59264-584-8, *hardcover*

Printed and bound in the United States

For Sivan

Contents

Foreword

God is eternal. The vast debating society that is the Jewish people endures. The voice from Sinai never ceases to call. The bundle of contradictions that is human nature abides. And history is moving and changing all the time. God, Torah, Israel – all draw their commanding power precisely from their challenge to the relentless flux of experience and time, their challenging us to pause in the mad flux, fix our sights and our actions on what truly matters and endures, while never trying to escape the necessities and obligations of life in this world and our immersion in the river of time.

The broad categories we use – like religion, nationalism, secularism – and the narrower ones familiar to this volume's readers – Modern Orthodox, Religious Zionist, Mizrahi, on the *derekh*, off the *derekh*, yeshivish, hasidic – are all attempts to capture lives in midflight, attempts as necessary as they are partial and ultimately doomed, the closer we get to how we actually live our lives.

But we have to start somewhere, and so gamely we move with our categories in hand, making the best sense of things we can as we go.

That's all right, so long as we periodically check reality to see how our familiar categories are holding up.

All of which is meant to say that thoughtful readers interested in the current fortunes of traditional Judaism in Israel, the United States, or anywhere else are deeply in debt to Yair Ettinger.

The slim volume you have before you is, as Ḥazal put it, "one of the places where a little held a great deal" (Leviticus Rabba 10:9), in particular, a procession of passionate, committed Israeli Jews who fracture our familiar categories: religious women who insist on serving in the IDF whether their rabbis like it or not, yet insist on halakhic scrupulousness; religious Jews who visit the Temple Mount in defiance of rabbinic authority; learned women who as *yoatzot halakha* lengthen the reach of rabbinic authority, and as advocates in rabbinic courts challenge it; egalitarian prayer groups that insist on *meḥitzot*; the first *kippa*-wearing prime minister, reviled by much of the Religious Zionist camp that once looked to him as a savior; and much, much more.

In all likelihood, some, perhaps even most all, of these stories and people will be familiar to readers drawn to this volume. Ettinger's achievement here is to bring them all together, with a journalist's ear for candor and cant, an historian's eye for context, and a believer's mindful recognition of genuine passion. He manages to enter sympathetically into the worlds of his protagonists without ever surrendering his own inquiring mind and common sense.

Ettinger discerns a crucial thread running through all these stories – and it pointedly isn't the familiar dichotomy of liberal/conservative, or the slightly less tired moderate/radical. What he sees is "The Privatization of Religious Zionism," challenges to monopolies (like the Chief Rabbinate) and leading institutions (the yeshivot that broke away from Mercaz HaRav); rabbinic authority having a vote but not a veto; do-it-yourself *minyanim*; nonprofit *kashrut* services appealing to non-Orthodox Israelis; and perhaps above all, a Religious Zionist community many of whose members, after the Gaza disengagement of 2005 and its tortured aftermath, no longer see themselves as the secular state's faithful supporters but as its new successors.

Indeed, one unmistakable feature of Ettinger's subjects, alongside their commitment to Israel and Torah, is deep self-confidence, or more accurately – and even when taking on new commitments and obligations – inner freedom.

It is that sense of freedom that enables people to take stands at variance from rabbinic authority and religious convention out of the conviction that doing so lives out a truer commitment that strengthens rather than endangers Torah and the people.

And it is here that one finds an especially valuable point of comparison between these figures and their counterparts abroad, especially in the United States. In an important study, Shlomo Fischer deftly illuminated the crucial differences between Israeli Religious Zionism, and Anglo Modern Orthodoxy.[1] His key insight is that "Israeli Religious Zionism is a Romantic Nationalist culture with a strong expressivist dimension; that is, a strong emphasis on self-expression and notions such as authenticity. American Centrist Orthodoxy continues the traditional Jewish pattern of emphasis on religious heteronomy; that is, the Torah and God's commandments are imposed externally on the Jew."[2]

A little unpacking will be helpful here. Zionism, like other modern Jewish movements and all kinds of nationalism, arose in response to massive crises of Jewry in the eighteenth and nineteenth-century community that shook community and authority to their foundations. With the collapse of the premodern *kehilla*, which enjoyed genuine even if not sweeping autonomy and authority and buttressed the doctrinal basis of Jewish life, Jews sought new kinds of communal structures (e.g., hasidic courts, Lithuanian yeshivot) from without, and new sources of commitment and meaning (e.g., *devekut*, existential commitment) from within. The broader currents of Romanticism, of which nationalism and Hasidism were each a part, met the seeming eclipse of God in heaven by finding God anew from deep inside, from the deepest echoes of national

---

1. Shlomo Fischer, "Two Orthodox Cultures: 'Centrist' Orthodoxy and Religious Zionism," in Elieizer Ben-Refael, Judit Bokser Liwerant, and Yosef Gorny, eds., *Reconsidering Israel-Diaspora Relations* (Leiden/Boston: Brill, 2014), 146–68.
2. Ibid, 146.

belonging, ethical life, and questing spirit – and bringing those echoes to expression.[3]

Zionism, like other nationalisms, encouraged Jews to actualize their own deepest impulses and creative energies, impulses and energies which to Religious Zionists, especially Rabbi Kook and his followers, were themselves features of God's revelation in the world and the royal road to the true freedom that the Rabbis said was the reward and goal of Torah (Mishna Avot 6:2).

Of course, it was not nearly as simple as that. For decades, Religious Zionism long contented itself with being the junior partner of secular Zionism, Labor Zionism in particular. Starting in 1967 and with mounting force after the earthquake of the Yom Kippur War in 1973 and ever since, Religious Zionism increasingly took hold of its sense of self as the true inheritor of the Zionist revolution. At the same time, the large, hegemonic stories and structures of the state establishment have given way to new ethnic, religious, and national groupings; the centralized state economy has moved largely to private hands (even if not to the same extent as in the United States); and this steady splintering of centralized authority has left its mark on Religious Zionism. Thus, neo-Hasidism seeks authenticity, the decisions of leading rabbis are for Nationalist Zionists not rulings but suggestions, and feminists are not afraid to challenge the rabbinic courts and to bear the wounds they suffer for it.

In America the situation has been different: a liberal, individualist society rather than a nationalist one, there the institutions which Jewish traditionalists have needed to define themselves in relation to are not Jewish secularism and the army, but non-Orthodox denominations, religion-state separation, and the university. This has yielded

---

3. Fischer's understandings, as well as this author's, are deeply indebted to the magisterial work of Charles Taylor, especially his *Sources of the Self: The Making of Modern Identity* (Cambridge: Harvard University Press, 1989). Fischer discusses this at length in his forthcoming, long-awaited volume on Religious Zionism, and this author has put forward his understandings in the introductory chapter to his work *Towards the Mystical Experience of Modernity: The Making of Rav Kook, 1865–1904* (Boston: Academic Studies Press, 2021).

a traditionalism in some ways more cosmopolitan and in others more hesitant and defensive, for better or for worse.

At the same time, American Jewry plays a subtle role in this volume too – any number of developments, especially as regards feminism and gender, charted in these pages, from Torah study to partnership *minyanim*, began in the United States, came to Israel with Anglo-Saxon *olim*, struck deeper roots there, and in turn have come to influence Jewish life in the United States.[4] This is an insufficiently noticed feature of us-Israel relations very worthy of further exploration.

Another dimension, implicit in, if not developed at length in, this volume, is the respective roles of Ashkenazic and Sephardic identities and traditions. The erasure of Sephardic identity in the early years of the state and its amalgamation into an undifferentiated, and regularly marginalized, Mizrahi identity, and its striking return, transformed into Ashkenazi-style ultra-Orthodoxy by the Shas Party, is a well-known tale. In a recent, penetrating study, Nissim Leon has observed that the Ashkenazic character of Religious Zionism is its own kind of erasure, its lumping together of religious traditions as varied as those of Germany, Lithuania, Galicia, and Italy into one homogeneous mass its own version of the then-ruling Zionist hegemonies.[5]

In other words, Mizrahim were not the only ones whose traditions were being erased in the nationalization of ethnic cultural traditions, even as they stayed religiously observant. In this light, Leon argues, the various fissurings of Religious Zionism, the neo-hasidic renewal, among Ashkenazim and Mizrahim both, is also a turning toward, or grasping for, a living ethnic heritage long since emptied by Zionist hegemony.

---

4. In addition to all that is gathered in this volume, see, for instance, Ellie Ash, "Observant Feminism: The Transnational Origins of Partnership Minyanim," *Modern Judaism* 42:2 (2022), 157–82; and Tamar Biala, ed. *Dirshuni: Contemporary Women's Midrash* (Waltham: Brandeis University Press, 2022).

5. Nissim Leon, "HaTzabar VeHaTzimmes: Leumiyut Mahapkhanit uMasoret Adatit BaTzioniyut HaDatit," in Yair Sheleg, ed., *Mi-Mashgiaḥ HaKashrut LeNahag HaKatar? Ha-Tzionut HaDatit VeHaḤevra HaYisraelit* (Jerusalem: Israel Democracy Institute, 2019), 191–212.

Indeed, while nationalism has proved itself time and again to be one of recent history's most powerful forces on the planet, the price exacted by its victories have been steep. Those prices have come in human lives, and in morals too.

One large subject whose absence sensitive readers will note in this chronicle of arguments is, ironically, the overwhelming focus of world attention on Israel, the painful and still unresolved conflict with the Arab world and in particular with the Arabs of Palestine. This was, to be sure, the subject of strong internal Religious Zionist debate in the past. But, as Ettinger notes in his introduction, the second intifada of 2000 and the Gaza disengagement of 2005 effectively removed the prospect of meaningful peace negotiations and the hard decisions those might entail as a live possibility, at least until a new and moderate generation of Palestinian leadership steps forward. (For that matter, the political dovishness of Israel's *haredi* parties is by now a thing of the past.) In particular, the Gaza disengagement and its aftermath effectively alienated and radicalized many younger Religious Zionists, leading them to conclude that rather than working within Israel's state and society they now had to wrest them from a compromised, globalized, flaccid elite. For them, the familiar image of the dash connecting Dati-Leumi as a bridge was to be replaced with a battering ram. While not all of the cultural struggles recorded in these pages were born out of Gaza, that newly combative stand is very much a part of them.

Yet more subtly, the peace process's sustained eclipse has in its very absence helped shape the contours and debates of Religious Zionism today. To begin with, one possible line of debate and demarcation has been largely removed. The deliberately porous borders of Religious Zionism have formed along questions of gender, halakhic norms, cultural openness, and rabbinic authority. In the absence of a meaningful political left to join, many have de facto stayed inside the camp. More deeply, the Palestinian leadership's rejectionism and inflexibility have largely mooted debates and discussions that raged as recently as the 1990s as to how Torah ethics can best comport with Jews' minority status and military strength. Finally, and disturbingly, among not a few Religious Zionist circles, including some very essential ones, the fusion of Torah and Zionism, of God's word and one national-political movement, has become so complete as to be in the minds of many one and the same thing, modernity's distinctive contribution to the Devil's dictionary of idolatry.

In terms of self-understanding, can one really say that the range of issues the people in this volume are actively, creatively exploring – be it women and men's changing self-understandings, new horizons of Torah study, longings for the Temple, activism on behalf of *agunot* – is remotely captured by the term "Religious Zionism"?[6] And to what extent does one's self understanding as a "Religious Zionist" subtly but ineluctably encourage an identification of nationalist ideology with religious truth, an identification driving its adherents perilously close to the idolatries of national chauvinism and worship of state power?[7]

 The stakes and ideas engendered by this book, in other words, go wide and deep.

Even as we keep these larger questions in mind, the book's vitality and charm lies in the striking individuals, one after another, whose voices are sounded on these pages, and who found, in Yair Ettinger, a listening scribe with a sensitive eye whose own participation in the currents described here, matched with journalistic acuity, make for a fascinating tour through vital happenings in Jewish religious life in Israel.

 Ettinger's writing, free from ideological anxieties and academic theorizing, opens a thrilling window into the vitality and richness, in celebration and struggle, of being a free people in the Land of Israel. And, like all good books, is an invitation to more conversation, among and within ourselves.

Yehuda Mirsky
Jerusalem
Author, *Rav Kook: Mystic in a Time of Revolution*

---

6. This point is powerfully argued by Baruch Kahane, "Al HaMigzar VeHaNigzar Mimenu," in Sheleg, *Mi-Mashgiaḥ HaKashrut LeNahag HaKatar?*, 435–56.
7. See on this the comments by Yair Assulin, "Laḥzor LeTafkid Masha"k HaDat," in Sheleg, *Mi-Mashgiaḥ HaKashrut LeNahag HaKatar?*, 381–94.

Introduction

Three Women

Bereavement struck three Israeli women. Three tragedies in the span of three years. And each blow brought a woman out of anonymity and into the spotlight, not just as a victim but as a hero. In their lifetimes, each played a decisive role in a field that had nothing to do with loss; a role related not to war or peace, but to what the modern world often downplays and frequently belittles: the formation of religious tradition.

In June 2014, Rachelle Fraenkel lost her son Naftali, who was kidnapped and murdered by Palestinian terrorists together with two other Israeli teenagers, Gilad Shaer and Eyal Yifrah; the three had been hitchhiking home. By the time the teens were laid to rest, after an excruciating eighteen-day manhunt, Rachelle Fraenkel and the two other bereaved mothers were household names. Many Israelis saw the three mothers, a constant presence in the media during the frenetic search, as symbols of dignity, inspiration, and faith. The boys' funeral, attended by tens of thousands of Israelis and broadcast live on television and radio, turned Naftali's mother into a religious symbol. Departing from conventional custom in Orthodox and traditionalist Judaism in Israel, Rachelle Fraenkel stood over her son's body, alongside the adult men in her family, and chanted aloud the mourner's prayer, the Kaddish. Although the act had been halakhically approved before by certain rabbinic figures, the sight of a woman saying Kaddish on TV was still a striking novelty for most Israelis – and especially most religious Israelis. Rachelle Fraenkel shifted the consciousness of Jews in Israel and around the world.

In October of the same year, Cpt. Tamar Ariel was killed in an avalanche in Annapurna, Nepal. She was on leave and due to return to her squadron. Before then, many Israelis had known her only by her initial – "T," the first religious female combat navigator in the history of the Israel Air Force. After she died, the army revealed her identity and personal story: she was not only a woman but a religious woman, who had swum against the tide to put herself through the most prestigious form of combat service in the Israeli military – IAF Flight School. Ariel had enlisted despite the staunch opposition of most Orthodox rabbis in Israel, who insisted that military service for women was a violation of halakha (Jewish law). In her life, Ariel was a role model for young religious women; but in her death, she came to symbolize a larger movement of religious girls who sought to serve, in uniform, in defiance of communal and educational public opinion. Tzahali, the women's religious pre-military academy, was renamed in her honor.

In January 2016, Dafna Meir was murdered at the doorstep of her home in the settlement of Otniel by a knife-wielding Palestinian terrorist. She was a mother of five, including two foster children, and a nurse by trade, who wrote prolific letters to relatives, friends, patients, and rabbis. Meir was part of a new culture in Israel's religious society, one that embraced an open conversation about femininity and sexuality. As a nurse, Meir advised religious women on delicate halakhic matters, such as the use of contraception and difficulties arising from observing the sensitive commandment of *nidda* – the prohibition on sexual intercourse, and even physical touch, during and shortly after a woman's period. This commandment is particularly onerous for women with a short menstrual cycle, who cannot get pregnant because abstinence forces them to miss their ovulation dates. Meir referred such women to rabbis who gave them special dispensation to shorten the period of sexual abstinence after menstruation. This guidance brought her into conflict with at least one prominent Orthodox rabbi, Menachem Burstein, the head of the PUAH Institute for fertility and halakha, who, like others, believed that she had crossed a red line.

These three calamities – of one bereaved mother and two young women killed in the prime of life – were not just the stories of high-profile victims on a long list of Israeli bereavement. They were seminal events. They shed a bright light on the cracks that were already running through the walls of consensus. Only later, after the fact, was their significance fully felt.

In all three cases, it was tragedy that made each woman a household name in Israel and inspired Jewish women around the world. But many Israeli women had already heard of them. All three had broken a thick glass ceiling in Israel's religious society: Tamar Ariel in the army; Dafna Meir in the realm of halakha, sexuality, and fertility; and Rachelle Fraenkel, long before disaster struck, by pushing the frontiers of female Torah scholarship and religious jurisprudence as a teacher at leading Torah institutes for women.

These three women belonged to the second generation of the feminist revolution in Orthodox Judaism. All three were unmistakably religious and committed to the practice and study of Jewish law. They neither emerged from nor mixed in modern feminist circles, and they were certainly not members of progressive Jewish denominations. They came from small religious communities outside of Israel's big cities, and two of them – Fraenkel (from Nof Ayalon) and Meir (from Otniel) – came from fairly conservative and religiously exclusive communities, on the more stringent edges of Orthodoxy. None planned on becoming an icon for a new religious avant-garde, but all, and each in her own way, departed from the rabbinic-mandated status quo and charted a path of change.

The fact that their life stories were suddenly intertwined with Israel's national story had two peculiar consequences. First, the grief moderated and effectively muted the reactionary criticism that their religious derring-do might have otherwise provoked. Second, the spotlight gave them an outsized public influence, especially on Orthodox Jewish women in Israel and abroad.[1] Their deeds, particularly those of Fraenkel and Ariel, resonated widely and won broad legitimacy.

In retrospect, each of these three women represented a particular side in polemics that have long thrummed through Israel's Religious Zionist society: the role of women in prayer, Torah scholarship, and religious jurisprudence; the role of women in the army and society; and the role of women at the juncture of halakha and medicine. But above all, the three women represented a sea change in the status of women as compared to men, and especially rabbis, and the old Orthodox order. Their personal stories told of the presence of a broad and diverse movement, which has neither a name, nor a leadership, nor a central address.

The three women's tragedies highlighted their trailblazing deeds, presenting them as not only legitimate but laudatory. It seems that even the most religiously explosive subjects in Judaism are rendered less flammable by the heartbreaking context of national mourning. The Religious Zionist movement in Israel may be fraying, but at its core there remains, always, a potent national sentiment.

The stories of Dafna Meir, Rachelle Fraenkel, and Tamar Ariel might have made a suitable ending to this book. Their tales blunt the blade of division; they are tales in which unity prevails. But in Israel's day-to-day reality, these three stories are windows into disagreements that risk tearing the Religious Zionist community apart and might already be doing so. No revolution, large or small, is waged without a battle, and this one is already well underway: in raging screeds on social media, in

---

1.   Dramatic cultural and religious developments taking place within Religious Zionism are occurring not only in Israel but in Modern Orthodox communities across the globe, particularly in the United States. The impact that these communities have on one another is amplified by the easy flow of information across the world. The presence of a significant number of English speaking *olim* situated in Religious Zionist communities throughout Israel also contributes to this cross-continental influence.

  Each of these communities is unique, yet they share many of the same challenges. They are each struggling to define the parameters of the role of women and LGBTQ people in Orthodox life. Similarly, they are each contending with the challenges of rabbinic authority, individual rights, and the proper relationships to non-Orthodox movements. We clearly see that the effects of globalization are felt throughout the Modern Orthodox world.

halakhic rulings and the official correspondence of rabbis, in funded campaigns and barbed discussions around Shabbat tables. This is a war over the identity of the Orthodox individual and the commandment-keeping community, over the very nature of Orthodoxy. Some of these battles have been resolved, or are being resolved, but the fundamental clashes rage on. These are confrontations over the role of women, the authority of rabbis, the attitudes toward the state and Western culture, the nature of prayer and the physical dimensions of synagogues, the appropriate educational doctrine, and what it means to be a an observant Jew, to be Orthodox, in the third millennium of Jewish life.

Yair Ettinger
May 2022

Chapter I

The Age of Bennett

THE IRONY

The inaugural speech of an Israeli prime minister looks nothing like that of an American president. There are no towering backdrops and no beautifully tailored coats. No plumes of cold January air and no poet laureates. And yet, it is festive and familial, with mothers and wives and husbands and fathers in attendance. Sometimes the men wear flowers in their lapels. Generally speaking, the audience in the plenum, all 120 Members of Knesset, are reasonably respectful.

This was not the case on June 13, 2021, when Naftali Bennett was called to the lectern. Wearing a blue suit and his trademark small knitted *kippa*, Bennett got to his feet and clasped hands with his new coalition partners MK Gideon Sa'ar, a former Netanyahu loyalist turned rival, MK Mansour Abbas, the head of the Islamic party, Ra'am, and MK Yair Lapid, the face of centrist secular Israel. Jauntily, he approached the podium.

No one in Israel expected the speech to go smoothly. After all, this was the last day of Benjamin Netanyahu's rule – severed by Bennett's crossing of the Rubicon, his willingness to serve alongside a hard-left party like Meretz and a distinctly non-Zionist party like Ra'am. But few imagined the mayhem that would ensue, and more importantly, the primary sources of it.

Bennett, who later that day would be sworn in as the first religious prime minister in the history of Israel, a nearly unfathomable development during the early years of the state, was heckled most severely not by Arab MKs who support a single state between the river and the sea, but by three members of his own community, two of whom had served under him when he headed the Jewish Home Party. In fact, the first three MKs to be thrown out of the plenum that afternoon were Bezalel Smotrich, Orit Strock, and Itamar Ben-Gvir. Settlers all, religious all. Shouting "shame!" and hoisting placards, the three protested the rise of one of their own to the highest post in the land.

The scene was raw with irony: The Mizrachi movement, founded in 1902, had at long last sent one of its sons to the very seat of political power in Israel, but once ensconced, he found that only a part of his own camp was behind him; the other wing, the more religiously and ideologically conservative part of the community, was waging all-out war against him, dismissive nearly to the point of excommunication. Once seen as the salvation of the Jewish Home Party by many within this conservative camp, he was now viewed as a disaster and as a danger to the state, a prime minister who had to be ousted at all costs. Some of this had to do with his political maneuverings, his violation of explicit campaign promises, but it went well beyond that, to the cleaving and privatization of a political home that was being split into ideological shards.

There is nothing quite like the age of Bennett to illustrate the rift within the Religious Zionist world in Israel, which had long ago shaken off the illusion of unity, its calling card for decades, back when there was only one Religious Zionist party – the National Religious Party. Bennett played a major role in the political rending of the party, but it was a process that had already started earlier, the result of deep-moving ideological currents. Bennett, who stepped down in June 2022, was merely the emissary.

In the span of two years, from 2019 to 2021, Israel went through four election cycles. All four can be viewed as a single, ongoing political event. The facts are many and muddled – and inextricably linked to a national referendum on Benjamin Netanyahu's fitness to continue to serve as prime minister – but sifting through them reveals the fissures that run through the length of the Religious Zionist community, which has become a kingmaker in Israeli politics.

At the close of the fourth election cycle, in the spring of 2021, thirteen political parties (including two Arab parties) were sworn in to the Knesset; six of them had representatives from the "knitted *kippa*" community. All garnered support from the community and all saw themselves as its authentic representatives. They spanned a spectrum of ideological views, from the hard right, where support for Jewish supremacy and the forcible transfer of Arabs from the Land of Israel has gained a following, to the stately right, to the political center – a large group of disparate politicians who all shared what might be termed "the ideological trinity" of Religious Zionist ideology: a devotion to the Land of Israel, the Torah of Israel, and the people of Israel.

These core principles were presented and ratified at the Mizrachi movement's founding conference in Vilna, Lithuania. The motto under which the conference was held was "The Land of Israel for the People of Israel According to the Torah of Israel." The three sides of this triangle have, over time, shifted in relative size and importance, with one occasionally overshadowing the others. Taking the measure of the dimensional shifts allows us to chart the evolution of Religious Zionism.

THE PEOPLE OF ISRAEL

For Naftali Bennett, the most important part of this trinity, if we are to judge by his public remarks, is this one, and although he, as an Orthodox Jew, is a minority in Israel, it seems that his primary identity is Israeli and his overriding ethos is one of integration.

When Bennett entered politics, he arrived as the great hope of the sectarian Jewish Home Party. But in actuality, his arrival marked the end of the political and ideological unity within the community.

In his first election campaign, in 2013, he revitalized a lagging party, quadrupling its tally of seats in Knesset, to twelve. Late at night, talking to a crowd of knitted *kippa*-wearing supporters, who greeted him like a rock star once the results of the polls were known, he said: "Today we've made history, we've ceased to be a sectarian political party."

He and his political partner, Ayelet Shaked, both of whom had once worked under Netanyahu, sought from day one to increase cooperation between religious and secular Israelis, of the sort who serve together in the same uniform and work together in the same high-tech firms. He sees himself as situated more on the Israeli axis than on the religious axis, and upon entering the Knesset he declared that he would not be taking orders from rabbis. The Israelis – the name of the party that he and Shaked sought to launch in 2012 before their takeover of the Jewish Home Party – is also shorthand for where Bennett feels he truly belongs.

He and Shaked – a secular, Tel Aviv-dwelling politician and a staunch supporter of the settler movement – were joint leaders from the get-go. Their agenda, advanced both within the Jewish Home Party and subsequently in their other political endeavors, was non-sectarian, or post-sectarian patriotism. Beneath the fluttering flag of nationalism, he placed on a lower height the flag of Judaism, representing a brand of religion that wasn't overly stringent, wasn't repulsive to secular Israelis, wasn't in favor of religious coercion and yet still served as a declaration of his identity and sense of belonging. The National Religious Party – the predecessor of the Jewish Home Party – used patriotism and settlement expansion in the service of religion; Bennett used religion in the service of his patriotism. The old NRP was a religious sectarian party, while Bennett, from his first day in politics, used the blurring of the old dividing lines between that which is religious and that which is secular as a wider stage upon which he could stand.

The party slogan that he used when entering politics was "Something new is starting." This was true of him personally, too, as someone who sparked both curiosity and suspicion as an idealist who was not an ideologue, an Orthodox urbanite from Raanana, a bourgeois who never tried to hide the fact that his commitment to halakha was less than complete. Unlike his predecessors at the helm of the NRP, he did not come up through the political ranks or the education sector and, in contrast to many of his peers, he had not studied at a yeshiva after high school. Before throwing himself into politics, Bennett was a high-tech entrepreneur who had made tens of millions of shekels in the industry.

At the outset of his political career, Bennett felt the sting of rabbinic critique, absorbing public barbs about the size of his *kippa* and comments about him "not having the scent of Torah." It's doubtful that the offensive remarks were wounding. They may actually have helped him early on, even within the community itself. The secret of his success was linked to his persona as a free-spirited and straight-talking individual who did not hide the fact that he was not observant for years after his army service, had married a woman who had been raised in a secular home, and, as a politician, that he would not be bound by rabbinic decree. These statements were codes, granting legitimacy to autonomous religious people who were not willing to accept the old hierarchy but nonetheless saw themselves as part of the community.

As prime minister, he did not fly a religious or messianic flag. He did not champion the settlement movement, which was once his chief cause. Instead, he advocated for unity and a "government of healing." In his inaugural address – which was written in advance, though it seemed to be tailored to the in-house hecklers – he drew inspiration from two characters, both active in the revolt against the Roman Empire in the first century of the common era.

"I see here right before my eyes Simon bar Giora and John of Giscala," he said, ticking off the names of two warring hawks, who split the people of Israel during the time of Roman rule and led inevitably to the destruction of the Temple. "Each was right, yet with all their being right, they burnt the house down on top of us. I am proud of the ability to sit together with people with very different views from my own. This time, at the decisive moment, we have taken responsibility."

That was Bennett in his own words, laying out his doctrine and justifying the abandonment of Netanyahu and the right-wing base by advocating for an Israeli-Jewish partnership of religious and secular, right and left, even if in reality his government was made up of only some swaths of the right and large chunks of the left, including, for the first time, an Arab-Islamic party, Ra'am. His decision drove a wedge into his own community, even while he, as prime minister, sought to fill the cracks within the wider mosaic of Israeli life.

By his own logic, in the name of avoiding a national rift and "destruction," a man of the right such as himself must serve alongside someone like Health Minister Nitzan Horowitz, the openly gay chairman of the Meretz Party, which has long advocated for LGBTQ rights and settlement withdrawals. He, he seemed to be saying, had chosen a thorny partnership over a comfortable sectarian isolation.

Bennett's inaugural address was interpreted, rightly, as an apologia for the covenant he made with his ideological rivals, violating explicit campaign promises. In truth, though, integration had been part of the Bennett ethos for years. In that he resembled the progeny of the founding fathers of the Mizrachi movement, who, unlike the other Orthodox sects – the Haredim – saw no inherent conflict between religious devotion and Zionism. But the founding fathers of Religious Zionism set themselves a more modest goal. They set out to serve as the *kashrut* supervisors on the mostly secular train of Zionism, which is to say to be a part of the larger community while ensuring that the Jewish tradition isn't pushed out the door. Bennett, unlike them, grew up in modern Israel. He passed through all of mainstream society's rites of passage: in the most elite field unit in the army, in the flourishing high-tech sector, and as a civil servant. As such, he was free of feelings of inferiority – both vis-à-vis the Haredim and the secular majority. He saw himself as a *kippa*-wearing Israeli, fit for leadership.

The outlook brought him to the top but also hastened his fall.[1] With the sectarian party disassembled, he found himself with scant support from the Religious Zionist community and little support of any other sector of the population at large. He was, for much of his year in office, an unpopular prime minister, lacking a base of support and hanging by a thread, and those who were most vocal in their appreciation of his service and who advocated for his government hailed mostly from the center-left of the political map, and did not, and will not, vote for him. Worse – Bennett, who has steadfastly put the people of Israel foremost

---

1. In July 2022, after handing over the reins to Prime Minister Yair Lapid, Bennett announced that he would not run in the November 2022 national elections. His one-year term as prime minister was the shortest in the history of the country.

in his ideology, is despised by large swaths of the right-wing public, and particularly the public in which he was raised.

THE LAND OF ISRAEL

Bennett, like Smotrich, like most of the Jewish MKs in the Knesset today, has been a staunch supporter of Greater Israel. His career as a public servant began with his tenure as the head of the Yesha Council, and as a politician he mainstreamed the once-radical notion of annexing parts of the West Bank and imposing Israeli law upon it. And yet, upon closer inspection, there are notable differences between the two leaders and their contingencies. Not as regards the central diplomatic question facing Israel – the vast majority of the Religious Zionist community remains staunchly opposed to withdrawals from territory – but rather the lengths one should go to in fortifying the settlements, even in the face of opposition from the establishment, the army, the courts, and the international community.

The settlement enterprise, from its inception, has had a complex relationship with the various governments of Israel – a frictional embrace. Although governments from left and right have endorsed the founding of settlements, it is also hardly unusual to see settlers and soldiers clashing on hilltops and dunes, both during the initial move onto the land and later while clinging to it in the face of an evacuation order.

The oracle of the revolutionary and messianic ideology of Religious Zionism, Rabbi Zvi Yehuda Kook, dictated the narrative of confrontation when he famously said: "Over Judea and Samaria, over the Golan Heights – it won't work without war." The notion of warfare was further entrenched during the days of the Oslo Accords and it brought waves of confrontation between the state and the settler movement.

The greater the friction, the greater the need for rabbinic rulings: What may be done to stop the evacuation of settlements, rabbis were asked, and may soldiers refuse to carry out evacuation orders? The questions were of a strategic or tactical nature and often the answers were issued in the language of halakha.

The friction guided Religious Zionist ideology down two divergent paths: that of the decorous right, which clung to the sanctity of the

Jewish army and the symbols of the Jewish state, and the hard ideological right, which, when its back was to the wall, was willing to violate secular law and the dictates of the state. The first sharp departure came in the early 1980s, when the Shin Bet revealed the presence of a Jewish "underground," which planned and executed murderous terror attacks against Palestinian targets. Its members were all of the Religious Zionist community. A decade later, in 1994, Baruch Goldstein, another member of the community, committed mass murder in the Tomb of the Patriarchs, gunning down twenty-nine Palestinians while in prayer. One year later came the assassination of Prime Minister Yitzhak Rabin at the hands of a Religious Zionist law student – a rupture within Israeli society, a long-reverberating trauma.

The NRP, despite its gradual acceptance of Gush Emunim's Greater Land of Israel ideology, was used to having smaller, more hawkish parties to its political right, while it clung to the center, managing, even, to serve in the reigning governments of the Oslo Accords era. This is the very same party that would later be headed by Bezalel Smotrich and change its name to the Religious Zionism Party.

Diplomatically speaking, the matter of settlements has been largely removed from the agenda. The doctrine of land for peace was eliminated from the Israeli consensus first by the bloody Second Intifada and then by the 2005 Gaza Disengagement, which buried the notion of a unilateral withdrawal and settlement evacuation. The political center shifted rightward and even when the Israeli left-wing parties were included in Bennett's governing coalition in 2021, after many years of exile in the opposition, it was blatantly clear that one of the central flags of their ideology would be left unfurled – conciliation with the Palestinians.

Although the right appears triumphant on the matter of the Territories, the question of force as a means toward a goal remains unresolved. Smotrich has adhered to a fiery and rebellious approach to many of the conflicts that have pitted his halakhic beliefs against the rule of law, an approach that Bennett and others on the right have condemned.

While Bennett on multiple occasions came out against nationalistic crime committed by Jews, Smotrich tended to denounce it in the gentlest of terms, if at all. In 2017, he called for the immediate pardon of

Elor Azaria, a soldier who had gunned down a long-since incapacitated Palestinian terrorist in Hebron, and two years before that, when most of the country was shocked by the torching of a home and the killing, by Jews, of a Palestinian family in the village of Duma, Smotrich published an opinion piece in which he argued that "the murder in Duma, for all its severity, is not a terror attack."[2]

Yet he was not the far-right marker on the political map of Israel and of Religious Zionism. Beyond Smotrich stood MK Itamar Ben-Gvir, the head of the Otzma Yehudit Party and a disciple of Rabbi Meir Kahane, whose party, Kach, was banned from Israel's parliament for its racist views. Otzma Yehudit was not similarly barred, but it too failed, until 2021, to cross the electoral threshold of the Knesset. That changed when Benjamin Netanyahu decided in the midst of a grueling election cycle that a religious nationalist party on the far right would serve his interests, ensuring that many thousands of votes were not thrown away in the course of yet another solo run by Ben-Gvir. Smotrich was only too happy to oblige. He brought Ben-Gvir's party, Otzma, into the fold, along with Noam, a reactionary party founded by the staunchly conservative rabbis of Yeshivat Har Hamor. Its platform was illiberal and anti-gay.

These splinter parties put aside their quibbling differences (over matters such as the Temple Mount) and set their sights squarely on Bennett, a common enemy. In a November 2021 speech in the Knesset, Smotrich said of Bennett: "When the body expels the pus and cleanses itself of the germs, it returns afterward cleaner and better." That "body," created by Smotrich and Ben-Gvir, and carrying the name "Religious Zionism," was infinitely more conservative and nationalist than any previous representation of the national-religious community. It did not reflect the movement at large, but it did prove that a Kahanist ideology of territory, placing the Land of Israel first and foremost, coupled with an Arab population transfer, long since excoriated by the stately wing of the right, had been whitewashed and normalized in swaths of Religious Zionist and Haredi society.

---

2. "Price Tag Is Not Terror," *BeSheva*, December 10, 2015.

THE TORAH OF ISRAEL

The State of Israel is both Jewish and democratic, two fundamental traits that are often at odds. Some might say they stand in diametric opposition to one another. The prevailing notion in Israel and abroad is that the majority of internal tension, the fault line within Israeli society, is the democratic nature of the state: human rights, nationalism, ethnocentrism, the authority of the courts, the status of the Palestinians, the left and right.

But times have changed, and for a multitude of reasons it has become clear that the front has shifted. Many of the battles being waged today are less about the democracy of the Jewish state and more about the democratization of Judaism. Jewish identity, religious affairs, the balance between religion and state, identity and culture: all lie at the heart of our domestic debates. In the wake of Netanyahu's departure and Bennett's arrival (and departure one year later), we've seen these simmering issues boil to the surface.

Take for example the ever-combustible matter of religious services, as provided by the Chief Rabbinate of Israel, and the effect of this monopoly on the Jewish identity of the state. During the Bennett government (2021–2022), pitched battles were waged, almost daily, between two principal camps: on one side, Haredim, Religious Zionists, and religious traditionalists loyal to the Netanyahu base and now serving in the opposition in the Knesset, and on the other, members of the coalition – secularists and liberal Religious Zionists. At the red-hot center of these debates stood Religious Zionists, from either camp, the new median of Israel, locking horns over matters of identity and the proper interpretation of the Torah of Israel.

The ringleader was not Bennett but his once brother-in-arms, Matan Kahana – a former special forces operator and fighter pilot whom Bennett drafted into the Yamina Party.

Over the years Bennett shied away from matters of religion and state. Those issues may not have interested him all that much. But Kahana is a different story. He defines himself as a "*dos*," as someone who is one hundred percent committed to keeping the Torah commandments, but who also has sought change in the religious services provided by the state. Speaking of Bennett, he told me: "He's from the knitted *kippa* community, but it isn't the thing that he's most interested in dealing with.

And then I came along, ostensibly on the security ticket, and I said: I want that. He said: There's no one better. Jump on it."

Kahana was a surprising pick for Minister of Religious Affairs. He met Bennett in 1990 on the grounds of the Sayeret Matkal recon unit. The two became friends. Bennett, having made it through the grueling training phase, chose to attend officers' school and to serve in a different unit as a platoon and then company commander. Kahana did his time in "the Unit," as it's known, and then, rather than return to civilian life, enrolled in the IAF Flight School. He graduated the grueling course as a fighter pilot and went on to command a squadron of F-16 aircraft. He retired with the rank of brigadier-general and, with no prior political experience, was recruited by Bennett.

Immediately upon taking office, Kahana launched an initiative that was nothing short of radical. Within five months, he had privatized *kashrut* supervision in Israel. Private entities could for the first time lawfully issue *kashrut* certificates that were once the exclusive domain of the Chief Rabbinate. The monopoly of the rabbinate had been broken.

This may seem like a formality, but it cut to the essence of the state. Kahana's initiative, passed into law, marked the beginning of the end of the Chief Rabbinate's exclusive grip on matters of personal status such as burials, weddings, and births. The Chief Rabbinate predates Israel, having been founded under British mandatory rule, and it had retained, by law, exclusive control of halakha for decades.

After *kashrut*, Kahana set his sights on other reforms: the state-run conversion courts, the appointment of rabbis and heads of religious councils (where he placed an emphasis on the appointment of women), and marriage registration. No previous minister of religious affairs had ever dared to make such sweeping changes to the state-run religious services, which since the founding of the state had been seen as a sort of dowry that the secular state paid to the religious public in return for industrial silence – at first to the NRP and later to the Haredi parties.

Kahana's overarching goal was the mitigation of religious coercion.[3] The means: the insertion of competition into fields that were by

---

3. In under a year as minister, Kahana managed to realize a small yet unprecedented part of the religious activists' agenda. He privatized *kashrut*, smashing the rabbinate's

definition monopolistic – *kashrut,* conversion, and more; a religious privatization that seized authority from a hegemonic group of rabbis. "The state of Jewish identity is very poor," he told me. "You cannot force an identity on people. I believe that with less coercion people will opt for Judaism, they'll want to be married 'according to the law of Moses and Israel.'" His comments were issued after years of Haredi control over all state-run religious services.

Within the opposition he was promptly marked not just as a political rival but as a religious adversary. "Antiochus," MK Moshe Gafni of the Haredi United Torah Judaism Party called him, likening Kahana to the first of the rulers who sought to annihilate Jews, 2,200 years ago, solely on the basis of their religion. This was but one of countless denouncements – in the Knesset, in rabbinic letters, in editorials and cartoons and social media posts, and in protests outside his house, where yeshiva students, wearing knitted *kippot* on their heads, cooked shrimp and other foods prohibited by Jewish law as a form of protest against his *kashrut* initiatives.

---

state-granted monopoly. He changed the regulations regarding the appointment of municipal rabbis. He tried to promote, albeit without success, a change to the state conversion process, pressing for competition to the established rabbinic courts, and he managed to appoint ten women to religious regional councils all across Israel while also securing funding for female halakhic advisors. These moves – which were long part of the synagogue and state debates in Israel, and which were met with approval in parts of the Religious Zionist community – were eventually overshadowed by the culture war surrounding the Bennett government. The narrative changed as the government began to teeter and fall. Kahana and his colleagues were increasingly seen not merely as trying to weaken the rabbinate, but as enemies of the state's Jewish identity. Smotrich began referring to the opposition, which included half of the Religious Zionist camp, all of the Haredi camp, and the religious and traditionalist voters of the Likud, who generally show respect to the rabbinate and to rabbis in general, as "believing Israel." The non-believers, he made clear, included all of the religious members of the government. MK Dudi Amsalem of the Likud Party declared: "We are in an insane six months, in which every member of the coalition is running to erase more than his peers of Jewish values. It's a competition.... I see it as an existential threat to the state of Israel." The Netanyahu-affiliated Channel 14 put Kahana on the cover of its print magazine. The headline: "The Undertaker." And beneath that: "This is how Matan Kahana is trying to bury the Jewish identity of the State of Israel." The legitimate difference of opinion was rendered illegitimate.

The political battle became religious and ideological, nearly theological, and it touched upon the historical differences between the Haredi and Religious Zionist communities, the validity of each ideological path, the preferred degree of isolationism and of halakhic severity. "We are no less careful in the fulfillment of halakha and no less God-fearing," Kahana bellowed at Haredi MKs from the Knesset podium in one of his speeches.

"Honestly, they were pushed from the sources of their power. They thought they had the deeds marked down in the real estate registry and it's eating them up, that's the reason. Power, power, power," Kahana told me when asked why he has so outraged the Haredim. But in the offing – and this was understood by both his supporters and detractors alike – was something far deeper than a thirst for power. For within the question of what is kosher food and what is a proper conversion lies the question of who gets to define the nature of Judaism.

Since the nineties, and all the more so during the years of Netanyahu's rule, it was clear to all to who had that right: the Haredi community. Gradually, during the Netanyahu years, an internal Orthodox opposition to the Haredi-Likud hegemony began to develop. It demanded less religious coercion, less severe rabbinic rulings, and a shedding of the corruption that has clung to the Chief Rabbinate.

In contrast with other previous battles, this was not a clash between religious and secular, but rather between two different types of commandment-keeping Orthodox Jews. Both saw Judaism as a top priority, but defined it differently. One supported a religious monopoly and a strengthening of the Chief Rabbinate; the other believed in competition. One stood guard over the Chief Rabbinate of Israel, which over the years had become a Haredi institution, and the other wanted to weaken it and give expression to other approaches. The Ashkenazic and Sephardic chief rabbis declared war on Kahana, and dozens of Religious Zionist rabbis joined their ranks. They especially emphasized the honor of the institution of the Chief Rabbinate, which to them held theological significance since the days of Rabbi Avraham Yitzhak HaKohen Kook, the first Ashkenazic chief rabbi. The campaigns took on the shape of a religious war.

Kahana managed to rally a handful of rabbis, some of stature, around his conversion reform, but hundreds of other rabbis signed their names to sharp rebuttals, often casting Kahana as "an uprooter of religion." In February 2021, at a conference organized by the leading Religious Zionist weekly newspaper *Makor Rishon*, a rabbi in attendance, Amital Bareli, refused to shake the minister's hand. "When facing the swindling destroyers of Judaism there is no room for niceties and decorum," he explained on Twitter.

WHO IS A RELIGIOUS ZIONIST?

Bennett's coalitionary government was populated by other members of the Religious Zionist community who were also eager to alter the balance of religion and state. These Orthodox politicians, hailing from a variety of parties, were keen to bring change to the Chief Rabbinate, the nature of the public Israeli Shabbat, the exemption from army service for Haredim, and even the rabbinic council that controls the cellular telephone market in Haredi communities. They acted individually, independent of one another, but their behavior, and the manner in which they addressed the ideological trinity of Religious Zionism, spoke to a deep and significant similarity.

Bennett and his cohorts continue to represent a new generation within the Religious Zionist community. They are idealists, they are religious, and they feel comfortable in their own shoes; they are financially secure, firmly ensconced in the middle and upper classes, and they are seemingly devoid of any feelings of insecurity vis-à-vis other more idealistic or more devout members of the community, who have devoted their lives to the classic routes of education or settlement or rabbinical studies.

What brought about the change? The list of reasons is long, including the rise of individualism and the prevalence of social media, all of which will be discussed in subsequent chapters, but it is worth highlighting the summer of 2005, the Disengagement from Gaza. That move, led by Prime Minister Ariel Sharon, struck a blow to the standing of rabbis in the community and, more significantly, put a dent in the theology of Religious Zionism. Specifically, it undermined the notion that messianic redemption, sparked by the return of Jewish sovereignty over the Land of Israel, was moving inexorably forward. From amid that rupture, new ideas were formed, new leaders rose to prominence.

Politicians come and go, and so we may look at Bennett's cohort as a parable. Even if they all shortly vanish from the political arena, the religious and social phenomenon of which they are part will not fade away. MKs Matan Kahana, Elazar Stern, Yoaz Hendel, Moshe Tur-Paz, and Bennett himself – all represent a certain phenomenon.

They were raised within the Orthodox community and in adulthood lived in bourgeois religious towns and cities generally within the Green Line. They hold academic degrees and have had careers in the high-tech sector, the media, or the Israel Air Force, fields that demand individual excellence and independence, and also require a constant mingling with religious and secular Israelis, male and female. In other words, unlike the Religious Zionist politicians of old, who were predominantly rabbis and educators and party apparatchiks, these men were raised far from the isolationist bubble of the community.

In previous parliaments there were several women who also prioritized matters of synagogue and state (Aliza Lavie and Tehila Friedman of the Yesh Atid Party and Rachel Azaria of the Kulanu Party), but for the moment our focus is on the men, who acquired status and money and served in combat roles in the army. This significant period in their lives also influenced their path as politicians.

Their religiosity, and this speaks volumes, is given outward expression solely by their *kippot* (and in Hendel's case, the *kippa* is transparent, though he was raised within the community, sends his children to religious schools, and considers himself a part of the Religious Zionist community). Beneath those *kippot* they comport themselves autonomously. They do not see themselves as bound by rabbinic authority, and certainly not by that of the Chief Rabbinate. When I asked Kahana about his position on rabbis, he reverted to the jargon of the squadron. "I certainly consult with rabbis and listen very carefully to what they say," he told me, "but it's me on the stick and the throttle. I decide." The old guard of educators, then, has cleared the stage for a generation of successful aces with no inferiority complexes, and perhaps no abundance of modesty.

What is the linkage between an interest in matters of religion and state and military service? Is it coincidence that so many of these politicians emerged from within the elite ranks of the army?

For years the working assumption within large swaths of the secular elite was that religious soldiers and officers, when put to the test, would obey their rabbis and not their officers. The matter of obedience, in the face of, say, an order to evacuate a settlement, was questioned repeatedly in the media and on university campuses (including a book devoted entirely to the topic, *The Divine Commander: The Theocratization of the Israeli Military* by Prof. Yagil Levy). But it missed a larger and far more prevalent trend: religious officers who not only adhere to the very letter of the law of the military hierarchy, but also challenge the rabbinic hierarchy on matters of religious law.

Maj.-Gen. (res.) Elazar Stern and Brig.-Gen. (res.) Matan Kahana are prime examples. Both used their standing as senior officers to challenge the religious status quo. Stern, as a general in uniform, launched a religious conversion track within the Israeli army, dealt extensively with the burial of soldiers who were not halakhically Jewish, and curbed the autonomy of the Hesder yeshiva students. Those moves put him in direct confrontation not with the IDF General Staff but with the rabbis of his own community, in the army and in the civilian world.

The brass they wore on their shoulders and the experience they had had as combat officers granted them legitimacy. It is far easier to lead a campaign of change when your social status is secure and your prestige, as someone who has risked his life repeatedly for the country, is unassailable. In Israel in general, and in the Religious Zionist community in particular, a security background is a shield against much opposition and invective.

But it isn't just immunity that military service provides. It's also motivation. For if you do not encounter religious problems in the field, from up close, if you live in a separate society, the issues seem distant and irrelevant. When Matan Kahana wanted to convince the public of the need for change in state-run conversions, he posted a video that told the story of a female soldier who had served under his command and who was not considered as halakhically Jewish. He introduced her to the public and said, "We must do everything to bring her home to Judaism."

That could not have been done by a man who served in a homogenous unit of other likeminded religious men.

Bennett's cohort is a novelty. Not for nothing are they seen by many as a threat to the old order and as a group that collectively shuns the intensive ideological temperament voiced by Rabbi Zvi Yehuda Kook and others. Not for nothing are they seen by the conservative flank of the party as rebels, revolting against the very idea of Religious Zionism. Smotrich sees himself as the keeper of the old flame, the one who will yet rehabilitate the political framework of the community. And yet he too is a novelty. He advances opinions that in the past were seen as beyond the pale and even took the unusual step of welcoming peripheral figures to the fold, first and foremost Itamar Ben-Gvir, the man who, weeks before Rabin's assassination, held up the hood ornament of his car and announced that "just as we got to the ornament, so too can we get to Rabin."

Two dramatic events with lasting consequences took place during the last week of the 2022 calendar year. The first was the return to power of Benjamin Netanyahu after years of political deadlock. Netanyahu's coalition is the most right-wing and religious government in Israeli history. In fact, his government includes the ultra-nationalist parties of Bezalel Smotrich and Itamar Ben-Gvir. These parties have fourteen Knesset seats and unprecedented legislative power.

Two days before the swearing in of the new government, Rabbi Chaim Druckman passed away at the age of ninety. Rabbi Druckman was a symbol of the Religious Zionist community, having served it as a rabbi, educator, and political leader. In the last years of his life, he transferred his political support from Naftali Bennett and Ayelet Shaked to the more sectarian Religious Zionist party of Smotrich. He was alive to witness the enormous growth of Smotrich's party as well as the near political decimation of the more moderate religious camp lead by Shaked. More importantly, he saw the heated rhetoric that occurred during the election cycle, culminating with Smotrich stating that synagogues should not welcome those who vote for Shaked's party. While Rabbi Druckman had no chance of preventing the eventual split within Religious Zionism, his continued presence still allowed for the illusion of possible communal unity. With his death, and the establishment of the new government, it seems that this divide within Religious Zionism will only deepen.

Who, then, is an authentic Religious Zionist?

The political arena serves as an illustration. In the chapters of this book, we will see the deep processes of change surrounding synagogues and schools, the army and the Chief Rabbinate of Israel. Smotrich, will assert that he is the authentic face of the community; so too will Bennett and Kahana and Stern and even Ben-Gvir. Each one sees himself as the honest reflection of the community, and each one is right and wrong in his own way. Once it was easy to say who is a member of the Religious Zionist community. Today, in the era of religious and ideological privatization, the mission is growing ever more complex.

Chapter II

The Privatization of Religious Zionism

*K*ippot come in all shapes and sizes, but the knitted *kippa* –
the symbol of Religious Zionists – is everywhere in Israel. In the
Supreme Court and the media, the government and the army, the top
brass of the police and the Shin Bet. Men and women from the Religious Zionist community have made a name for themselves in academia,
business, and practically every walk of life in Israel. The list of Religious
Zionists at the top of Israeli society reads like a who's who of the country's movers and shakers: from Prime Minister Naftali Bennett to former
police chief Roni Alsheikh; from Attorney General Avichai Mandelblit
to multiple Supreme Court justices; from Channel 12's political analyst
Amit Segal to Prof. Menachem Ben-Sasson, the president of the Hebrew
University of Jerusalem. Sensing that a revolutionary change is afoot, the
journalist Ari Shavit dubbed them "Israel's new ruling elite."[1]

---

1.   Ari Shavit, "Successors of Rabbi Kook Are Israel's New Ruling Elite," *Haaretz*,
     August 16, 2016, available at https://www.haaretz.com/opinion/.premium-

And not just any elite. In a far-reaching and eye-opening study from 2014, the Israel Democracy Institute found that roughly one fifth (22 percent) of Israeli Jews identify as Religious Zionists. Together, they are known as the "national-religious" (*dati leumi*) community because of the unique fusion of Zionism and religion in their identity – a fusion that sets them apart from secular Zionists, on the one hand, and non-Zionist Haredi Jews on the other. The comprehensive study, which questioned a representative sample of 4,600 men and women, revealed that many Israelis who do not necessarily practice a national-religious lifestyle (be they secular, Haredi, or traditionalist) are coalescing around the social nucleus of the Religious Zionist community.[2]

Religious Zionists are everywhere, and this ubiquity is fostering within the community a sense of euphoria. One advertising campaign launched in 2016 for the biggest Religious Zionist youth movement declared: "One day, you too will be a graduate of Bnei Akiva!" The campaign in 2016 featured pictures of Orthodox men and women, politicians, rabbis, military officers, academics, and other famous people who had passed through its ranks. Another Bnei Akiva notice urged Israelis: "Let's shine the great light – so proud of the impressive graduates illuminating our common future!" Bezalel Smotrich, a member of Knesset and chairman of the far-right Religious Zionism Party, set an even more ambitious goal on the eve of Israel's April 2019 election: "When was the last time we told the Religious Zionist community that all the people of Israel would become Religious Zionists? We form the nuclear reactor that provides electric power to all the people of Israel."[3]

Meanwhile, on the far bank of the river that cuts through Israeli society, there is mounting anxiety over the increased prevalence of Religious Zionists in positions of power. According to the Israel Democracy Institute's annual democracy index, as of 2017, no fewer than 79 percent of secular Israelis agreed with the statement that "religious people are

successors-of-rabbi-kook-are-israel-s-new-ruling-elite-1.5423330.

2. Tamar Herman et al., *The National-Religious Sector in Israel in 2014*, trans. Karen Gold (Jerusalem: Israel Democracy Institute, 2015), available at https://en.idi.org.il/media/4663/madad-z-english_web.pdf.

3. Interview in the synagogue magazine *Olam Katan*, March 29, 2019.

gradually taking over the country."[4] This figure can be attributed to the rising profile of religion and religious individuals in the Israeli public sphere, but also to the popularization of a relatively new word that originated in academia: *hadata* – "religionization." This term carries a coercive connotation; the trend indicating an invasion of secular space by religious Jewish content, and even by religious Jews themselves. "One Israeli civilization is evaporating and another is taking over," Shavit wrote. "While almost nothing remains of David Ben-Gurion's heritage, the heritage of Rabbi Zvi Yehuda Kook has pretty much succeeded in taking over the State of Israel."[5]

Concern that secular Israelis are about to be vanquished by their national-religious compatriots has induced panic in some quarters. The columnist Yossi Klein provoked national outrage when he wrote in *Haaretz*, the newspaper identified with the Israeli secular left: "The Religious Zionists are dangerous, more dangerous than Hezbollah, hit-and-run drivers, or girls with scissors. Arabs can be 'neutralized'; Religious Zionists can't. What do they want? To take over the country and cleanse it of Arabs. If you ask them, they'll deny it. They know it's premature to be so candid. But don't believe their denials. Their religious nationalism is extreme nationalism wrapped in hypocritical fear of heaven. It percolates through the education system, grows stronger in the army, and even affects the Supreme Court. They're already headed our way; in another moment they'll be breaking down the door." The online version of the article featured a caricature by the cartoonist Eran Wolkowski, depicting a stereotypical Religious Zionist man in a knitted *kippa* pointing a gun through a Torah scroll. Like the Bnei Akiva movement, Klein and Wolkowski also saw the "Religious Zionists" as a single, ascendant monolith.

The Religious Zionists' newfound power, whether a blessing or a curse, is only part of the story. In reality, Israel's "new ruling elite" is being

---

4.   Tamar Hermann et al., *The Israeli Democracy Index 2017*, trans. Karen Gold (Jerusalem: Israel Democracy Institute, 2017), available at https://en.idi.org.il/media/10545/the-israeli-democracy-index-2017.pdf.

5.   Shavit, "Successors of Rabbi Kook Are Israel's New Ruling Elite."

heated from within and is quite close to the boiling point. Beneath the surface of what looks like a community on the rise, a fierce religious and cultural battle is raging. A battle that, as a journalist who has covered this story for two decades, I believe will be the most significant struggle within contemporary Judaism: one that pits observant Jews against other observant Jews.

In the summer of 2016, many Israelis heard that Rabbi Yigal Levinstein, the head of the flagship Bnei David pre-military academy in the West Bank settlement of Eli, gave a speech denouncing the IDF's tolerant attitude toward homosexuals, whom he called "perverts." Many also heard that in 2017 the same rabbi gave a class to young men who were about to enlist in the Israeli army, mocking female soldiers in combat roles. Levinstein denounced the enlistment of religious women, saying, "They've driven our girls crazy." Other rabbis at the academy also made headlines, including Rabbi Yosef Kalner, who told his students that "female spirituality is nonsense" and that females in positions of power were "femorillas."[6]

Such remarks are usually taken as evidence of a radicalization in the Religious Zionist community, but they are merely ripples across the surface of the water. Down below, beneath the seabed, the tectonic plates of Religious Zionism are rapidly shifting. The Orthodox world is in flux. To put it crudely, it is being redistributed along an axis from traditionalist to Haredi. The heritage of Rabbi Zvi Yehuda Kook, one of the founding fathers of this movement, whom we shall touch on later, never really enjoyed hegemonic status in Israeli religious society. And just as it seemed, in the view of outside observers, to be poised for total victory, it is actually losing its internal grip.

For years, the Land of Israel – or rather, the settlement movement in Judea, Samaria, and the Gaza Strip – was the Religious Zionists' chief political cause. The majority of the community saw the Jews' return to their ancient biblical heartland as an unmistakable sign that the era of messianic redemption was nearly upon us. Many Israelis, secular and religious alike, assumed that if anything might divide the Religious

---

6. A video clip from the lesson was broadcast on the nightly news on Channel 12 by religious affairs reporter Yair Cherki.

Zionists, it would be the heated battle over the settlement enterprise. But in recent years, fault lines have emerged elsewhere, on questions of culture and religion, synagogue and state, society and capitalism. The greater the consensus on the old topics of debate, the greater the dissent around the new issues.

Israel's four consecutive elections in 2019–2021 exposed just how much the iconic knitted *kippa* is fraying into its constituent religious and cultural threads. This cycle of national elections revealed the fault lines dividing the politicians identified with Religious Zionism: the cracks dividing liberal Orthodox and the more conservative group known as "Dati-Torani" or "national-Haredi"; and the cracks between liberals who wish to open up to the secular world, and the conservatives who wish to remain a self-isolated religious vanguard.

Politics is a window, but it offers only a limited view of the drama within the home. A more comprehensive look around the house reveals the sort of partitions that not only belie the notion of a single, unified, socio-political camp, but also call into question the notion of a single common identity or coherent religious denomination.

For nowadays, when someone speaks of "Religious Zionists," there is no escaping the question: *Which ones?* Which rabbis do they obey, if at all? Do they believe in equality, and specifically gender equality, and if so, to what extent? Are they in favor of having female religious leaders? Are they open to women-led synagogue services? What about women in the military? Are they willing to accept homosexuals as fully equal members of the community? What are their attitudes toward the Chief Rabbinate of Israel? What do they think about non-observant Jews? Haredi Jews? What about Reform and Conservative Jews, or members of other religions? How do they present themselves to the outside world, and how do they define themselves from an expanding menu of intra-communal identities? Questions of identity, ideology, and halakha are dividing the national-religious community from top to bottom and from side to side.

This unraveling is the proper context for understanding much of what is happening in Israel's religious Jewish society. It is also the epic story at the heart of this book. A story about religious lifestyles in a community that is losing its internal cohesion, torn between highly charged poles: the national-Haredi camp and the liberal-Orthodox one. In the middle ground there is a thriving mosaic of sects, including the "post-Orthodox," "the spectrum Orthodox," "the religious-lite," "the new traditionalists," "the selectively religious," "the bourgeois religious," and plain old national-religious. The definitions of these groups are hazy and in constant flux, but the proliferation of identities reveals that the Religious Zionist community is fraying into increasingly diverse and colorful threads.[7]

These transformations have not been peaceful. They have emerged from a culture war raging in the Religious Zionist world concerning the contours of religious law and of the religious community itself. They revolve around questions such as "What is Orthodox Judaism, and who gets to be included in it?" Both factions are essentially conservative: both place themselves squarely in an ancient tradition defined by God, the Torah, halakha, and binding authority. Their culture war is about shades of conservatism, about the balance between conservatism and other values, Jewish or otherwise. The culture war is being fought on the confined battlefield of the slightly-more and slightly-less conservative.

From the perspective of the more conservative faction, the greatest threat to all that is sacred to them is not secular society, as in the past, or the Reform and Conservative movements; it comes from fellow observant Jews, most of whom grew up like they did in Bnei Akiva, and all of whom identify as Orthodox – the rightful heirs of the small conservative denomination in Judaism.

In the summer of 2019, for example, the more conservative faction tried to block the appointment of Dr. Ayelet Seidler, a religious academic, to a position in the Israeli Education Ministry overseeing Bible studies in religious schools. Her opponents sent a blitz of anonymous text messages alleging that she wanted to introduce the study of

---

7. The Israel Democracy Institute's study on the national-religious sector revealed not only the power of the community, but also its internal fissures, breaking down into distinct core groups: the national-Haredi community (also known Dati-Torani) comprises 6 percent of the total population that identifies as national religious; the liberal-Orthodox comprise 12 percent; and plain-old "national-religious" make up 31 percent of the total.

Christian commentaries to the Hebrew Bible; one rabbi sent a letter of protest to Education Minister Rafi Peretz of the Jewish Home Party, a high-profile leader of the more conservative camp. The rabbi decried Dr. Seidler as "a woman whose thinking, lectures, and articles all take a secular-literary and critical academic approach." The revolt failed; Seidler got the job. But heads did roll: further up the chain, the official who appointed her, the head of religious education within the Education Ministry's national-religious wing, Dr. Avraham Lipsitz, who was disliked by many within the conservative camp, lost his job.

One year earlier, the liberal faction was incensed by a video released by Chotam, an umbrella organization associated with the more conservative faction. It smeared liberal religious groups, in the parlance of the community, by calling them agents of the New Israel Fund – an organization that is considered beyond the pale by many right-wing Israelis. The clip was the last and most provocative segment in a series that was produced to delegitimize liberal religious voices by linking them to an alleged anti-religious conspiracy. This offensive in the intra-religious culture war has continued to reverberate in an endless series of articles, social media debates, letters from rabbis, and sermons – supporting and opposing – from synagogue pulpits.

Local disagreements have also helped shine a light on the fissures running through the Religious Zionist world. Zeitlin High School in Tel Aviv, one of Israel's oldest religious boys' schools, opened a new track for liberal Orthodox girls. In 2018, this island of educational autonomy sparked a fierce dispute. Some teachers and parents were outraged by the appointment of Dr. Chana Friedman, a leading Orthodox feminist and supporter of LGBTQ rights, as the principal of the new girls-only track. Others grumbled about the newfangled curriculum, including Talmud studies – traditionally reserved for boys – and separate, female-led prayers. At the peak of the controversy, stickers appeared around the campus decrying the girls as "Reform" and as "goys." As the school descended into a religious, social, and political culture war, the Education Ministry officials in charge of the religious school system tried to sidestep the issue and project business as usual, even though in the knitted community, as it's sometimes known, there was no longer anything ordinary. By the summer, the principal of the boys' school, who had objected to the merger, had paid with his job. By winter, the girls' school was searching for new premises.

The ferocity of the debate is evident in the rhetoric used by community leaders in recent years. In 2009, Rabbi Yehoshua Shapira, the head of the Ramat Gan Hesder Yeshiva, blasted the leaders of the liberal-Orthodox movement as "neo-Reform." His comments were aimed at congregations that had embraced joint prayer quorums in which women could lead services, as well as rabbis who allowed unmarried women to use sperm donations. Shapira opined that the Religious Zionist world was on the brink of a "justified schism," which would overshadow the political split between the Religious Zionist parties.[8] In 2016, the chairman of the Jewish Home faction on the Jerusalem City Council, Dov Kalmanovitch, predicted: "In ten years, write this down, we'll find ourselves facing a huge Reform movement, joined by many devout Jews, including graduates of the state religious education system." This is the rhetoric. These are the sentiments. In both the spoken and written word, this is the wind that is blowing through the Religious Zionist camp.[9]

---

8. Rabbi Yehoshua Shapira's remarks were reported by Kobi Nachshoni on Ynet News. The report prompted Rabbi Eliyahu Zini, who taught at the Technion Israel Institute of Technology, to say, "They're not neo-Reform, but totally Reform.... We must urgently examine what has led us to this point, how to stop this spiritual hemorrhage."

9. Two separate organizations were set up in 2013 – Liba Yehudit and the Chotam Forum (an umbrella organization for various institutes and groups) – by national-Haredi rabbis with the express purpose of combating liberalization in Israeli society, especially in religious circles. The rabbis leading these organizations, and the donors bankrolling them, believe that the order of the day is to fight for what they consider "authentic" Jewish identity, through position papers, public campaigns, and investigations against their ideological rivals. Their foes include religious organizations at the other end of the spectrum, such as the feminist Kolech, the private kosher certification initiative Hashgacha Pratit, the liberal Orthodox Ne'emanei Torah Va'Avodah, the liberal religious advocacy organization ITIM, and others. These organizations will appear throughout this book in various contexts, but for now we note that they all work in fields that touch on questions of religious law. Chotam's campaign against groups and activists supported by the New Israel Fund in 2018 was the most blatant example of its battle against liberal organizations.

The Religious Zionist community usually attracts Israeli public interest in the context of politics. The settlement enterprise, after all, has been the number one priority for two generations of Religious Zionist leaders and remains a fundamental bone of contention in Israeli society. Recently, Israelis have started noting the proliferation of Religious Zionists in positions of power – counting the *kippot* (and headscarves) in the Prime Minister's Office, the Knesset, the IDF top brass, the media, and the Supreme Court. This too is an extension of politics – a focus on the sectors of Israeli society and their relative power.

But these tired debates, which religious and secular Israelis are so eager to recycle, ignore a whole world of content that interests and concerns religious men and women: the world of religious practice. It is impossible to understand Israeli society, and certainly its religious society, without this. Yet even the most rigorous reporters and authors, standing at the ramparts of Israeli society, tend to overlook this critical dimension of religious Israelis' lives, downplaying it, or reducing it to a simple story about power relations. The discourse about "religionization," for example, treats the practice of religion as a sideshow for the main event – the coercion that religious Israelis allegedly plan to inflict on their secular brethren. Questions of identity and faith, religious law and *Yiddishkeit* – the core issues within the knitted community, the ingredients which define its internal relations and its relations with the outside world – are largely absent from discussions of religious society.

This book places religion, and the related concerns of religious Israelis, center stage.

For many national-religious Israelis, their nationalism is undoubtedly an integral component of their Judaism. But this book will barely address their Zionist politics. The question is not about their brand of nationalism – their attitudes to the State of Israel and the settlement enterprise – but their brand of religion.

Over the next few pages I'd like to sketch out a rough guide to the forces fueling the struggles within Religious Zionism today, a broad topographical map of the issues at hand. The Religious Zionists form an ideological and religious movement with considerable pedigree, enmeshed in a complicated web of relationships with religious and non-religious groups alike, past and present; a current snapshot of the Religious Zionist community includes a plethora of key figures, ideas, political parties, organizations, and events, all of which are pertinent to a discussion about the community's religiosity. For now, for the sake of clarity, I will paint the story in broad brushstrokes, illustrating mainly that which is necessary in order to proceed to the following chapters, where I'll more vividly chart the ideological fissures that have riven this society.

PRIVATIZATION

Many take the measure of the Religious Zionist community with a ruler that has moderation on one end and radicalization on the other. Expressions of radicalization have flourished in recent years, especially in regard to sexual matters, which are all placed under the banner of "modesty." Some branches of Bnei Akiva, a co-ed youth movement, have imposed a separation between boys and girls. Some national-Haredi schools have dramatically cut back on the core curriculum in favor of religious content, and their rabbis are demanding greater censorship of general literature, including ordinary children's books. In the summer of 2018, the Ramat Gan Yeshiva, which belongs to this more conservative faction, presented the public with an innovation at its annual conference: men and women would be kept apart not only in the lecture halls, but also in the elevators.

In most cases these episodes attest not to a general radicalization, but a radicalization among the already radical. Those who build the highest barriers, wishing to live within the walls of their own fortifications, toil to make them even higher. This conservative camp is the politically dominant faction, and it is a faction that has often enjoyed government support, but it does not represent the majority of Israel's religious population. In this culture war, the liberal and conservative extremes represent two separate poles, and the battle for the center-ground has not yet been won – or rather, sometimes one side wins on a particular issue, and sometimes the other side prevails.

But rather than radicalization or moderation, the main force within Religious Zionism is privatization. It affects the liberal flank no less than its conservative counterpart. In order to understand these processes and upheavals, I propose regarding the national-religious community – especially after the trauma of the Disengagement from the Gaza Strip in 2005 – as a centralized economy that has, over time, turned toward the free market. Needless to say, there is a global context: the whole world is in the throes of a crisis of authority and legitimacy, old borders dissolved, hierarchies erased.

Similarly, Israel's religious monopolies are collapsing. Much of their power is shifting from the establishment to religious entrepreneurs and "consumers." Among these declining monopolies is the Chief Rabbinate of Israel, which has deep theological roots within the Religious Zionist community, but is today, internally speaking, a controversial institution, and the Mercaz HaRav Yeshiva in Jerusalem, which exercised a direct and indirect influence on the whole national-religious community for decades. Have other rabbis replaced these monopolies? Have new hegemonic institutions taken their place? It's complicated. There are new Religious Zionist "corporations," such as Yeshivat Har Hamor and a raft of pre-military academies, but like the most influential rabbis of the generation, they play a somewhat different role from their predecessors. The system has changed.

When new ideas emerge and old ideas are cast into doubt, the privatized market becomes a place of ideological and religious ferment. As the Religious Zionist enterprise expanded and diversified, as it became more politically and culturally powerful, as many of its members gained self-confidence, something almost paradoxical occurred: it became less religiously cohesive. No longer can rabbis, politicians, or youth movements claim exclusive control of the narrative.

But the revolutionary element of this wave of privatization is not to be found in discourse and debate; it resides in religious practice, in the way people worship and serve God: in prayer, in marriage, in the observance of dietary laws, and in their customs regarding the ritual baths. Terms such as competition, private initiative, freedom of choice, and self-determination have penetrated into the realm of the religious world in Israel. The same is true of equality. In this privatized world, each religious subgroup defines its own limits on the boundaries of religious law. Behind the self-classification of being "religious" or "Orthodox" lies a more diverse array of identities and behaviors than ever before. All across Israel's religious society, this is the privatization generation.

Kvutzat Yavne, near Ashdod, is known as the "mother of religious kib-butzim." It is an economically and socially successful collective and one of the few kibbutzim – secular and religious alike – to have survived a wave of privatizations. But shortly after becoming the community's religious leader, Rabbi Ilay Ofran told me that the first enterprise to be privatized in Kvutzat Yavne would be the synagogue. Not the dairy farm, or the communal dining areas, or the animal feed production plant, or even the pickle factory – but the house of prayer, which was supposed to serve the entire kibbutz as a collectivist community.

Kvutzat Yavne was founded in 1941 by German-Jewish immigrants and became a symbol of success. It neither succumbed to the winds of change nor diverged from its austere founders' defining values. But it may struggle to absorb without change the recent multiplicity of Jew-ish religious identities.

In recent years, families on the kibbutz have started asking for permission to hold their own one-off services in which, for example, girls might celebrate their bat mitzva by reading from the Torah. Such bat mitzvas are increasingly common in Israeli cities and even some communal villages and towns but remain far from conventional in most Orthodox communities. The first families did not even ask to use the synagogue, just a separate hall, and Ofran chose not to resist. Perhaps he understood which way the winds were blowing. In this bastion of conservatism and idealism, the greatest challenge would be to preserve religious cohesion.

The rabbi's forecast of privatization was realized faster than expected. Within just a few years, after a series of stormy debates and kibbutz-wide policy meetings, new prayer quorums, all a departure from the founders' norms, started to crop up. The first was a "partner-ship *minyan*" that met every few weeks on Shabbat, in which women read from the Torah and led some of the prayer services. Ofran moni-tored the process, declining to veto any side of the argument. Once the dam burst, it was inevitable that a third quorum would arise. In another departure from the founders' vision, this one included the recitation of the Priestly Blessing on all days of the week, as is com-mon in Israel, and not just on Shabbat and festivals, as the kibbutz founders had done.

In a synagogue, in any synagogue, changes are major events, and the changes at Kvutzat Yavne did not pass without protest in kibbutz member meetings and in opinion pieces penned for the local newsletter. "Do we really want to resemble Conservative communities in Israel and abroad?" asked one opponent of the partnership *minyan*.

But the time for change had come. The prayer services dictated by the kibbutz founders more than eighty years earlier were no longer the only form on offer. It's a brutal game at which no one can win, Ofran said after the fact. "If Kvutzat Yavne doesn't manage to change, there will be no more good old Yavne," he explained, "and if it does change, it will no longer be good old Yavne." The winds of religious privatization swept through even this culturally homogeneous, collectivist community.

The upheavals that rocked Kvutzat Yavne are transforming many other Religious Zionist communities, including those that are led by a rabbi and those that are not. The status quo is changing, and the pioneers of those changes often have no formal or traditional authority to assume this role: they are not rabbis. Sometimes the trailblazers are ordinary men and women, well versed in halakha and Jewish texts. Rabbis no longer are the sole bearers of the treasure chest of Torah knowledge, and to extend the privatization metaphor, the "religious capital" has been diversified across the board, spread throughout the community thanks to generations of graduates of yeshivas, women's seminaries, and academic Jewish Studies programs, as well as unrestricted access to religious literature online. Men and women without rabbinic ordination are insisting on interpreting halakha for themselves, or at least on following their conscience.

For Rabbi Ofran, this period is reminiscent of the greatest Jewish religious revolution of all – the aftermath of the destruction of the Second Temple in 70 CE, when Judaism changed from being a religion of sacrifices to one of Torah scholarship, prayer, and religious observance. Rabbi Yoḥanan ben Zakkai "privatized Temple Judaism and transferred it to everyone's personal domain," he said, speaking of the monumental first-century sage who refocused Jewish life on study and prayer in Yavne after the Romans destroyed the Temple in Jerusalem. "He saved Judaism but transformed it completely. We lost a lot because of him, but there was no alternative." And yet, there is a difference: "Even after

Rabbi Yoḥanan ben Zakkai's privatization, there was still an accepted regulator – the Sages. Nowadays, there is no accepted regulator."

Privatization did not come out of thin air. It was the result of a new, volatile, religious discourse at odds with the traditional conception of halakha. Jewish religious law, to put it bluntly, demands devotion. It is total and hierarchical; it sets red lines; it determines who is in and who is out; and for the most part, it cares little about the sensitivities of individuals and minorities who may feel excluded, marginalized, or oppressed.

The greatest challenge to this mentality over the past two generations has come predominantly from within the ranks of Orthodox feminism, which first sprouted as a fringe movement in American Jewish life and is currently surging into the mainstream of Israel's national-religious scene. Orthodox feminists did not demand, at least initially, that religious law be altered. One founding mother of Orthodox feminism in the United States, Blu Greenberg, famously said: "Where there's a rabbinic will, there's a halakhic way." Their activism to promote women in leadership positions and liberate others trapped in miserable conditions, such as those refused a religious divorce by their husbands, was often quite conservative in terms of its interpretation of religious law.

But Orthodox feminism contains a fissile core: namely, its discourse about rights and self-determination for individuals and for groups within the larger society. It has championed the overarching value, which is not to be taken for granted, that all humans are created equal. Following in their wake, LGBTQ groups and individuals and others started demanding recognition and a voice in Orthodox communal frameworks. They wished to remain inside the ideological and practical boundaries of the religious community while remaining true to themselves. Some Orthodox Jews felt religiously obligated to accede to these demands; others maintained they had a religious duty to reject them. To insist on certain red lines. This is the core of the dispute.

Makor Rishon, Israel's leading national-religious newspaper, caused a stir in 2013 with a feature on young religious Israelis, including some famous individuals, who took a selective approach to religious observance and even texted on Shabbat. It came as a surprise to no one that some members of the community were hardly sticklers for the rules, but the report and the ensuing uproar hinted that something new was afoot: these "new traditionalists" were out and proud about violating Shabbat but still insisted on claiming a legitimate place in religious society. Four years later, Channel 10 reporter Akiva Novick aired a report showing how widespread this phenomenon had become, introducing the wider public to those who identified as "on the religious spectrum," a newly charted swath of gray between "religious" and "formerly religious." Orthodox Jews who are "on the religious spectrum" are open to the secular lifestyle, with the possible exception of publicly violating Shabbat, but remain within the blurry boundaries of the knitted community.

Until fairly recently, the natural choice for sinners and heretics was to abandon religion, leave their religious communities, and become "formerly religious" – or *datlash*, to use the common Hebrew acronym.[10] Another option was simply to accept a socially inferior status. Now, however, they are demanding, often successfully, a place of their own in religious society. Unmarried religious men and women who text on Shabbat or have pre-marital sexual relations no longer feel that they have no place in the synagogue. It takes two to tango: the sinners and Shabbat-texters do not want to leave the community, and the community, for the most part, no matter how much some members disapprove, refuses to throw them out.

This "soft" religiosity, which is not the focus of this book, would probably not have rankled the more conservative members of the religious camp had they not noted that even devoted Orthodox Jews were

---

10. In the spring of 2018, an educational-theological debate about the boundaries of halakha erupted at Yeshivat Otniel. One of the more senior rabbis announced that he would scale back his own attendance at the yeshiva in protest against an article published in its internal newsletter by a fellow educator promoting inclusion, including of students who had lost their faith in God. The teacher had written to the parents and rabbis: "If someone comes to you and says he thinks there's no such thing as divine providence, or prophecy, or God, or that the Jews are not the Chosen People – don't tell him he's a heretic. He may believe that he has no place in Orthodox Judaism, but you can always tell him that he agrees with Maimonides, or with much more radical Jewish philosophers. The truth is that there have been many wiser figures who thought just like him and remained practicing religious Jews, and there's no reason for him not to follow this path." The senior rabbi protested that the yeshiva was failing to set red lines against what he saw as heresy.

accommodating these dissenting voices. The Orthodox status quo is under assault not just from those who are culturally committed to Judaism yet take a more lenient approach to religious law – but also from those who are fully committed to the Orthodox Jewish way of life.

In the summer of 2016, many religious men and women sought to protest Rabbi Levinstein's speech denouncing homosexuals as "perverts." Hundreds of them joined the Gay Pride Parade in Jerusalem. Around the same time, three hundred rabbis signed a statement of support for Rabbi Levinstein, writing that "rabbis in Israel have a duty to address halakhic or moral issues clearly and bluntly." For the latter group, Judaism sets red lines. For the former group, Judaism permits and perhaps even demands interpretive flexibility and the inclusion of minority groups. For the conservative wing of the religious camp, male homosexuality is an "abomination," as per Leviticus. For the progressive wing, this attitude is a reflection of homophobia. Both camps emerged from the same population, but with time they are increasingly incapable of understanding each other's language.

THE DISENGAGEMENT

in June 2005, I stood among a thousand people in mass prayer in Neve Dekalim, the largest community in Gush Katif – the cluster of Israeli settlements in the southern Gaza Strip. The Israeli military was about to carry out the Gaza Disengagement and unilaterally withdraw troops and settlers from the Gaza Strip, forcibly dismantling twenty-one Jewish communities and evicting some eight thousand civilians. Next to the commercial center, in the glow of a setting sun, a huge crowd gathered to cry out to the heavens. Local residents had come seeking a boost in morale, hoping that by reciting Psalms and blowing a shofar they could cancel the decree of withdrawal, which had already been approved by the Israeli government and the Knesset.

Israel's elderly chief rabbi, Mordechai Eliyahu, widely seen as the spiritual leader of Religious Zionism, climbed up onto the stage. He urged the doubters to stay strong, guaranteeing or promising that the withdrawal would not go ahead as planned. "It shall not be," he chanted three times, repeating the mantra that many took to be a sacred vow, and others reinterpreted in hindsight as something more of a wish. For within two months, "it" did indeed happen. Neve Dekalim was laid waste, its houses demolished. Rabbi Eliyahu died five years later. Never since has anyone been called "the spiritual leader of Religious Zionism."

The national-religious community had experienced political upheavals before: the withdrawal from Sinai, the murder of Prime Minister Yitzhak Rabin (by one of their own), the waves of terror. But none of these came close to the trauma of the great eviction of 2005. Something snapped, especially for the younger generation, and especially in its regard for the state and its leadership and the process of messianic redemption, which, they had always been taught, was meant to progress and certainly not regress.

The Disengagement did not create the divisions in the Religious Zionist world, but almost all of them were sparked or intensified in the years that followed. The atmosphere of crisis fanned the flames. It was only after 2005 that controversial religious fashions forced their way from the margins into the mainstream – from the Temple Mount movement, which demands Jewish prayer rights on the Temple Mount, to the partnership *minyanim*. The political rift between conservatives and liberals deepened after the Disengagement. In many respects, the rubble of Gush Katif was ground zero of the Religious Zionism of today. It was a turning point, separating the world before from that which emerged afterward.

By the end of the summer of 2005, thousands of Israeli evacuees were left emotionally crushed and homeless, but even worse – defenseless, with no conviction left unshaken. This may be one of the reasons why rhetoric about the Jewish people, the Land of Israel, the settlements, and the longed-for redemption – causes that have excited the Religious Zionist imagination since at least the first attempt to settle Sebastia in the mid-seventies – slipped off the agenda. It was replaced, at least outwardly, by a litany of grievances about government failures to rehabilitate the evacuees, about temporary solutions that became permanent, and about compensation that was never paid or did not go far enough. Without getting into the merits of these complaints, it is important to note that the big buzzwords – destiny, mission, devotion, good and evil – were supplanted by a long list of injustices. Without a formal leadership, the evacuees demanded their rights from the government or perhaps the nation. The discourse of individual rights seeped into the political debate about the settlements, and for Religious Zionists, this was a significant novelty.

Naturally, the language of rights focuses on individuals and minority groups and not on the collective. And it can be heard from surprising quarters, not just from the women's gallery in synagogues. For example, the rhetoric of the Temple Mount movement, which is making its way into the national-religious consensus, is replete with arguments about individual freedom of worship. Ever since Israel conquered the Old City of Jerusalem from Jordan in 1967, it has banned Jews from praying on the Temple Mount. The activists are using the language of rights to challenge this restriction. Even though we are a minority, they claim, we have rights. Another common argument: If progressive values dictate that the Women of the Wall have a right to pray at the Western Wall as they wish, with Torah scrolls and tefillin, why should Jews who wish to sway in silent prayer on the Temple Mount have their rights infringed upon?

YESHIVAS

In the beginning there was Mercaz HaRav. The yeshiva was founded by Rabbi Avraham Yitkzhak HaKohen Kook and later passed to the leadership of his son, Rabbi Zvi Yehuda. The Mercaz – "the Center" – was much more than a yeshiva. It was the most influential higher education institute in the Religious Zionist world, an incubator in which its revolutionary messianic philosophy was refined and the theology of the settlement movement was born. A whole generation of rabbis and leaders of the religious right passed through its ranks. Then, after nearly seventy years, Har Hamor was founded as a breakaway institution, following a leadership struggle combined with an ideological spat. Led by Rabbi Zvi Thau, the splitters protested a decision to open a teacher training academy alongside the main yeshiva, which would offer instruction not just in religion but pedagogical studies.

Like Rabbi Zvi Yehuda Kook, Har Hamor also treated the secular state of Israel and its institutions with sacred reverence. It too became a superpower, surrounded by a satellite network of yeshivas and women's seminaries known as *yeshivot hakav*: the "line yeshivas." These institutions sent clusters of dedicated religious families (each was known as a *garin torani*: a Torah-based nucleus) to settle underdeveloped areas, and whole communities in Israeli settlements and towns were molded in their conservative image. In time, the Har Hamor network's influence on Religious Zionist elites surpassed that of the original yeshiva, Mercaz HaRav. Its more isolationist approach – its hostility to general studies, opposition to liberal values, and stringency on matters of "modesty" – was embraced, in a more diluted form, by pre-military academies associated with Har Hamor, which would gain a critical influence on many young Israelis before their military service.

Mercaz remained an icon; Har Hamor, thanks to its pre-military academies and *garin torani* system, became the more politically powerful. But both yeshivas, adhering to the ideological teachings of Rabbi Zvi Yehuda Kook, maintain a sort of monopoly on the waning spiritual leadership of the Religious Zionist camp.

The religious scene is full of yeshivas and communities that have never been "Team Mercaz" or "Team Har Hamor." Much of the national-religious public has rejected the stringent religious demands and general conservatism of the leading rabbis of those institutions. The two "flagships" have always sailed alongside much smaller vessels, which were never particularly interested in Rabbi Kook's brand of messianism. Yeshivat Har Etzion, known colloquially in the US as "the Gush," has always been more focused on scholarship and open to modern academic thought. There is also the Religious Kibbutz Movement and local institutions, such as the Pelech Religious Experimental School for girls and the Shalom Hartman Institute, both in Jerusalem. But none could hold a candle to the dominance of Mercaz HaRav till a new, exciting movement – Hasidic in nature – emerged from within the yeshiva world itself.

At the vanguard of the revolution were three teachers – Rabbi Shimon Gershon Rosenberg, Rabbi Menachem Froman, and Rabbi Adin Steinsaltz – who built Hasidic-like institutions within the national-religious community. The three, all of whom have since passed away, encouraged women to study Talmud, which was bold in the 1980s but not altogether unprecedented. Instead, the heart of the teaching they tried to convey was based on sincerity, religious intensity, and individualism. This was a departure from the collectivist goals and personal restraint taught by Mercaz HaRav. Hasidic Zionism, as advanced by these rabbis, took a conservative approach to Jewish law but encouraged in its students doubt about the possibility of absolute truth. It nurtured personal and emotional self-expression in religious worship and study (Rabbi Rosenberg, in his scholarship, focused on religious life in a postmodern world).

Rabbi Zvi Yehuda Kook took a dim view of the Hasidic Zionist focus on individual worship; Mercaz HaRav placed the grand themes of the people of Israel and the Land of Israel above private spiritual affairs. Yet the success of Hasidic Zionism pointed to a weariness within the national-religious world, a fatigue with its sectarian wrangling about existential political issues and an appetite for spiritual renewal. This aspiration was common to many twentieth-century Jewish thinkers, from Martin Buber to the American progressive movements. And in this way the pioneering trio of Rosenberg, Froman, and Steinsaltz brought neo-Hasidic spirituality to the beating heart of the Religious Zionist world.

Even if it was not their original intent, it's easy to see how a spiritual focus on individual worship coincided with a growing legitimacy given to the proliferation of independent religious voices. It was this shift that paved the way for women to recite the Mourner's Kaddish over loved ones, a practice that Rabbi Froman supported in the settlement of Tekoa, where he was the local chief rabbi.

Hasidic Zionism emphasized the individual as much as the community and the Jewish national collective. Hasidic Zionist yeshivas started teaching not only Talmud and Rabbi Kook's messianic thought, but also classic Hasidic texts and poetry (including writings by Rabbi Kook the elder that were downplayed, if not censored, by his son's generation); they taught Jewish melodies and music; and they focused on the experiential side of prayer. This new language served, indirectly, to weaken the grip of Mercaz HaRav (the alma mater of both Rosenberg and Froman), and to shift the center of gravity to a new network of national-religious yeshivas that responded to the Hasidic calling. Among them was Yeshivat Otniel, which became one of the biggest in the Religious Zionist world, the Makor Chaim Yeshiva, and many more.

When Rabbi Froman died in 2013, some six years after Rabbi Rosenberg, he left behind a national-religious world transformed from what he had known in his youth. A world in which superlative titles such as "leaders of Religious Zionism" and "the most senior rabbis" started to sound anachronistic. The Mercaz was no longer the center. Its monopoly had been crushed.

URBANISM

The city of Jerusalem, between Mercaz HaRav in the north and Har Hamor in the south, offers a smorgasbord of religious choices, liberal and conservative alike. The Israeli capital is the main laboratory of the religious Jewish world, and practically every spiritual trend in contemporary Orthodox synagogues and in religious life has sprouted in its soil.

Jerusalem is the home of the Chief Rabbinate and many of the dynastic Hasidic courts and a large Orthodox Jewish population. Precisely because it is so vast, the margins are so wide. Some neighborhoods have produced urban varieties of Judaism that exist nowhere else in the Jewish world, including an eclectic array of religious academies and diverse forms of spirituality, from the Secular Yeshiva to the radical Hasidic sect of Toldos Aharon. It is a colorful entrepôt, a hub of religious innovation. While rural communities might have a few lone synagogues (or one central synagogue, with a fixed way of doing things), Orthodox Jews in the big city are free to take their pick and sample different synagogues without committing exclusively to any particular community. This is a new conception of religious identity and belonging, which accepts that people are free to move around and be flexible, popping up here one Shabbat and there on a specific holiday – just like urbanites in any big city are free to move between cultural institutions, bars, and cafes.

New prayer services can spring up in a big city without provoking resistance. Shira Hadasha, the first self-identifying Orthodox congregation in which women could lead services, emerged from the conservative city of Jerusalem. It started inside a liberal Ashkenazic bubble and has proliferated widely. The small community in the German Colony of Jerusalem, populated mostly by new immigrants from the United States or their children, went from being a local neighborhood affair to a genuine global trendsetter. Part of the reason was that the synagogue drew visitors from all across the world. Tourism made the Shira Hadasha model global. That said, these avant-garde *minyanim*, whether in Melbourne or Modiin, have thrived mostly in upper-class, largely Ashkenazic communities. The significance of this, in a country that is so Jewishly diverse, is certainly worth exploring in greater detail, but for now we may say that those who expected, or hoped, that the moderate and accepting nature of the Sephardic Jewish tradition would lead to a bridge between those communities and the communities of religious liberalism, were mistaken. One apparent barrier is the autonomy and individualism evident in this new religious scene, elements that clash openly with the principle of *emunat ḥakhamim*, or faith in the learned, a central element in religion in general and in the traditionalist Sephardic communities especially. It will be compelling to see whether the prevalence of the avant-garde *minyanim* in certain mainstream schools, for example, will have an effect on communities outside of its current sociological bubble.

The urban bubble dynamic was at play with the advent of alternative *kashrut* services, too, in which the official rabbinate's monopoly on certifying kosher food and restaurants was openly defied. It started as a local Jerusalemite initiative, based on trust and born of frustration with the rabbinic establishment. Slowly but surely, the initiative branched out of Jerusalem until in 2018, it made its big exit, backed by the Tzohar organization of Religious Zionist rabbis, and presented a serious challenge to the rabbinate's monopoly on kosher certifications.

Many of the developments described in this book began in small social bubbles in Jerusalem, and then expanded or were exported in a kind of "globalization" process of religious taste. Israel's Chief Rabbinate and local rabbinic councils did their utmost to thwart many of these initiatives and safeguard their monopoly, whether by penalizing wayward communities with budget cuts or slapping fines on restaurants that used private kosher certification. There are surely many battles ahead. But the rabbinate and its acolytes discovered in Jerusalem that their powers to police a metropolis are very limited indeed.

NETWORKS

This introduction would be incomplete without touching on the decisive impact of the internet on the Religious Zionist community. Social media has been one of the main drivers of the privatization of religious authority. It has blurred hierarchies and geographic and communal borders; it has connected people and groups who would previously have never known of each other's existence; and it has given outsized prominence to fringe groups, on both the left and right. Thanks to the internet, rabbis' lessons with students in pre-military academies are now regularly shared with the wider public online, knocking down the walls of the study hall and exposing rabbis to public criticism.

In 2012, a closed group appeared on Facebook called "I'm a *religious* feminist, and I too lack a sense of humor." Deborah Aroshas, one of the group founders, wrote a post early on that surprised many of the other members and led to internal debate and fissures within the group. Her bottom line was that feminism and Judaism can no longer go hand in hand. "It's true, we saw the smoke screen," she wrote, but "we told ourselves that so long as we spotted it and pointed it out – then we'd managed to beat the system. But we missed the main point: the very existence of this forum here is in and of itself another smoke screen across the surface of reality: a reality of inherent, basic, and essential inequality between man and woman in Judaism. This group itself is like a relaxant drug, anesthetizing and dulling, screening."

The group's membership skyrocketed as it fostered an open conversation about the role of women in halakha and within the national-religious community. It later spawned several spin-off religious groups before finally closing in May 2021.

The first Orthodox Jewish feminists came mostly from liberal hothouses in Jerusalem and New York in the 1970s and were treated as radical fringe elements. Many women from these "wilderness years" of Orthodox feminism paid a social price for their opinions or activism. Orthodox feminism existed on the margins and certainly did not threaten the national-religious status quo. But with some 16,000 male and female members, the "I'm a *religious* feminist" Facebook group is a little public square of its own, hosting critical and often seething discussions about education for religious girls, increasingly strict "modesty" requirements at religious institutions and youth movements, the role of women behind the *meḥitza* (partition) in synagogues, men who refuse to grant their wives a divorce, and sexual abuse. The group is also a meeting place for biting discussions about rabbis' comments. It has even contributed a new word to the national-religious argot: *fadlaḥushiyot*, the Hebrew acronym of "humorless religious feminists." This group and others, such as the more conservative "Halakhic Feminists," brought feminist discourse into the homes of national-religious Facebook users across Israel and expedited the maturation of religious Jewish feminism the world over. These groups cultivated a new agenda from the bottom up, often without the rabbis knowing or understanding what was growing right under their noses.[11]

Thanks to Facebook groups, Simḥat Torah has become an unmistakably feminist holiday in the Religious Zionist world. Every year there are dozens of posts about which synagogues plan to allow women to dance holding Torah scrolls, and which intend to be even more audacious and let women *read* from the Torah, whether in front of a limited audience of women or the whole congregation.

As soon as night fell on Simḥat Torah in 2016, one woman took to "Halakhic Feminists" to describe dancing with a Torah scroll as "a strong feeling of the messianic age … truly! An excitement that hasn't abated." She reported to her friends: "It was moving and meaningful, personal and feminine, full of new, refreshing voices. Exciting ideas that could make you cry. Women going up to read from the Torah (history! 'Fear and trembling,' honestly. In tears and choking up, couldn't even finish the blessing!). For the *hakafot shniyot* [the procession with Torah scrolls at nightfall after Simḥat Torah], a Torah scroll was passed over

---

11. Events in 2016 proved the power of social media. The Israeli reporter Roy Sharon revealed in an exposé on Channel 10 that the head of the Gush Etzion Regional Council, Davidi Perl, had paid hush money to a woman who had accused him of sexual harassment, as part of a deal reached through mediation by the Forum Takana, which includes rabbis and other public officials. Even after the deal became public, local rabbis stuck by the deal and their support for Davidi, but then the Facebook group of religious feminists swooped in. The unrest online spilled over into the real world, and Perl was ultimately forced to resign, despite the support of rabbis and other public officials.

the partition and stayed with us the whole time. Girls, young women from Bnei Akiva, mothers, grandmothers. The whole community stayed on its feet dancing. Our girls (and boys!) will treat this as obvious, like it always should have been. I watched from the side for a moment, my face hurting from all the smiling, and I was amazed. *This is the day G-d made, let us exult and rejoice in it!"* She posted this from her personal account with her full name and picture, from her home in Kfar HaRo'eh, a religious community that hosts a Bnei Akiva flagship yeshiva that has produced some of the previous generation's leading rabbis. She thanked the group for giving her "so much strength to dream and create change," and the next day, she updated her post, noting the insults she'd heard from neighbors.

This is but one example, regarding Orthodox feminism. But social media plays a role in practically every form of religious revolt against the rabbinic establishment.

What has changed? Social networks are, by their nature, social – places for the masses to talk, listen, react, and share content. Official position holders in the real world have no inherent advantage on Facebook or Twitter. The rules of the game are such that national-religious Facebook groups, with their countless members, are a powerful force preventing rabbis from regulating the conversation. The constant stream of public posts creates an ongoing dialogue between the demands of the rabbis and the personal wishes of their congregants. These groups are a steady and religiously explosive source of friction, as ordinary people are pushing new values, aspirations, and fiercely critical language all the way to the top, with a knock-on effect for fellow citizens' religious behavior. Facebook has allowed a critical religious discourse, which for years was confined to liberal academic circles in Jerusalem, to spread like wildfire and define the Orthodox conversation from liberal Tel Aviv to conservative settlements in Samaria, including communities where the rabbinic leadership is vehemently opposed to these new trends.[12]

---

12. The national-religious media scene had grown before the age of Facebook and Twitter, long before the Disengagement, with the popular Jewish channel on the NRG website, which discussed a range of issues from being single in the religious world to leisure culture. Later, the *Makor Rishon* newspaper launched its *Motzash*

Not everyone has joined the conversation. The feed is still a relatively elitist and Ashkenazic place. Nevertheless, or perhaps therefore, it can no longer be ignored. The internet, social media, and YouTube are changing the religious marketplace in Israel, mostly to the rabbis' detriment: the rabbi of a pre-military academy in a West Bank settlement might become the top story on the nightly news because someone posted a video of him saying something derogatory about women or homosexuals or non-Jews. Social media can also be a boon: an unknown rabbi from a remote community can become an internet sensation if he is sharp-witted, snappy, and understands the medium. The current era has turned some rabbis into online personalities, such as Chaim Navon from Modiin, Amnon Bazak from Yeshivat Har Etzion, and Avraham Stav who teaches at the Sha'arei Tzion *beit midrash* for city rabbis. When they first studied the ins-and-outs of Jewish law in yeshiva, there was no such thing as an "influencer" and they had no idea what it meant to have tens of thousands of online followers. But they learned fast.

Will the polemics in the Religious Zionist community, specifically around the role of women and rabbinic authority, necessarily trigger a religious and tribal schism, resulting in two distinct denominations? Or will a desire for reconciliation, a devotion to *shlom bayit* (peace within the home), win the day and bring the arguments down to a simmer, as often happens in religious communities? What changes are in flux within Orthodox Judaism? How long can the label of "Orthodox" continue to apply to both a married, full-time yeshiva student at Mercaz HaRav and a woman wearing a tallit and reading from the Torah in a Tel Aviv or Jerusalem synagogue?

It is too early to declare that the Religious Zionist world has split forever, but it is essential to understand this challenging period in the annals of the religious community.

To my mind, this is the scene of the most important and intriguing culture war in the contemporary Jewish world. It is not a war of

---

weekend magazine, which gave a permanent voice to millennials and their concerns. There were also more serious publications, such as the *Akdamot* and *De'ot* journals, and *Makor Rishon*'s weekend supplement, *Shabbat*.

succession or a battle for hegemony, as often happens in some Haredi communities, and it is not a conflict fueled by economic or material interests or a thirst for power. It is a struggle over opinions and principles, articles of faith and ideals. A battle over values between two brands of conservatism, between participants who almost all still self-identify with the derivative of a single word that comes to us from the Greek: Orthodoxy.

Chapter III

The End of the Rabbinic Era

For a moment, there was a genuine fear that the young men in the big woolen *kippot* would wreak havoc – not on the Israeli soldiers hunkering down in their vehicle, its tires slashed and windows broken, but on the elderly rabbi who was trying to calm the situation. It was just after midnight and a hot summer's wind swept through the road outside the biggest Jewish settlement in the Gaza Strip, Neve Dekalim, two and a half days before the withdrawal in August 2005. Rabbi Shlomo Aviner, the head of a well-known yeshiva and one of the biggest names in Religious Zionism, had come to Gush Katif from his home in the West Bank settlement of Beit El precisely to contain situations like these, in which the fanatics were liable to dictate the height of the flames.

The rabbi had set out in the dead of night toward the main road outside the settlement, hoping to persuade the enraged youth to clear the way and let the Israeli army evacuate the trapped jeep. But they refused and the situation escalated. "We can't fight a two-headed battle, we mustn't quarrel!" he shouted. "There are rabbis here in these settlements.

They decided that tires are not to be slashed, so don't slash tires! If you don't listen to the rabbis, how can you expect the national leadership to listen to them? Please, let this vehicle through."

Several youths retreated; others refused. "My rabbi told me to stay put!" someone shouted, and then suddenly, without warning, someone shoved Rabbi Aviner. The rabbi, sweating and red in the face, grabbed the assailant, or his friend, I can't remember which, and hollered: "Do you obey your rabbis, or not?!" He repeated this cry again and again, refusing to release the young man from his clutches.

I was on the ground in Gush Katif in the moment of truth, and it was an event I shall never forget. It exposed a vast gulf between the ideal of respect for rabbis, which both the Israeli public and their national leaders supposedly held dear, and the ugly truth, which would play out in the barrage of curses that the youngsters rained on the rabbi. Aviner's failure was twofold. He did not manage to get the situation under control, and he did not manage to play his trump card – his rabbinical status, which fell battered and bruised to the hot asphalt. His failure, understandable as it might have been in the tumultuous circumstances (and it is notable that there was relatively little violence during the withdrawal), raised some questions: Can the rabbis still demand total deference from the national-religious community, and if so, in what circumstances? Is Rabbi Aviner's question ("Do you obey your rabbis, or not?!") still relevant to the lives of religious Israeli youths and what significance do the leadership titles regularly affixed to the names of people like Aviner even have in today's world?

At first glance, the status of the rabbis in Israel in on the rise. Every year, hundreds of yeshiva graduates take the Chief Rabbinate's exams and receive rabbinic ordination. Some find communities in Israel and enjoy the privilege of presiding over a synagogue, for a modest salary or on a voluntary basis. Others join the education system. Most religious kibbutzim have scrapped their old rule against employing spiritual leaders and now hire "kibbutz rabbis." But by far the biggest employer of rabbis in Israel remains the state, including local authorities, with rabbis on the payroll in towns and neighborhoods and settlements and government ministries and *kashrut* authorities and ritual baths and a long list of associations that receive taxpayer support. Most state-run religious schools in Israel have their own in-house rabbi, and in recent years so do some kindergartens.

The Religious Zionist community, across the spectrum, has produced many rabbis and Torah scholars. Some are role models in their local communities, admired leaders and orators with broad leadership authority on questions of education and morality. Many Religious Zionists seek rabbinic guidance on personal and public affairs, and the Israeli general public is also interested in what rabbis have to say. Rabbis are frequently interviewed and quoted, at times under headlines about "extremism," but occasionally in a positive light.

On the face of it, the ubiquity of rabbis in Israel ought to be interpreted as a sign of their growing status and authority. That would be a mistake. As always, the situation differs from place to place, and the settlement of Beit El, where Shlomo Aviner served as the community's rabbi, is quite different from a major city that is home to a mosaic of religious identities. Nevertheless, Aviner's authoritarian presumption – his "thou-shalt-do-as-instructed" attitude – is divorced from reality. The status of rabbis is not being eroded. It is being revolutionized. Less and less can the relationship between the rabbis and the Religious Zionist communities be described in terms of authority; at best, the right terms would be respect, choice, and partnership. All this, of course, is connected to a much broader modern crisis of leadership.

Some national-religious rabbis enjoy great public prestige but do not call the shots alone. It is easy to see how a rabbi loses control of a highly charged event like the uprooting of a settlement, but the persistent tension between rabbis and non-rabbis is also evident in essentially religious matters. In Orthodox circles, increasing numbers of women and men with no formal ordination are taking halakha into their own hands and interpreting it for themselves. So in order to understand what is happening in any particular religious community, it is important to observe changes happening from the bottom up, and not just the rabbis' actions and pronouncements.

In the winter of 2013, for example, Rabbi Yaakov Ariel – the well-known Religious Zionist chief rabbi of Ramat Gan – sparked a firestorm on social media when he decried the possibility of women delivering sermons in synagogue as an unacceptable "desecration of sanctity." The outrage and the charges leveled at him for extremism and the ostracization of women was predictable, and perhaps understandable, but it rather missed the point.

The chief rabbi of Ramat Gan had not taken an extremist turn. He had never had the slightest inclination to let a woman speak in the middle of a prayer service, and in the old world, his congregants would probably never have entertained such thoughts. But the year he put his opposition in writing was the year in which he became aware of a steady trickle – the beginning of a torrent – which might have begun with a lenient rabbi's initiative or a grassroots movement. In any case, women had started delivering sermons from the *bima*, the central platform, in several synagogues, either after or in the middle of services. Rabbi Ariel was writing as a man whose grip had been loosened; not as the representative of a hegemonic order.

The hardline rabbis are facing opposition, bordering on open revolt in all but name, both from the self-identifying "religious-lite" (who belong to Orthodox society but do not lead fully observant lives) as well as from the new Orthodox, feminist Orthodox, post-Orthodox, and liberal Orthodox, who are committed both to Jewish law and to a shifting of its status quo within the borders of religious Judaism. There are rabbis who are partners to these changes (for example, regarding the Temple Mount and the inclusion of women in synagogue life) but they are not leading the charge. And those rabbis who seek to stop it cold, have frequently met with outright failure.

In the words of Rabbanit Idit Bartov: "The Torah is consistently around twenty years behind the science. We're reactive, not proactive, and that applies to every field. Every social matter that arises, for instance the whole discourse on homosexuality, that's something new that has come up in recent years on account of a public and social awakening. It's not because halakha suddenly turned in the direction of something we hadn't heard of on Mount Sinai. Part of the equation is social pressure and a bottom-up awakening, and then the rabbis in the end say, wait, wait for me."

This game of catch-up can be partially explained by the fact that rabbis, conservative by definition, tend to react to social change rather than initiate it, but their efforts to impede change have had an eroding effect on their status. Chana Godinger Dreyfus, the head of Yeshivat Drisha (a women's yeshiva) on Kibbutz Kfar Etzion and a halakhic authority at the Pelech school in Jerusalem, points to the desperate battle that rabbis are waging to halt the enlistment of post-high school girls in the army. "Stopping them is all that you have to offer? That's a battlefront that won't hold," she said in an interview with Roy Sharon on Channel 10 about religious female enlistment in the IDF. In her analysis, observant youth feel alienated from the rabbis who regularly serve as "brakes" on social change, fighting a futile rearguard battle.

Perhaps we ought to dwell for a moment on the institution of rabbi and how its standing has been shaken in recent years. Judaism is a hierarchical religion, which expects obedience to community "elders" and rabbis. Observant Jews usually have a figure to whom they can turn for counsel, a particular rabbi who can offer guidance at critical moments in life. In Haredi communities, the identity of one's rabbi is an essential part of one's personal identity. And to borrow a phrase – the personal is political. The Haredim have a concept of *daas Torah* ("Torah wisdom"), an idea around two centuries old, which revolves around the notion that rabbis possess absolute knowledge about the correct Jewish approach to everything, even issues that have no obvious connection to Jewish wisdom. This doctrine gave rise to a class of rabbis known as "the greats of Israel," who supposedly have access to a rich reservoir of ancient wisdom.

For Israel's Haredi parties, namely Shas and United Torah Judaism, deference to *daas Torah* has long been official and absolute. Their members of Knesset are meant to serve as emissaries of their rabbis. This terminology has not been accepted in the Religious Zionist community, but in recent decades, to varying extents, there have been mechanisms of consultation with rabbis. Some of the more conservative elements of Religious Zionist society have tried to emulate the Haredi model in the political arena. But as we shall see throughout this book – it remains a matter of dispute within the community.

Who are the "greats" – the *gedolim* – of our generation?

The guest of honor at the opening event of the annual conference of the Jewish Federations of North America in Washington, DC, in 2016 entered to rapturous applause. "We can't think of anyone more inspiring than our next speaker," said the host as she invited (the since deceased) Rabbi Lord Jonathan Sacks, the former British chief rabbi, to the stage. "An internationally acclaimed Judaic scholar and authority, a thought leader and award-winning author, and truly a major personal inspiration for us all." Rabbi Sacks richly deserved those accolades, yet the British rabbi, knighted by the Queen, was a guest of honor at many major American Jewish events. Are there no American rabbis who can similarly address and inspire Jews in their own country?

Indeed not. In the United States, as in Israel, very few rabbis can unite large swaths of the public behind them. There used to be the Lubavitcher Rebbe (Menachem Mendel Schneerson), Rabbi Abraham Joshua Heschel, Rabbi Joseph B. Soloveitchik, and a few others. But nobody since has been able to fill their shoes. Whatever the reasons, as a rough generalization, rabbis are increasingly finding that their influence is factional, limited to the immediate group from which they emerged. You can count on one hand the rabbis who could be invited to deliver the keynote speech at an event with a diverse Jewish audience.[1]

The same rule applies to the Haredim, who used to have "greats" whose influence transcended sectarian borders – such as Rabbi Eliezer Menachem Shach and the fifth Gerrer Rebbe, Rabbi Yisrael Alter. The last Haredi rabbi whose influence extended beyond his immediate community was Rabbi Ovadia Yosef, the late spiritual leader of the Shas Party and great halakhic authority, who found an exceptionally diverse Jewish audience, beyond the Haredi world.

In the fall of 2013, as Rabbi Ovadia Yosef lay on his deathbed, Rabbi Benny Lau shared an interesting interpretation of the timeline of Jewish history broken up into large chunks of roughly five hundred years since the destruction of the Second Temple, describing distinct rabbinic periods: the mishnaic and talmudic era (ending in the late sixth century); the period of the *Geonim* and the Babylonian academies (till

---

1. This exclusive club includes Rabbi Israel Meir Lau, the chairman of Yad Vashem and a former Israeli chief rabbi who is respected by a range of communities, and of course Rabbi Lord Jonathan Sacks, one of the select few rabbis embraced both by Orthodox and progressive Jews as both a scholar and a moral voice.

the eleventh century); the period of the *Rishonim* (till the fifteenth century); and the period of the *Aḥaronim* ("the latter ones"), from there on. In theory, we are still in the period of the *Aḥaronim*, but in Rabbi Lau's thesis, Rabbi Ovadia Yosef marked the end of that chapter, rounding off another five-hundred-year era. A new and unknown chapter in Jewish history has begun.

Rabbi Benny Lau of Jerusalem, widely known for his intellectual independence and openness, wrote his doctorate on Rabbi Ovadia Yosef's halakhic philosophy. He draws a direct link between Rabbi Joseph Karo, the sixteenth-century author of the monumental code of Jewish law, *Shulḥan Arukh*, and Rabbi Ovadia Yosef, as transitional figures between rabbinic epochs.[2] His assertion that Rabbi Ovadia Yosef was the last of the *Aḥaronim* – the last rabbi to enjoy broad authority – is based on an observation of public, not rabbinic, perceptions. The end of the era of Rabbi Ovadia Yosef, he reasons cautiously, may mark the dawn of the era of the democratization of halakha. Religious Jews follow and will continue to follow halakha, but in an era when leadership authority has crumbled everywhere and direct and full access to information is available to nearly all, the Orthodox public is shunning the yoke of authority and making decisions for itself. After the era of the *Aḥaronim*, the spotlights will swing from the rabbis to individuals or new groups of elites.

Back to the present and the Orthodox community. The challenge to rabbinic authority did not end with the Gaza Disengagement. In the ensuing years the community was subjected to further upheaval, including, first and foremost, the serial sexual abuse committed by one of its best-known leaders.

No rabbi from within the knitted community has ever fallen from grace as dramatically as Rabbi Moti Elon. Born to a family that was practically national-religious nobility, he became a darling of the Religious

---

2. Lau resigned as the rabbi of the Ramban Synagogue in Jerusalem in 2019 after nearly two decades in the role. His academic research was published as Benjamin Lau, *From "Maran" to "Maran": The Halachic Philosophy of Rav Ovadia Yosef* (Tel Aviv: Yediot Books, 2005) [Hebrew].

Zionist community. He enthralled youth and adults alike with his sermons, books, charming moderation, and decorous right-wing style. But
in 2006, feted as a religious and political leader, he suddenly disappeared
from the public eye. He explained his disappearance to his students as
a retreat for spiritual reflection, as "doctor's orders," instructions to take
it easy. Some whispered that the honorable rabbi was traumatized by
the withdrawal from Gaza.

The truth only came to light in 2010. Elon had left his home in
Jerusalem and his senior educational roles at the behest of the Forum
Takana, a sort of informal tribunal, involving rabbis and public officials,
established to address offenses within the community that might otherwise not come to light. Years earlier, the forum, with the knowledge
of state prosecutors, had investigated allegations from several boys that
Elon had sexually assaulted them. The complaints were made public in
2010, a consequence of the rabbi having violated the agreed-upon restrictions that had barred him from all public and teaching roles. Moreover,
there were new claims of assault. The police launched a criminal investigation and Elon was convicted of sexual offenses against two of the
complainants. In 2018, it came to light that Elon, who had always protested his innocence, had relapsed: another youth, who had turned to
him for guidance, filed a complaint with the Forum Takana. Elon did
not deny what had happened behind closed doors.

This time, the allegations also tarnished the reputation of the
chairman of the Bnei Akiva yeshiva network and practically the elder
statesman of the Religious Zionist rabbinic world, Rabbi Haim Druckman. Despite Elon's conviction and despite the calls of protest, of which
he was well aware, Druckman insisted on letting Elon teach at Yeshivat
Or Etzion, the seminary that he headed. When the controversy resur-
faced in 2018, a group of rabbis from the Orthodox Union in the United
States censured Druckman, and rabbis in Israel also voiced criticism.
Malka Puterkovsky, a halakhic authority, publicly accused him in a
radio interview of "not taking a stance against Moti Elon and thus letting him harm others." She urged Druckman to seek forgiveness from
Elon's victims. The fact that a rabbi of Druckman's stature, a member of
the founding generation of modern Religious Zionism, was implicated
in the Elon affair was hugely consequential. Druckman had enjoyed a

unique status as practically the only consensus figure in the national-religious community. Now, that too was gone.

The Elon affair was a lesson in shock therapy. Every Religious Zionist rabbi and notable figure was involved in one way or another. After the initial shock, more stories came to light, including details about sexual assault by another well-known rabbi, Ze'ev Kopolovitch, in the 1980s and 1990s, similarly with the knowledge of a tight-lipped Rabbi Druckman. The revelations did nothing to enhance the prestige of rabbis who had always been seen as leaders of the national-religious community. A few days after the Elon affair exploded in 2010, the journalist Anshel Pfeffer, formerly a student of Rabbi Elon's, did some honest soul-searching. He wrote: "It is almost impossible to put in words what Rabbi Mordechai (Moti) Elon meant to me and still means for thousands of youngsters and grown-ups who learned from him and took his advice at every step of their personal lives…. As a father, the only lesson I can impart to my children from my years close to Rabbi Elon is while they have a duty to respect their teachers, never suspend your critical faculties toward figures of authority; do not become dependent on objects of admiration; and beware of charisma, as if from fire."[3]

The *De'ot* journal, published by the liberal Ne'emanei Torah Va'Avodah movement, released a special issue about the status of rabbis. The halakhic scholar Dr. Ariel Picard, formerly a community rabbi, urged the public to "grow up and move beyond rabbis." For his own part, he had stopped using the hard-earned title of "rabbi" and criticized the tendency in more hardline Religious Zionist circles to treat rabbis as omniscient: "It is not right for so much power to be concentrated in the hands of a single man for so long. The present levels of rabbinic authority are an open invitation for various kinds of corruption (like in any other case of excessive authority). But besides this, it is also problematic from a spiritual perspective because it absolves ordinary people of responsibility. Why think for yourself when you can send a text message or an email to the rabbi and receive answers to your questions: 'Where was

---

3. Anshel Pfeffer, "The Crucial Role Rabbi Elon Played in My Life," *Haaretz*, February 22, 2010, available at https://www.haaretz.com/1.5031896.

God in the Holocaust?'; 'Is it OK for me to have a girlfriend?'; or 'What does the rabbi think of Obama?'"

Rabbis came under sustained criticism, especially from liberal circles. Then, shortly after Elon completed his six months of community service, another devastating scandal broke. Ezra Sheinberg, a graduate of the finest Religious Zionist yeshivas, was the respected rabbi of the Orot HaAri community in Safed. He exploited his reputation as a mystic with "supernatural powers" to sexually assault several women, including members of his community. In July 2017, two years after he was charged with rape, sodomy, and other sexual offenses, he confessed in the context of a plea bargain that saw some of the serious charges against him toned down. He was sentenced to seven and a half years in jail.

Sheinberg was initially able to get away with his crimes thanks to the near-absolute deference that he enjoyed, especially as a man who supposedly possessed magical powers. "As far as I was concerned, he was God," one of the complainants told the reporter Emily Amrousi. "I'm not ashamed to say so."[4] Some saw him as the successor of former chief rabbi Mordechai Eliyahu, as the guardian of the secrets of Kabbalistic mysticism. He had developed such an extreme cult around him, one of total dependence and self-abnegation, that his innocent victims were willing to believe that his sexual assault was a kind of spiritual rebirth.

Rabbi Shmuel Tal – the head of Yeshivat Torat HaChaim and the leader of the large, reclusive community that coalesced around it – had a personal relationship with a woman who came to him for guidance. She asserted that the pressure that led her to divorce her husband stemmed from his directives, which were subsequently explained as direct instructions that Tal had received from "the *Ruaḥ HaKodesh*." This notion of mystical revelation was one that he invoked repeatedly as an explanation for untoward acts committed behind closed doors, a world away from the public reputation he had cultivated. In 2019 the mounting evidence, including from journalistic investigations and rabbinic forums, ripped his community asunder and compelled leading rabbis to sharply denounce him. As with Sheinberg a few years earlier, this episode came to light

---

4. Emily Amrousi, "The Rabbi Told Me: If You Tell Anyone About Our Relationship, You'll No Longer be Blessed," *Israel Hayom*, November 30, 2017 [Hebrew].

after Rabbi Shmuel Eliyahu of Safed, who had received complaints about his colleague, blew the whistle.[5]

Blind obedience to rabbis is a rare commodity in the Religious Zionist world. These cases were outliers. But as the stories emerged, more and more reputations were tarnished. Time and again, rabbis let their communities down – either through their personal deviancy or tacit complicity, or their empty promises to stop the Disengagement or their controversial or embarrassing remarks.[6] And if that were not enough, all this unfolded after the turn of the millennium, as young people all around the world, religious and secular alike, opted to govern their own affairs rather than have them governed by their elders.

If the situation is so grim, why are there so many more rabbis? The title of rabbi is still a coveted prize, or personal challenge, for so many Religious Zionist yeshiva students, who will go on to fill a growing number of rabbinic posts in Israel's Chief Rabbinate, in schools, and in synagogues across the country.

---

5. The Rabbi Tal affair was exposed by Roy Sharon on Israel's Channel 11. Yehuda Yifrach published a subsequent investigation on Tal's misdeeds in *Makor Rishon*.

6. As a rabbi in Gush Katif, where his yeshiva, Torat HaChaim, was based, Rabbi Shmuel Tal was exceptional in his hardline opposition to the Disengagement. He opposed any contact with the army and the government, open or covert. As a result, his students and others refused to prepare to be evacuated, arousing extreme concern from the Israeli security forces. Tal seemed to be an ideologue who would pay any price to maintain his position. But immediately after the evacuation, I was tipped off that while preparations were underway and he was urging his community to refuse to cooperate, he himself had reached a secret understanding with Defense Minister Shaul Mofaz. The agreement, which I revealed in *Haaretz*, ensured the peaceful eviction of hundreds of yeshiva students in exchange for a package of financial and bureaucratic benefits that enabled the yeshiva to reestablish itself with relative ease, compared to the other evacuees. The new community that Tal built in Yad Binyamin flourished, until his illicit behavior came to light, which caused a rupture in 2019. Although Tal declared de facto independence from the State of Israel and Israeli society, and indeed Religious Zionist society, back in 2007, it was Religious Zionist youth who continued to sign up to his institutions.

    Yair Ettinger, "Mofaz Struck Secret Deal with Gaza Rabbi to Ensure Orderly Pullout from Yeshiva," *Haaretz*, September 8, 2005, available at https://www.haaretz.com/1.4940255.

Rabbi Chaim Navon, previously a community rabbi in Modiin, totally rejects the claim that the rabbinic age is over. He recalls that when he was made the rabbi of his community, the city had just one other rabbi, who also headed a synagogue. By the time he stepped down, there were dozens of congregational rabbis in Modiin alone. Although most of them serve in a volunteer capacity or for a symbolic salary, and although Modiin is home to many new immigrants who hail from countries where every synagogue has a rabbi (which is not the rule in Israel), Navon believes that the numbers attest to a growing demand for rabbis and their leadership. The reason that more synagogues are appointing rabbis, he argues, is "not because people want rabbis to issue halakhic rulings for them, but because they feel that in religious communities, rabbis reinforce the community as the focal point of their lives. Synagogues with rabbis offer many more study sessions. They are much more diverse, and they have become much more vibrant places."

What is the role of rabbi in a changing world? Rabbis in Israel and abroad are currently discussing new, less dictatorial models for community rabbis and others. Navon, as one who has started writing a popular newspaper column, and as an intensive Facebook user, whose posts can attract hundreds of responses, faithfully represents this change. He speaks to and chats with his congregants as equals, not shying away from fierce arguments in which he criticizes others and absorbs a great deal of criticism in return.

Some rabbis have started practicing new forms of engagement. In an article titled "The End of the Rabbinic Age," the Jerusalem-based community rabbi Aaron Leibowitz, one of the founders of the alternative kosher certification "Hashgacha Pratit," argued that rabbis must start rethinking the parameters of their role: "Millennials are losing patience. They feel that we do not respect them or value them. We stopped being relevant the moment we stopped listening and got used to simply talking. We are too invested in giving instruction, but we need to go back to being students. They have no need of our knowledge and no interest in our halakhic rulings but from my experience, there is a great appetite for our wisdom, our perspective, so long as we approach the conversation as equal partners, not from a position of hegemony."[7]

Being a rabbi is a matter of leadership, authority, and charisma, but it also requires professional aptitude: it is a rabbi's job to issue halakhic rulings, following a strict hierarchy and clear set of rules. However, knowledge that was once considered the exclusive domain of rabbis is now being outsourced to independent actors, men and women alike. What follows are a few examples of alternative halakhic jurisprudence. They all come from the margins of the national-religious world, on the left and right, but are far from marginal in their importance. They pose a challenge to halakha and to the rabbis on critical controversial issues, in ways that most likely could not have been possible in the past.

In 2006, an Orthodox gynecologist and Torah scholar, Dr. Daniel Rosenak, set out on a journey to spark "new thinking," as he put it, about a particularly sensitive halakhic issue: the laws of *nidda*. He raised the matter of women with short menstrual cycles, who are unable to get pregnant because they are required by halakha to abstain from sexual relations for nearly two weeks after the start of their period. They suffer from an artificial infertility: a halakhic infertility. Some women only discover this truth after reaching menopause. Rosenak advocated annulling "Rabbi Zeira's stringency" – the 1,500-year-old rabbinic norm mandating "seven clean days" after the period has ended, for a total of eleven or twelve days of sexual abstinence. Instead, he proposed returning to the original letter of the law, as written in Leviticus: a single week of abstinence. Rosenak first made his case in the now-defunct conservative national-religious newspaper, *HaTzofe*. It was an attempt to speak to the public, over the heads of the rabbis. "I admit I don't expect change to come from above," he said in an interview. "I think when the public becomes aware of the issue (and I don't think it's aware at all right now!), the rabbis will hear what people are saying and reevaluate the situation."[8]

7.   Rabbi Aaron Leibowitz, "The End of the Rabbinic Age," *De'ot* 73 (2016) [Hebrew].
8.   Rivka Shimon and Daniel Rosenak, "Rabbi Zeira's Stringency – Time for a Rethink," *HaTzofe*, November 3, 2006 [Hebrew].

Rabbi Yoel Catane was one of the many rabbis from the conservative flank who tried to suppress Rosenak's revolt. "There have always been those who have tried to mitigate and whittle down halakha, and in every generation the causes and their advocates change, but the principle is the same," he said.[9] Some liberal rabbis also joined the opposition, including Rabbi Benny Lau and his wife Rabbanit Noa Lau, who maintained that this was a fundamental point of halakha that could not be dismissed, but that individual solutions could be found for women in need. Rosenak did not induce any rabbis to publicly change their positions, but he did set the agenda, and soon rabbis started privately advising women suffering from halakhic infertility to shorten the period of mandatory abstinence. National-religious newspapers started providing a platform for tough questions, such as whether it was legitimate for rabbis to refer healthy women to gynecologists for medically unnecessary hormonal treatments to fix a problem created solely by halakha. Instead of the radical move of abolishing the stringency, as advocated by Rosenak, others have recently called for various intermediate solutions that were never previously offered to halakhically infertile women (the late Dafna Meir's involvement in this subject was briefly mentioned in the introduction to this book).[10]

Another example of halakhic outsourcing, which has swept the whole Jewish world, is "partnership *minyanim*," in which women are able to lead parts of services for a congregation of men and women. Chapter v will examine this matter in greater detail, but for now I wish to point out the process that led to their establishment: the institution of "halakhic committees," which determine what is allowed and what is forbidden, and the decision to do so without rabbis.

Shira Hadasha, the first such synagogue, was founded by a group of Israelis in Jerusalem, including several immigrants from the United States. Tova Hartman, a professor of gender studies and education, makes a point of saying that it was founded by a group of women and

---

9.   Yoel Catane, "Leave Rabbi Zeira!" *HaTzofe*, November 17, 2006 [Hebrew].
10. The polemic sparked a war of words, and in 2011 two halakhic advisors, Tova Ganzel and Dina Rachel Zimmerman, published a halakhic article on the subject, and the dean of Yeshivat Maale Gilboa, Rabbi David Bigman, also waded in.

men, and that halakhic decisions are made by committee. Some committee members have extensive training in Jewish law, and some even have formal rabbinic ordination, but the structure is democratic rather than hierarchical: a popular vote settles matters of halakhic law. The Hakhel *minyan* in the Jerusalem neighborhood of Baka followed suit a few years later.

These halakhic committees convened to set policy, and in time to change it. Over the years, these communities began to make more roles available to women, such as leading the festive *Hallel* prayer or leading the *Kabbalat Shabbat* service on Friday night. The decision-making process usually involved a period of dedicated learning. Shira Hadasha set up a committee of five: three women, and two men. After the study stage had been completed, one committee member, who happened to be an ordained rabbi, wrote a position paper on behalf of the committee, explaining why halakha permitted women to lead evening services. In the next stage, the whole community was invited to attend a series of classes, and only then was a vote scheduled.

Rabbi Dr. Meir Ben Shahar, a member of Shira Hadasha's steering committee, explains that the halakhic process is conducted in good faith, not in an attempt to retroactively justify decisions that have already been made. He says, "It mattered for the community that there were people who had gone through this process and could articulate it to any educated individual. It was also important for us as a community to know that the mechanism for change was not 'change for the sake of change' and was completely anchored in the texts. Reading and learning. This was very important to us."

For our purposes, this democratic mechanism matters not just because of the halakhic conclusions that were reached. Ben Shahar, who holds a PhD in Jewish history, is unaware of any precedent for halakhic decision-making by popular vote. There were "councils of sages," but halakhic committees are something else altogether: "What there has never been before is coming to a community and saying, Folks, what do you propose? Even Reform congregations had rabbinic assemblies, and the formalities were so cumbersome that nobody even imagined asking the lay people what they thought. Nobody asked the Conservative rank-and-file before the rabbis allowed them to drive to synagogue on

Shabbat. As a halakhic committee, we sketch the borders, without laying down the law like rabbis have always done. It's a new model. It's based on a recognition that the distance between the *poskim* [the arbiters of Jewish law] and committee members and the congregants has shrunk, and that this is a communal institution that ought to be community-run, as per its own needs and wishes. The democratic tradition has trickled into these institutions."

The decision to manage their daily affairs without a rabbi was the natural choice for members of most partnership communities.[11] They were founded by two groups of Orthodox Jews, those born in Israel and those who had grown up in the United States, and they were, to a great extent, the religious community's generation of freedom and flexibility.

In reality, this model was not a complete innovation but a limited return to the not-so-distant past. For decades, most Religious Zionist synagogues did not have their own in-house rabbis. The congregations were intrinsically independent and belonged to their members. Many Religious Zionist synagogues still function without their own rabbi, not even one serving in a voluntary capacity. Only in recent years have many congregations started hiring rabbis, and they were mostly volunteers.

The American-born founding generation of Shira Hadasha came from a different world, one in which each congregation had its own rabbi, who was an essential part of each synagogue's landscape and often of its members' religious identity. In the United States, practically every synagogue has a rabbi on the payroll – a system the American immigrants in Israel wanted to break free of. "In Jerusalem, we shook off the yoke of the American rabbinate," explains Tova Hartman, daughter of the late Rabbi Prof. David Hartman, who founded the Shalom Hartman Institute, a progressive religious think tank, and a pair of religious

---

11. Several exceptions include the Darkhei Noam congregation in New York, which appointed Rabbi Prof. Daniel Sperber from Israel as its rabbi, although as one congregant told me, "It's no coincidence we chose a rabbi who lives in Jerusalem, 10,000 km away." Another exception is the Zemer HaZayit congregation in Efrat, which appointed Rabbi David Bollag, and Shirat HaTamar, also in Efrat, under the leadership of Rabbanit Shira Marili Mirvis. Rabbi Mishael Zion and his wife Ilana founded and lead the Klausner congregation in Jerusalem, but he is not a congregation rabbi in the full sense of the term.

high schools. "At Shira Hadasha, the founders had confidence: some of us came from homes of Torah scholars and we wanted to shake off the burden of needing a rabbi to tell us what was allowed. That's what I felt personally as the daughter of a rabbi, and I was not alone. We freed ourselves from the question: *What will the rabbis say?*"

The Israeli-born Ben Shahar recalls that when he was a child, synagogues did not have rabbis: "Nowadays, many Religious Zionist synagogues have their own rabbi, but in our generation, the absence of rabbis from synagogues strengthened the community. People realized that they could run the synagogue by themselves, they didn't feel a need to turn to a rabbi for every question."

Shira Hadasha was given approval to establish a halakhic partnership *minyan* from Mendel Shapiro, a member of its founding core. Shapiro was an ordained rabbi but did not take the role of rabbi, and in 2001 he wrote an informal halakhic paper in English asserting that there was no halakhic restriction preventing women from reading from the Torah. Only in 2007, after at least three partnership *minyanim* started operating around the world, was the first official halakhic paper published formally, asserting that women are permitted to lead certain parts of the prayer service.[12]

Exactly twenty years after Shapiro's paper was written, a religious congregation in Efrat, south of Jerusalem, appointed a female rabbi. Shirat HaTamar, as the congregation is known, does not call women up to the Torah and does not have women lead the prayer services; however, women are in charge of reading the weekly *haftara* portion during Shabbat services, they do lead the congregation through certain parts of the service, and girls, like boys, do sing the *Anim Zemirot* song at the end

---

12. In 2007, Rabbi Prof. Daniel Sperber published *The Path of Halakha, Women Reading the Torah: A Case of Pesika Policy* (Hebrew). This comprehensive halakhic discussion was the first Orthodox document to allow women to read from the Torah, as long as the halakhic principle of *kevod hatzibur* ("communal dignity") is preserved. In March 2016, Rabbi Ysoscher Katz of Yeshivat Chovevei Torah in New York published a comprehensive treatise, which also allowed women to read from the Torah, and a year later Rabbi Ethan Tucker and Rabbi Micha'el Rosenberg released their own short book with more far-reaching conclusions, titled *Gender Equality and Prayer in Jewish Law*. Each book provoked reactions for and against.

of the service. The *meḥitza* runs right down the middle of the hall and sermons are given by men and women alike.

Nonetheless, it was a surprise when they appointed the Israeli-born Rabbanit Shira Marili Mirvis to head the congregation. "Many Religious Zionist congregations don't even want a rabbi," she told me, "and the same is true of our community. If you were to ask if they want a congregational rabbi, the answer would be a categorical no. And if you were to ask if they want a rabbanit, I think the answer would again be negative. But when they asked who's in favor of appointing the Rabbanit Shira, the answer was yes. I don't know if it was a one-time thing, but it was a bottom-up process and I was there."

Marili Mirvis grew up in Jerusalem and began studying for ordination not as a means of breaking a glass ceiling and not as an agent of change, but simply, she says, "out of a love of Torah and a love of prayer and it just happens to be that I'm also a woman. The gender element is not the be-all and end-all, at least not in my case. It's not like there was a rabbi and we moved him out of the way and I inherited his spot as a feminist act. I was just a person who loves the community and loves learning and teaching. There is something significant in that we are breaking new ground but not breaking in."

She joined Shirat HaTamar as a regular member of the community who had left a more established synagogue in which she felt she had reached a dead end. At a synagogue meeting, convened in order to discuss certain demands for change, she realized that the opposition to expanding the women's place in the synagogue had nothing to do with halakha. "I prepared detailed halakhic sources, but someone said to me, 'Just don't come in with halakhic sources, because the only thing that people care about is that they want to pray in the synagogue of their grandfathers.' But for me, even my own grandmother didn't want to pray in the synagogue of my grandfather, so should my daughter and I want to pray there?"

At that meeting it was decided that women would not be allowed to deliver a *devar Torah* in the synagogue. "And I said: I can't go on. Not because I felt a pressing need to deliver a *devar Torah*, but because there was no way I was going to have my children see, Shabbat after Shabbat, only men on the *bima*. There was no way they'd not see women delivering *divrei Torah.* The whole thing was not even about reading from the Torah, but about the core issue, the voice of women, and where the *meḥitza* is drawn. In a reality in which I don't have the ability to touch the *sefer Torah,* I cannot pray."

The opposition, she said, is not engaged in a halakhic dialogue. "That doesn't interest them. It drives me crazy. Because if it isn't about halakha, then what is it? Conservatism? Conservatism is good, if it's pleasant, if it grants you a space, but what about me, for whom it's not good and not pleasant – what do I do? What do I do if the current space I'm in doesn't grant me a place? So it comes from a lack of choice and a love of prayer and an understanding that I will not give up my place and my belonging to the community. I realize that we're walking on thin ice, but we have a duty to walk on that thin ice. I can't be left with 'This is what there is, and so this is what we'll continue to do.'"

Self-confidence or shirking of duty, democracy or anarchy, these bones of contention are not the sole preserve of religious liberals. The spirit of independence is also strong among Temple Mount activists (as we shall see in chapter VII) and the radical right. Just consider Meir Ettinger. A distant relative I have never met, he has been called the Shin Bet's "most wanted man" in the media. Far more than any rabbi, Ettinger is the chief ideologue of the group known as "The Revolt," which seeks to topple the State of Israel's secular system of government. Ettinger was influenced by such figures as Rabbi Yitzhak Ginsburgh and perhaps also his grandfather, the extremist leader Rabbi Meir Kahane. But the ideology of The Revolt is his own, and he wrote it out, as a manifesto, only after drifting away from his rabbis. For it is also an uprising against them, against those rabbis he considers to be excessively moderate.

Ettinger, who is not a rabbi, became in his twenties a religious authority for members of Israel's hardcore, anti-government, anarchist right. He has many followers, avid readers of his work. His insights and lectures, often delivered in the rabbinic form of a *devar Torah,* are published on his blog and on Twitter and even without the formal title of "rabbi," he represents a challenge to rabbinic authority on political and even religious affairs. What would he, this grandson of Meir Kahane, say, if Rabbi Aviner looked him in the eye and implored: "Do you obey your rabbis, or not?!"

Chapter IV

Rabbi, Rabba, Rabbanit

A winter storm battered the Matan Women's Institute for Torah Studies in Jerusalem as a large crowd of religious Israelis gathered for a sort of summit meeting of female Torah scholars. Some in attendance that evening were men, most were women. Many held titles such as "rabbanit" or "halakhic advisor." Many had been immersed in the study of Torah for years. They were an elite group, well established and no longer as peripheral as they had once been, but still, in January 2014, they were still looking of for a way to influence wider Orthodox society.

The hosts of the gala event, Matan, Beit Morasha, and Midreshet Lindenbaum, had started years earlier to offer advanced halakha courses for women. The first graduates were issued certificates of ordination, although no Israeli state authority had even the slightest intention of recognizing them. It was clear to everyone that the Orthodox world was on the brink of a seismic change in its attitude to female religious leadership. Where, asked one of the speakers at the event, will this high-speed train stop next?

The future sat on the dais in the form of a young eloquent woman in a full head covering, flanked by several rabbis (men and women) and two politicians. Rabbanit Idit Bartov was described in terms that still sound like science fiction – a student for the bench, for *dayanut*, for service as a female judge on a rabbinic court.

Rabbanit Bartov was a member of the first class at Midreshet Lindenbaum to graduate as *morot hora'ah*, "halakhic guides," a title akin to "rabbi," and over the past year had started studying in a new program for female religious judges: year one of a ten-year plan. The target date: 2023. There were two women in the class. They were embarking on a long journey of hundreds of lessons, thousands of self-study sessions and assignments, and countless articles and exams, before they could be ordained as *dayaniyot* – a new title that even Hebrew struggles to accommodate, not to mention the rabbinic establishment. Distant as it seemed then, Bartov and her colleague had set the course for the train's next station: recognition and legitimacy from the rabbinic world, and appointments as judges on the benches of Israel's state-run rabbinic courts.

Bartov sounded self-assured. When she and other women completed their studies, she reasoned that evening, the rabbinic courts would accept them even without a legal challenge. "There is, uh, *ample* cause for optimism," she said, smiling as she punned the word for female rabbi and ample. "It all happened so quickly for me, and I'm talking about society's response, which will obviously only accelerate as time goes by and we become accustomed, as a society, to there being a creature of this sort." She maintained that the dispute was not halakhic, but sociological. "When I worked in the midrasha writing halakhic responsa, I wrote my last reply about female religious judges. Even the most hardline figures understand that if you open up the texts and debate them seriously, you can't say it's impossible. Honestly, it's a social problem, and society is changing."

It certainly is. And yet demands for official recognition of female religious leadership – particularly when paired with a rabbinic title – is still a recipe for discord. And that is the subject of this chapter.

By the spring of 2015, it was clear that this high-speed train was not to be stopped. Several seminaries in Israel and the United States, founded only a few years earlier, ordained a dozen Orthodox women as religious leaders – an all-time high. Some used the honorific *rabba*, as the feminine form of "rabbi." After years of study, six of the women were ordained at Yeshivat

Maharat in New York (its name is the Hebrew acronym of the official title it bestows: Halakhic Spiritual Torah Leader), and another six in Israel – two at Lindenbaum, two at Beit Morasha, and two at Beit Midrash Har'el, a small outfit that also ordained two men at the same time.

Each institute emphasized a different aspect of what it means to be a rabbi, and as we shall see there is a fundamental difference between the more academic Israeli institutions and Maharat in New York, which focuses more on training women as synagogue leaders. But these separate institutions had become a movement. A dozen women is a lot, especially considering that there was no guiding hand or single philanthropist funding their training. They were taught simultaneously at four independent institutions (by male rabbis), and even if some of them knew each other, the substantial graduating class was the result of a slow process that had started from the ground up and would go on to smash record after record.

The women had different backgrounds and their sights were trained on different destinations. Yet every woman who spoke at a graduation ceremony, or gave an interview, or posted on Facebook, understood that this was a historic moment. And with good reason. Twelve is a relatively small number compared to the masses of men ordained as rabbis every year, but the figure is brought into sharper focus when compared to the goings-on in Conservative Judaism.

Conservative Judaism, a world-spanning empire with hundreds of thousands of constituents, started ordaining female rabbis long ago. Yet in that same year, 2015, the institution ordained just twelve female rabbis from all its seminaries and rabbinic training programs: nine from the Jewish Theological Seminary in New York, and three from the Ziegler School of Rabbinic Studies in Los Angeles. The Schechter Institute in Israel had zero graduates. A Conservative rabbinic college in Argentina ordained one rabbi – a man.[1] Indeed, 2015 seemed to be the Spring of Orthodox Jewish Women.[2]

---

1.   This comparison does not include unaffiliated liberal rabbinic colleges, which did ordain women in 2015. One of them was Hebrew College in Boston.
2.   As an aside, it is worth noting that in non-Orthodox Judaism in the United States, the institution of the rabbi is being feminized: rabbinic colleges are attracting grow-

In her graduation speech at Har'el in Jerusalem, Rahel Berkovits managed to deliver two or three sentences from the *devar Torah* she had prepared before her tears got the better of her. "Real rabbis cry," she said, taking a deep breath, and the tension dissipated as everyone laughed along with her. That marked the beginning of a speech that focused less on Torah and more on Berkovits's personal experience as a woman who had received, in her words, "the great privilege, which I surely don't deserve, of being part of this significant moment in the history of the Jewish people."

"I'd have liked to tell you all that what's happening here is the fulfillment of a dream, but that's not true. I never, ever dreamed of being ordained as a rabbi. In fact, I never thought it would happen, and I still can't believe it's happening. For those of you who know me, this might sound strange. I have devoted most of my life to thinking, learning, teaching, and writing about the status of women in Judaism. So why didn't I dream about this moment?"

Berkovits explained that in her personal and religious life, she had managed to put her egalitarian ideals into practice, "but *semikha* [ordination]? Honestly, it's connected to a long rabbinic tradition, spanning many generations, involving Torah scholars who are part of the male rabbinic establishment. I think you can understand why I simply never thought it would happen."

Naturally, 2015 also saw the emergence of a counterreaction, which showed just how divisive the debate over Orthodox women in leadership positions would be. It was fiercest in the United States, where the women who were ordained at Maharat had expected to receive rabbinic appointments in Orthodox synagogues.

The Rabbinical Council of America (RCA), the largest organization of Orthodox rabbis in North America and perhaps the world, scrapped its policy of inclusion in the fall of 2015 and announced in unambiguous terms: "RCA members with positions in Orthodox institutions may not ordain women into the Orthodox rabbinate, regardless

---

ing numbers of women. Quite often, women comprise the majority of graduating classes in progressive rabbinic colleges.

of the title used; or hire or ratify the hiring of a woman into a rabbinic position at an Orthodox institution, or allow a title implying rabbinic ordination to be used by a teacher of Limudei Kodesh [Jewish studies] in an Orthodox institution."[3]

A year and a half later, the Orthodox Union forbade its synagogues from employing women as clergy. It was a dramatic announcement, because some Orthodox Union synagogues had already hired female rabbis and refused to fire them.

The policy was designed to send a signal to the female graduates and the rabbis ordaining them: The Orthodox establishment will not recognize rabbinic titles for women, and nobody holding such a title will receive communal appointments or legitimacy from the observant public. The Rabbinical Council of America and the Orthodox Union threw down the gauntlet: the threat of a community-wide schism was made plain. The Orthodox establishment in the United States would cut off liberal congregations that hired women as rabbis.

But not all Orthodox congregations were deterred from appointing women to leadership positions. Rabbi Shmuel Herzfeld, of Ohev Sholom – The National Synagogue in Washington, DC – had already employed, and continues to employ, a female clergy member. He responded to the statement by the Orthodox Union, which also runs the world's biggest kosher certification authority, by quipping: "The OU [Orthodox Union] should stick to tuna fish."[4] Facing such a backlash, after a period of deliberation, the Orthodox Union decided to keep the threat on the table but not follow through on it just yet. It held off on excommunicating synagogues like Ohev Sholom in Washington, but its leaders hoped that the unequivocal warning would deter others from following suit. If they employed female clergy members, the Orthodox Union reserved the right to expel them, depriving them not just of their

---

3. Cited in Uriel Heilman, "With Resolution Against Hiring Women Rabbis, RCA Votes for Confrontation," *Jewish Telegraphic Agency*, November 3, 2015, available at https://www.jta.org/2015/11/03/united-states/with-resolution-against-hiring-women-rabbis-rca-votes-for-confrontation.
4. Josh Nathan-Kazis, "Exclusive: Orthodox Union Adopts New Policy Barring Women Clergy," *The Forward*, February 2, 2017, available at https://forward.com/news/362043/orthodox-union-adopts-policy-barring-women-clergy/.

link to a vast network of Orthodox congregations, but mostly of a sense of belonging, legitimacy, and political support.

In Israel, women who had earned titles akin to that of rabbi (such as "halakhic advisor") faced a different career path. But here too, the issue cleaved religious society, splitting it along its conservative and liberal flanks. In 2015, Rabbi Shlomo Riskin, the municipal chief rabbi of Efrat and chancellor of Ohr Torah institutions, appointed one of his students in the halakhic leadership track, Dr. Jennie Rosenfeld, to the post of *manhiga ruḥanit*, "communal spiritual leader," alongside him. Several months later, the Chief Rabbinical Council made an attempt to oust Riskin from his role as community rabbi. The official reason was his advanced age, but Riskin's positions toward women in religious spaces and other issues were known to be anathema to the Chief Rabbinate. Some rabbis on the conservative flank of Religious Zionism lent their support to his ostracization.[5]

No such efforts were made, nor were they possible, at Ramban Synagogue in Jerusalem, which appointed Rabbanit Carmit Feintuch as a spiritual leader alongside Rabbi Benny Lau in 2016. The Chief Rabbinate held no sway over a community that had decided on and funded the appointment by itself, but the divisions in the Religious Zionist world, nonetheless, rose to the surface – Feintuch's appointment was met with resistance from within the congregation and she stepped down two years later. Rabbi Lau later followed suit.

In recent years, though, there has been a notable shift within the middle ground. In 2021, for example, Bar-Ilan University, a flagship academic institution affiliated with the Religious Zionist community (though its student body is heterogeneous), appointed Rabbanit Devorah Evron to the post of "spiritual leader," filling a new slot alongside the school's rabbi. That same year, Rabbanit Michal Tikochinsky, who has a doctorate in Talmud studies and, like Evron, is from the old

---

5. When the controversy erupted, Rabbi Micha HaLevi, the municipal chief rabbi of Petach Tikva, who was associated with Har Hamor, gave an interview for the telephone news service *The Haredi Voice* (a recorded news service that can be listened to over the phone, to avoid the need for television or secular radio), and listed what he considered Rabbi Riskin's defects, such as "trying to compel the rabbinate to follow his position on questions of conversion."

guard of female scholars of halakha, was appointed to the board of the Tzohar Rabbinical Organization. Rabbanit Shira Marili Mirvis, who was ordained by Rabbi Shlomo Riskin, made history that same year by becoming the first female leader of an Orthodox congregation, Shirat HaTamar, in Efrat. These three women, all Israeli born, all raised within the mainstream of the community, are evidence of a deep shift within the heartland of Religious Zionism.

Since the 1980s, Israel has seen many attempts to get women appointed to public positions in the state-run religious services. The typical route involved petitioning the Supreme Court, against the stiff resistance of the Chief Rabbinate, the local religious councils, and the Haredi parties. One trailblazer was Leah Shakdiel, who was appointed to the religious council in Yeruham in 1988 after a legal battle. But it would be years before women were able to sit on the committee that appointed religious judges, and before the courts ruled that women could apply for the role of director-general of the religious courts, and before anyone tried to get women included in the body that elects Israel's two chief rabbis and to seriously increase female representation on municipal religious councils. In 2014, the Chief Rabbinate was forced to allow nine women to take its tests for *kashrut* supervisors and to give them diplomas when they passed with flying colors. In 2022, during his brief term as minister of religious services, Matan Kahana appointed ten women as heads of local religious councils.

Each of these campaigns had an indirect effect on religious life, as well as political repercussions. But much more consequential were the fights for appointments in the heart of religious life – leadership roles in synagogues, in Torah study, and in Orthodox communities. The battle over whether women can serve as arbiters of halakha is first and foremost a political and social question, but also has implications for Jewish law.

Past generations were witness to female Torah scholars and even ritual slaughterers and circumcisers. But they were a select few, the rare case that was the exception to the solid historical rule. Judaism had traditionally reserved a place for female influence in the home, and to the extent that women were assigned any public, communal religious role, it was the sort that was performed behind the partition, in the women's gallery. Traditional Jewish culture, from the Hebrew Bible to contemporary rabbinic literature, was home to millennia of male supremacy in the public sphere.

Both halakha and history were largely written by men, and Orthodox Judaism makes no attempt to erase this: across the full gamut of religious perspectives in the Orthodox world, the liberal side broadly accepts the conservative rules of the game. It does not want to annul or change religious laws, but to foster social and moral changes based on existing religious jurisprudence. It is a matter of negotiation within the contours of halakha, and even for those inclined to be lenient, the halakhic case for change must be made by isolating the halakhic principle in question from the broader historical and social context.

This is the perspective of the more lenient rabbis, such as Rabbi Prof. Daniel Sperber, who has conferred rabbinic ordination on several women in Israel and the United States in recent years, especially at Yeshivat Maharat. In an article for the religious feminist organization Kolech, Sperber explained his support for conferring ordination to women, stipulating his admission criteria: "Any wise, God-fearing woman who has studied a great deal of Torah, and has studied halakha in a deep and systematic manner from distinguished Torah scholars, and was tested by them and/or by any other experienced teacher, and has undertaken or will undertake a rabbinic apprenticeship, is certainly fit to be crowned with the crown of the Torah and to be considered a sage who is worthy of answering halakhic questions and delivering halakhic legal rulings in the halakhic subjects on which she was tested and found competent, and may God shield her from any mistakes."[6]

Sperber, an Israel Prize-winning professor of Talmud and a former head of Bar-Ilan University's Institute for Advanced Torah Studies, was addressing whether women could be empowered to deliver halakhic rulings – a sensitive and prestigious part of the role of rabbi. *Poskim* (or in the feminine, *poskot*) are authorized to answer halakhic questions by referring to the body of halakhic literature and using their judgment to settle disputes between competing authorities in the Jewish tradition.

---

6.   Rabbi Prof. Daniel Sperber, "Can a Woman Be a *Poseket Halakha*?" Kolech.org.il.

Such rulings are considered binding, because when Orthodox Jews approach a rabbi for guidance, they are expected to obey his word, not shop around till they get the answer they want.

Being a *posek* is not a part of every rabbi's job description. Some rabbis hold the title in virtue of their Torah scholarship, in recognition of their intellect and expertise, regardless of their position; congregation rabbis have a clerical function, which varies from place to place – from teaching classes and organizing prayers, to providing individual and collective pastoral care, to officiating at weddings and funerals; there are also in-house rabbis at yeshivas and religious high schools, whose role is mainly educational; and religious judges, *dayanim*, are also rabbis, whose job is to adjudicate personal or financial disputes based on Jewish law.

In any case, the main bone of contention is whether women can be *poskot* and deliver halakhic rulings. Rabbi Sperber's position is politically audacious and certainly at odds with conventional Orthodox jurisprudence,[7] but the idea that women can deliver halakhic rulings is nothing new. Since the Middle Ages, this view has been shared by many leading rabbis, who distinguished the role of *posek* from that of a religious judge, which was still off-limits.[8] Among those who allowed women to deliver halakhic rulings were three Israeli chief rabbis – Rabbi Ben-Zion

---

7. Many rabbis reject the idea that a woman can deliver halakhic rulings, quoting a section in Bamidbar Rabba that seeks to elucidate why, in the book of Judges, Manoah insisted on hearing directly from an angel that his barren wife would bear a son, Samson, and did not rely on his wife's word that the angel had told her exactly the same. The Sages said that Manoah knew that he should not rely on his wife because "women are not to decide [matters of halakha]."

8. One relatively straightforward case of authorizing the exercise of halakhic authority by women is that of *kashrut* supervisors. The approval is based on the late American rabbi Moshe Feinstein, one of the most influential halakhic scholars of the twentieth century, who would be quoted years after his death by the Israeli Supreme Court in its judgment about *kashrut* supervisors in 2014. Feinstein's collection of halakhic decisions, *Igrot Moshe*, includes his legal response to a question about a woman whose husband was a *kashrut* supervisor and died. The woman inquired whether she was halakhically permitted to take over her husband's job as a *kashrut* supervisor to support her family. This halakhic question raised two issues: whether a woman was fit to attest on matters of *kashrut*, i.e., whether the public could trust her, and whether a woman could be placed in a position of authority (*serara*) over men. In both cases, the rabbi's bottom-line answer was Yes.

Meir Hai Uziel, Rabbi Isaac HaLevi Herzog, and Rabbi Eliyahu Bakshi-Doron, who was the most explicit of them all: "Women and converts can serve as leaders and even *gedolei hador* – the greats of the generation. Women and converts can serve as *poskim* and teach Torah. These are roles in which authority is based on the candidates' skills, and their authority is nourished by their skills."

The debate over the ordination of women did not begin in a vacuum. It can be traced back to a specific time and place: 1970s America, when women first started studying Talmud on a large scale. The women's revolution in Talmud scholarship began in the United States, including at the Drisha Institute in New York, as a phenomenon on the margins, and only when it reached Israel – and more specifically, Jerusalem – did it become a mass movement. This was the gift of the first generation

---

A more complicated case, halakhically speaking, is whether women can serve as religious judges – an even higher rank than rabbi. The debate centers on the prophetess Deborah, who according to the book of Judges, "led [lit., 'judged'] Israel at that time .... And the Israelites would come to her for decisions" (Judges 4:4–9). The verse seems to open judicial posts to all women, but how can a sweeping approval be reconciled with the unambiguous rule in the Talmud that women cannot even be called as witnesses in rabbinic courts? If a woman's word cannot be trusted at the witness stand, how can it be trusted on the judges' bench?

The Tosafists, the talmudic scholars of medieval France and Germany, offer several lines of reasoning to reconcile the seeming contradiction. According to one, Deborah was an exception, inspired by a special divine presence; according to another, Deborah was not actually a judge but had enough halakhic knowledge to train judges without being one herself. Could such a woman, in theory, make halakhic rulings for others?

The answer comes from the *Sefer HaḤinukh* ("Book of Education"), a thirteenth-century work that seeks to explain the reasons for religious laws. The book describes the prohibition on halakhic decisors to give halakhic rulings when inebriated, and mentions in an aside that the prohibition applies not just to men but also to "wise women worthy of deciding [matters of halakha]." From this aside, it is clear that the possibility exists of a woman giving halakhic rulings, and the first to state so in no uncertain terms was Rabbi Chaim Yosef David Azulai (1724–1806), who lived in Italy and the Land of Israel, and who ruled that "although women are disqualified from adjudicating, a wise woman can nevertheless deliver halakhic rulings."

of Orthodox feminists, which shaped the second generation, which is now demanding a role at the level of community religious leadership.

It is essential to understand this point, because Orthodox feminists were not pioneers. The Reform and Conservative movements in the United States had already appointed women to positions of spiritual leadership and given them the coveted title of "rabbi" or "rabba." After Regina Jonas, who was ordained as a rabbi in Germany in 1935, the Reform movement ordained Sally Priesand as the first female rabbi in the United States in 1972; Amy Eilberg joined her as the first Conservative female rabbi in 1985.

Many Orthodox Jews viewed the Reform and Conservative changes in the twentieth century as bold precedents, sometimes for the better but much more frequently for the worse. So when Orthodox women searched for role models, they preferred to invoke not the liberal trailblazers but women from different periods in Jewish history: women who were both Orthodox and considered Torah scholars. They drew inspiration from Bruriah, the studious wife of the second-century sage Rabbi Meir; from Osnat Barazani, the head of a yeshiva in seventeenth-century Kurdistan; from the contemporary Bible scholar Nechama Leibowitz; and from Sarah Schenirer, the founder of the first school for Haredi girls in early twentieth-century Poland, Beis Yaakov, which became a global franchise and transformed Torah scholarship and education among girls from being the preserve of a privileged elite to the birthright of the masses. The conclusion from these examples was that female leadership represented a direct continuation of this spirit of scholarship and was not motivated by an unseemly hunger for power or domination.

The choice of these role models had another context: the growing importance of Torah study in Religious Zionist society, starting around the 1970s. It was then that national-religious men started signing up in their masses to hundreds of advanced yeshivas, including Hesder yeshivas and pre-military academies. In time, national-religious women were also swept up in this wave of scholarship. It is no coincidence that most of the Orthodox rabbinic study programs for women were established in the framework of Jewish higher learning institutes, rather than rabbinic colleges, as is the norm in the Reform and Conservative movements (Yeshivat Maharat in New York is the notable exception to this rule).

From conversations with women studying to be rabbis and women educating others who seek to serve as rabbis, the desire to lead, influence, or settle halakhic questions seems to have arisen much later than the initial interest in studying for study's sake. A few days after the conference at Matan, in January 2014, I met Rabbanit Rachelle Fraenkel, who had just been appointed (around half a year before her son's tragic murder) as the head of the Hilkhata program, offering advanced halakhic studies for women. She said: "The general trend is that women who have gained a foothold in Talmud are now moving on to master halakha. And if the world was afraid of a slippery slope, then there is definitely a slope, but it's an ascent. Up the mountain. People were afraid of opening the door to us, they said, if you do this, you'll want to do that, and also that. And they were absolutely right. You opened up a little bit, we wanted more and more, because whoever tastes from the Tree of Knowledge develops an appetite for more. But it's not a downhill slope, there's no threatening abyss, there's a summit. It's a process of *tikkun olam* – repairing the world."

At the Matan conference, Rabbanit Idit Bartov described the difficult grind of halakha and Talmud programs, of studying for study's sake despite the financial sacrifice, unable to work, without any hint of a career path, without any assistance from the public purse of the sort male rabbinic students enjoy. "The level of self-sacrificing devotion," she said. "I don't know how many men have faced the same test."

The women's Talmud revolution, which initially enjoyed support from just a handful of rabbis,[9] underpins a much broader leadership

---

9. Only very few rabbis responded favorably to the demand from women to study Talmud. Among them were the late Rabbi Yosef Qafih, a Yemenite-Israeli authority on Maimonides and high-profile rabbi in Jerusalem, and the late Rabbi Aharon Lichtenstein, the head of Yeshivat Har Etzion, who held sway in both Israel and the United States. Lichtenstein was a disciple of Rabbi Joseph B. Soloveitchik, one of the towering rabbis of the twentieth century, and the most influential rabbi in Modern Orthodoxy in the United States. Although Lichtenstein allowed women to study Talmud in practice, he did not issue a sweeping halakhic ruling authorizing the practice.

revolution – a point that both liberal and conservative rabbis agree on. Mordechai Willig, a well-known American Orthodox rabbi halakhic authority, and a senior Talmud instructor at Yeshiva University, wrote that Orthodox women's growing leadership ambitions prove that it was a mistake to allow women to study Talmud. He called for a reconsideration of women's Talmud studies – a winding back of the clock.

In contrast, supporters of the ordination of women argue that for women to issue halakhic rulings is the natural next stage of the biggest change of the generation: the widespread study of Torah by women. They quote the Babylonian Talmud, which stipulates two cardinal dangers – incompetent people issuing halakhic rulings, and competent people who refrain from doing the same: "What is the meaning of that which is written: 'For she has cast down many wounded; and a mighty host are all her slain' (Proverbs 7:26)? ... This is referring to a Torah scholar who has not yet attained the ability to issue rulings, and yet he issues rulings. 'And a mighty host are all her slain'; this is referring to a Torah scholar who has attained the ability to issue rulings, but does not issue rulings and prevents the masses from learning Torah properly" (Sota 22a).

When precisely was the linkage between halakhic learning and leadership forged? The first sign of change seems to have been an institute founded in Israel in the 1990s to train female "rabbinic advocates," a role equivalent to attorney at a rabbinic court. The next step was a program that started in 1999 at the Nishmat seminary in Jerusalem to train women as *yoatzot halakha*, "halakhic advisors," on the laws of *nidda*. That is, to do something extremely similar to issuing halakhic rulings, but strictly limited to female matters. The track was founded by Rabbanit Chana Henkin and her husband, Rabbi Yehuda Herzl Henkin *zt"l*, both of whom emerged from mainstream Modern Orthodox circles in New York.

The Henkin family, like the Fraenkel family and others, suffered a tragedy. Their son Rabbi Eitam Henkin and his wife, Naama, were murdered in a shooting attack in the West Bank in 2015. Following the attack, their work gained greater public recognition in Israel, beyond Orthodox circles in Jerusalem, and Rabbanit Chana Henkin was invited to light an Independence Day torch at the official ceremony in 2017. By then, *yoatzot halakha* of the sort trained by Rabbanit Henkin attracted little controversy, and nowadays their work is increasingly accepted by rabbis from the conservative flank of the Religious Zionist world. The reason is that Nishmat's curriculum is extremely conservative regarding the role of women in interpreting halakha. It answers a very specific need – halakhic advice about marital relations – and steers clear of anything politically controversial. The founders of more daring programs, which train women to give halakhic advice on all matters, consider Nishmat to be a pioneer, the first to have broken through the wall, but insist that it did not go far enough.

These new programs are more demanding and offer more. The three Jerusalem-based programs (Matan, Beit Morasha, and Lindenbaum), another at Midreshet Ein HaNatziv in the Jordan Valley, and Maharat in New York differ in the intensity and rigor of study, but all require an in-depth halakhic and talmudic knowledge of the laws of family purity, dietary restrictions, *eiruvin*, festivals, Shabbat, conversion, mourning, and more. At the close of their studies the students must pass final exams; at Lindenbaum, the exams are identical to those that men take to be ordained by the Chief Rabbinate. Needless to say, these exams are not recognized by any official body, so their purpose is more declaratory than practical. Maharat, which prepares its students to work in synagogues in the United States, places its emphasis on spiritual support in the community, for life-cycle events and day-to-day life, in times of joy and grief. The Israeli programs are more oriented toward religious law, while Lindenbaum, which is especially onerous (a five-year course, involving twenty-six hours of weekly study), does both: besides Talmud and halakha, students are required to devote additional hours to the fields of psychology, rhetoric, mediation, and so forth.

Each Orthodox women's seminary gives its graduates a different title: rabbanit or rabba; halakhic instructor or responder or advisor or arbiter; Torah scholar or community leader or spiritual leader or religious leader; *marta de'atra* (an Aramaic honorific meaning "mistress of the locality"), or maharat – a neologism based on the Hebrew acronym meaning "female halakhic, spiritual, and Torah leader." Each is a convoluted feminine alternative for the simple, bi-syllabic word: rabbi.

What should the female equivalent of a rabbi be called, given that this is not just a day job but implies a certain social, spiritual, and even legal status? Some women are tired of this question. "It's flogging a dead horse," says Fraenkel. She prefers to focus on the content, not the label. Another female scholar says that men and women should focus more on women's "contribution to and influence" on religious seminaries and halakhic discourse than on the question of their title.

But names carry meaning. They shape how people think, define directions of change, and can be expected to provoke certain social reactions, as the past few years have proven. Ever since Orthodox women started undertaking rabbinic studies, the question of how they should be addressed defied simple explanation. The two obvious feminine forms of "rabbi" – "rabba" and "rabbanit" – were already taken. A "rabbanit" generally means a rabbi's wife, also known as a "rebbetzin," and she derives her power and authority from her husband's title. As a rule, there is no such thing as a rabbanit without a rabbi. The other option is "rabba," which has a distinctly Reform and Conservative ring.[10] In 2009, Sara Hurwitz, an Orthodox woman, was ordained by Rabbi Avi Weiss in New York. Other Orthodox women had received ordination privately before her, but Hurwitz was the first to have done so in a public, institutional, and festive manner. Rabbi Weiss initially gave her the made-up title of "maharat," the acronym of the study program he had founded, but a few months later, in early 2010, he retroactively declared her a "rabba."

The ordination of the Orthodox world's first rabba brought Rabbi Weiss into conflict with the Rabbinical Council of America, of which he was a member. He was rebuked by rabbis from Agudath Israel of America, who called for his excommunication from the Orthodox world, and tension grew with Yeshiva University, the flagship institution of Modern Orthodoxy. Facing such a backlash, Rabbi Weiss announced that he would no longer ordain women using this title.[11]

---

10. In the United States, Reform congregations commonly use the term "rabbi" for men and women alike, and in Israel, some Reform women wished to be called "rav" ("rabbi" in Hebrew) as an ungendered title. "Rabba" is a kind of intermediate solution for some ordained Orthodox women, as simply the feminine form of "rav." This distinction from Reform rabbis, in any case, did not placate their detractors.

11. Rabbi Weiss was not expelled from the RCA (although he walked out of it at one point), but there were many in the Orthodox establishment who thought that he

Rabba Sara moved on, joined the rabbinic team at Rabbi Weiss's synagogue in New York, and was later appointed the dean of Yeshivat Maharat. As expected, she was not recognized beyond the limited circle of Open Orthodoxy. For a few years, Hurwitz was the only Orthodox woman in the world with the title "rabba," as other women preferred less eye-catching titles, such as "maharat," "halakhic instructor," or "spiritual leader." But then came 2015, when a large cohort of Maharat graduates chose to be called "rabba." The hardline policy adopted by Orthodox institutions in the United States that year against the ordination of women was linked, in large part, to the rhetorical choice made by this graduating class.

Unlike "rabba," the title *yoatzet halakha* (used by Nishmat in Jerusalem) provoked virtually no resistance from the conservative flank of Orthodoxy. Rabbanit Henkin explained her choice of the term in an article for *Makor Rishon*: "When we set out … to train *yoatzot halakha*, we deliberately chose a modest and minimalistic term to describe this new role…. The choice of a *yoatzet halakha* was an educational choice. As we undertook to make a historic breakthrough, we wanted to emphasize to our [female] students the need to shirk arrogance and excessive independence, and to consult with halakhic decisors when making rulings."[12]

Beit Hillel, a Religious Zionist organization in which men and women hold internal deliberations and write halakhic rulings and position papers together, decided to call its female participants *talmidot ḥakhamim* – a title that evokes the traditional (male) reverence for Torah scholars (*talmidei ḥakhamim*), but tweaked to use the feminine form for the pupils themselves (*talmidot*). Malka Puterkovsky prefers to be called *eshet halakha*, "a woman of halakha" – using a grammatical structure in Hebrew that turns a noun into a profession, much like *eshet ḥinukh* (woman of education) is simply a female educator. Dina

---

had placed himself beyond the Orthodox pale. In late 2013 it was revealed, almost by chance, that the Chief Rabbinate had stopped recognizing Weiss's conversions and ordinations, citing doubts about his "commitment to accepted Jewish law." The decision was only revoked after Weiss revolted, with the help of politically powerful actors, including Alan Dershowitz and the Tzohar organization of rabbis, but in Israel the use of "rabba" caused alarm in the rabbinic establishment.

12. Chana Henkin, "Fortifying Halakha in Israel," *Makor Rishon*, October 2, 2015 [Hebrew].

Najman, who was privately ordained and established her own congregation in New York, describes herself as *rosh kehilla* ("head of community") or the Aramaic *marta de'atra*. Jennie Rosenfeld, who was appointed a spiritual leader in Efrat, preferred to dodge the question by using her academic title – "Dr." – instead. Carmit Feintuch, from Jerusalem's Ramban Synagogue, was officially a "spiritual leader" but was called "rabbanit" in day-to-day life.

"I think if we'd insisted on titles, we'd have had much less of an actual influence," Rachelle Fraenkel once said, dodging a question from the journalist Yair Sheleg. "Perhaps even the concept of a hala-khic advisor would still be considered unnatural."[13] This observation might account for attitudes on the conservative flank of contemporary Orthodoxy, which is open to a degree of female leadership as long as the title contains no whiff of rabbinic aspirations. In 2015, British Chief Rabbi Ephraim Mirvis fought to dissuade a major Orthodox synagogue from employing Dina Brawer, a feminist activist studying for the rabbinate at Maharat in New York. But a few months later, he inaugurated a new training scheme for women to serve as halakhic advisors of sorts. Many rabbis have understood the need to integrate women in such roles, and this may attest to the extent that the trend is sweeping the Orthodox world.

The winds of change can also be felt on the threshold of the national-Haredi community, which has opened seminaries and religious studies programs for women, such as the halakha program run by Tzurba M'Rabanan. This is a small step forward for women, under the tight supervision of rabbis, and it does not encompass the whole of conservative society, but it is worth remembering the hardline corner that national-Haredi rabbis had originally boxed themselves into: no advanced halakha studies whatsoever for women.

De facto female rabbinic leadership, albeit without titles such as "rabba" or "leader," is a fact of life for mainstream Religious Zionist society in Israel. The acceptance and normalization of female leadership, even in minor leadership roles such as halakhic advisors, was a rapid process

---

13. Yair Sheleg, "Torah Is Their Heart's Desire," *Makor Rishon*, October 2, 2015 [Hebrew].

in all but the hard national-Haredi flanks of Orthodox society, where assimilation of the idea has come slowly, and with difficulty.[14]

But what stands in the way of Orthodox female leadership is not only institutional barriers but a number of glass ceilings installed by Orthodox Jews who are themselves enthusiastic supporters of female leadership. The primary challenge of female leadership lies in practical encounters between halakhically trained women and the communities and individuals they wish to lead. These encounters often reveal a gulf between aspirations and reality, between enthusiastic rhetorical support for female halakhic leaders and their practical manifestations: in an era when the authority of rabbis is being eroded more broadly, for whom exactly can female Torah scholars serve as sources of halakhic authority?

Many Orthodox Jews avidly support the idea that women should be able to give halakhic rulings. The Israel Democracy Institute study on Israel's national-religious society asked respondents what they thought about the bold possibility that "women should be allowed to serve as judges on religious courts." Remember: many who welcome women as *poskot* still bar them from being judges (*dayaniyot*). This is an important nuance, because obviously nobody who welcomes female judges will object to women authoring halakhic rulings.

Among all self-identifying national-religious Israelis (including a range of more specific religious identities, from Haredi to traditionalist and "religious-lite"), 48 percent supported appointing women as judges on religious courts (26 percent "strongly supported," 22 percent "somewhat supported"), versus 42 percent who opposed it (30 percent strongly, 12 percent "somewhat"). Ten percent did not know or preferred not to answer. Notably, the more advanced a religious education the respondents had, the more likely they were to oppose women as religious judges. Nevertheless, a sizable proportion of graduates of Religious Zionist adult yeshivas (43 percent) and one third of Hesder graduates

---

14. This is not to mention Torah classes, such as those given in recent years by Rabbanit Yemima Mizrachi or the journalist Sivan Rahav-Meir to packed houses in Israel and abroad. This too is an example of female leadership in religious circles, and it is particularly prominent in the conservative camp.

(35 percent) were in favor. The stiffest resistance was registered among those who identified as Haredi (82 percent) or national-Haredi (80 percent). Among the core group of national-religious society, support for female judges stood at 46 percent, and among liberal and Modern Orthodox Jews, the rate stood at 60 percent.[15]

The data shows that national-religious society in Israel is ready to recognize women's authority on halakhic matters. But attitudes are only part of the picture. When push comes to shove, those who most reject women as halakhic authorities are also those who take halakha most seriously, those who, in the first place, are more prone to consulting their rabbis on halakhic questions in their personal life. The biggest cheerleaders of the female breakthrough, meanwhile, are those who are least likely to use their services, or, in fact, those of any rabbi at all. They simply consult rabbis less frequently. Some of them know enough to get along by themselves. Others, including those who identify as religious-lite, do not tend to ask for halakhic rulings to begin with.

When Beit Hillel launched a new initiative in the summer of 2018, offering halakhic responsa by women, it provoked hardly any reactionary pushback. Under the scheme, some two dozen female Torah scholars, including some graduates of advanced halakhic studies programs, invited women to consult them on halakhic and spiritual questions, just as rabbis have done for generations. Their answers were tailored to each woman and backed up with detailed evidence from halakhic sources.

The initiative was designed to introduce national-religious society to the professional women who had graduated from halakhic study programs, and to gain its trust. Many Orthodox Jews liked and supported the initiative. When its directors crowdfunded for a website, national-religious men and women alike donated generously. Within a short while, the initiative raised 315,000 NIS (around $95,000), more than the target sum. During the donation drive, many Israelis posted the link on Facebook and Twitter and urged their friends to share it as a means of "sanctifying God's name" or "repairing the world." The project passed the

---

15. The population sample included 1,012 people who self-identified as national-religious (representing 22 percent of a population sample of 4,600, which was representative of the Jewish population in Israel).

trial phase with flying colors, but its true test, and the test of other similar projects, hinges on a practical matter: Will members of the religious public, in their hours of need, turn to these women of halakha or not?

One of the participants in Beit Hillel's project was Rabbanit Bartov. In a conversation a few years ago, she told me: "By and large, the people I see as my relevant address, don't see me as theirs." Nevertheless, she said, there were signs that female halakhic authority was starting to trickle down into what she called "our community, the Orthodox community, which is more committed to halakha," adding: "I receive questions, mostly but not only, from women, and they're of course mostly about *nidda*."

Bartov is not the urbane feminist that you might imagine. She lives in the West Bank settlement of Talmon, has worked as a halakhic affairs advisor in the legal department of ITIM (a support service for people who need help dealing with the Chief Rabbinate), and is part of a women's activist group that lobbies for Jewish prayer rights on the Temple Mount. She is a teacher in her day job and a volunteer firewoman. "There's a popular dichotomy that if you're a woman who studies [halakha], you must be Reform, left-wing," she says. "People find it hard to digest that I'm right-wing. It doesn't match the image. I don't know how many women are caught in the same trap."

Rachelle Fraenkel is also acutely aware of the tension between the rapid pace at which women are claiming their place in religious spaces and the much slower pace dictated by those who need their services. Women trained in halakha, she told me in 2014, are already being asked questions on every subject, but most commonly about the laws of family purity – "women's issues." This is a consequence of the seriousness with which observant Jews treat these laws, and also of the need to feel comfortable with the person they are consulting on intimate matters.

Fraenkel insisted that this dissonance is not a fact of life: even members of her own community, Nof Ayalon, which is considered relatively hardline, were consulting women trained in halakhic questions, including her and Rabbanit Dr. Michal Tikochinsky, an educator at Herzog College and a board member at Tzohar, who also lives in Nof Ayalon.

Fraenkel, Bartov, Tikochinsky, and others who joined the Beit Hillel track wish to focus on the right-of-center of Religious Zionist society – those Bartov refers to as "our community, which is Orthodox, and more committed to halakha." Their challenge is complicated, however, by the fact that halakha programs include women who are more "halakhically lenient." For Bartov, "that's a shame, because it paints how people view these training programs in specific colors. As if they're all about Reform 'rabbot.' Very few women are fully committed to this complexity, both to halakha and to opening up whatever can be opened up."

In other words, some of the female religious leaders, who are at the vanguard of a rather radical undertaking, have distinctly conservative leanings. For some of the women, scholars who have spent years studying halakha and see it as the beating heart of religious life, conservatism is not only a theological and moral imperative but a practical condition for the success and broader recognition of the whole enterprise.

There remains another challenge, one related to the women's ordination programs. The most scathing criticism I have heard of them was from Malka Puterkovsky, in the week that women were ordained at Yeshivat Maharat in New York and Beit Midrash Har'el in Jerusalem. Puterkovsky was livid that the graduates had chosen to assume the title "rabba" after a four- or five-year course. "It's an own goal," she told me. "Do you know how long a man has to study for? A successful, bright yeshiva student with a solid background in Talmud – eight years, minimum. If you're willing to settle for less when it comes to women, you're basically saying you don't take any of this seriously. I'm completely against this."

Puterkovsky opposes the idea of giving women the same ordination as the one given to men by Israel's Chief Rabbinate. In her view, the Chief Rabbinate's standards are too low, and the whole sanctification of exams is anti-traditional. "How did they ordain all through the years? You used to have to be under the watchful eyes of the rabbi who taught you, and he had to check you're also a good human being. It's basic. We've gone and copied this miserable system [from the Chief Rabbinate] for women.... Add to that their willingness to make do with a sub-minimalist level of knowledge, and you've got a pretty problematic creature."

Puterkovsky dreams of a longer training track for women, lasting several more years and including rigorous personality tests and exams on halakha and jurisprudential skills, as well as on the general knowledge that she insists any rabbi or female halakhic authority must possess, including English literacy and basic psychology and economics, "because when a couple comes to me in distress and wants advice because they took too big a mortgage, I have to understand the subject."

As for the graduation ceremonies at the women's rabbinic seminaries: "Besides being an empty ritual that simply shoots us in the foot, there's nothing to it. For a simple reason: the burden of proof for women is higher than for men, so when a woman speaks on a subject on which she's not an expert, or doesn't express herself correctly in her behavior and speech, it's an own goal for the whole process. It's time that if there's something we truly believe in, we should do it seriously and thoroughly. You have to honor the method, and the halakhic method is complicated; it demands a high level of expertise, knowledge, and especially – 'I set the Lord ever before me.'"

Can Puterkovsky's demands be met? They are certainly not easy, not least because for Orthodox women, after an onerous and arduous journey, and the costs to their families and finances, there is no guaranteed gainful career waiting at the end of the road. Most of them end up teaching at women's seminaries or other institutions, in jobs they could have done without devoting years of their lives to advanced studies.

What about official, institutional recognition of these women's expertise in professions that require their halakhic skills?

Only in two cases has institutional recognition ever been forthcoming, once voluntarily and once under the threat of legal action. The first instance revolved around the admission of female halakhic advocates in rabbinic courts, after Rabbanit Nurit Fried opened a special training institute in the early 1990s. Despite opposition from the Haredi camp, the initiative took off because the management of the rabbinic courts, along with the chief rabbis at the time, Rabbi Avraham Shapira and Rabbi Mordechai Eliyahu, lent their cooperation.

The next instance came some twenty years later, after the religious women's movement Emunah and another group of religious women led by Avivit Ravia filed a class action lawsuit, demanding to be allowed to take the Chief Rabbinate's exams for *kashrut* supervisors. The role does not demand rabbinic ordination yet in practice had always been reserved for men. The Israeli rabbinate's admission criteria for *kashrut* supervisors stipulated a minimum of four years of yeshiva study – a box that women, barred from attending the necessarily all-male yeshivas, had no way of ticking.

The role of a *kashrut* supervisor demands knowledge of the Jewish dietary laws and the exercise of halakhic judgment. The Chief Rabbinate refused to let the women take the exams, but in 2014, when the Supreme Court seemed poised to order it to open its doors, the rabbinate dropped its opposition. Nine women took the test and passed; in 2019 the IDF Military Rabbinate followed suit and admitted female soldiers to its *kashrut* supervision course. Despite the festive atmosphere, however, none of the women who passed the test were subsequently employed by the rabbinate, and despite the legitimacy they had gained, they were forced to pursue careers elsewhere. Three of them joined Hashgacha Pratit, the alternative kosher certification agency that is challenging the Chief Rabbinate's monopoly. But they started a trend. In April 2019, six national-religious female Torah scholars petitioned the Supreme Court, demanding to be able to register for the Chief Rabbinate's regular halakha exams, which no woman had ever taken. In the wake of this petition, in June 2020, the state announced that for the first time, it would allow women to take the rabbinate exams and gain official recognition of their religious scholarship, although this would not include a formal certificate or rabbinical ordination.

This brings us back to the training scheme for *dayaniyot*, female religious judges, and the question of whether women might one day serve on Israel's state-run rabbinic courts. In 2015, Lindenbaum's track for religious judges had six women enrolled. They were backed up by a halakhic ruling stating that Jewish law permitted them to serve as judges in the future, so long as they met all the requirements. The author of that ruling was Rabbanit Idit Bartov, one of the students. She wrote a nine-page document analyzing the halakhic grounds for barring women. "The thrust of the rationale for the prohibition on women testifying and adjudicating," she wrote, "is rooted in societal norms, as are the formalistic halakhic reasons." In her analysis, the fact that a woman's testimony is admissible in certain cases demonstrates that "nothing invalidates its basic credibility, and a woman's testimony is necessary for the functioning of a proper legal system, which aspires to true justice, and which aims to remain a relevant alternative to other tribunals. Throughout the generations, as social norms changed, so did halakha, as needed, which presently opens up the possibility of reconsidering the prohibition and ... waiving it for those who wish [to do]."

The ruling did not suffice. The year that Rabbanit Bartov penned it, Lindenbaum suspended its *dayanut* course. Bartov maintains that the program was the victim of rabbinic politicking, and in any case the students were struggling with the prospect of investing years without an income or the promise of a career at the end of it. At any rate, the demand was not very high. Whereas women who completed rabbinic studies were able to get jobs as rabbis in all but name, there is no other way to be a religious judge in Israel other than in the state-run rabbinic courts. After the program was suspended, Bartov said: "I feel like a dream has been shattered. I can't see when the next window of opportunity will open. This is a setback for generations, truly for generations. I thought the redemption would come quickly, and now I understand that it will come step-by-step. It'll happen for our daughters, and if not for them, then for our granddaughters."

Chapter V

A New Song

Ayoung girl in Shabbat finery, perhaps in second or third grade, stands on a stool at the front of the synagogue and sings *Anim Zemirot*. The ark containing the Torah scrolls is open, the curtain moved aside, and the girl chants the beautiful liturgical poem at the top of her voice: "*I sing hymns and compose songs because my soul longs for You…*" The congregation responds in song – she sings one verse, and they sing the rest.

The scene is sweet and innocent, and today it seems wholly natural for many girls and boys growing up in the Orthodox community. But for this girl's parents, and for any Jew born in the twentieth century and taken as a child to synagogues where prayers were led exclusively by men – this is a revolution. It has its supporters and detractors, but all agree that this is an epoch-changing transformation. Until quite recently, girls did not sing *Anim Zemirot* – only boys did. Nowadays, in some synagogues, girls come to the front and lead the congregation in song.

The *Anim Zemirot* revolution is relatively tame, however, compared to some of the upheavals in many Orthodox communities in Israel. Yet it is these seemingly modest changes that are entering the mainstream and may prove especially explosive. Orthodox worshipers have begun demanding ostensibly minor changes, such as repositioning or remaking the *meḥitza*, passing the Torah scroll through the women's section during its procession around the synagogue, allowing women to deliver sermons from the front of the synagogue or dance with a Torah scroll on Simḥat Torah, or even allowing women to recite the Mourner's Kaddish during the service. Bit by bit, these changes have ruffled the feathers of previously placid synagogues. Sometimes disputes are settled by consensus; other times, they provoke such fierce arguments that members walk out and establish their own breakaway congregations.

Hakhel, the partnership *minyan* in Baka in Jerusalem, was set up by a group of worshipers who splintered off from another congregation in the neighborhood. They had wanted to open up a conversation about the role of women in the synagogue and proposed a series of what they considered modest reforms, both halakhically and in terms of the community's social norms: they wanted girls, like boys, to be able to sing *Anim Zemirot*, and women to read prayers that had been modernized anyway, such as the prayer for the State of Israel. But they opened a Pandora's box, which proved impossible to close. Before they walked out, one of their critics told them that he wanted to keep the synagogue exactly as it was, so that his "dead grandfather" could come and pray with them. In synagogue, a place which at its essence harbors a yearning for antiquity and for what once was, there is no such thing as a minor change.

This chapter is about more radical change than letting girls sing a twelfth-century poem at the end of the service, but it serves as an example of how much pent-up energy there is inside synagogues, and how issues that might appear inconsequential and peripheral from the outside are of enormous moral and symbolic significance for those within the community, at times to the point of being "make or break."

Synagogues are institutions that unite and divide communities, because everything about them, from their architecture to the format of the prayer services, reflects a very particular sense of belonging and identity. Often synagogues are defined by what they are not (a *shul* I would never set foot in …) and are animated by an aversion to change – the lifeblood of traditionalism. There have always been quarrels in synagogues about the liturgy, renovations, and even minor issues such as the location of a piece of furniture – but now they are touching the core of the synagogue experience: the prayers themselves.

The debate, as we shall see, is taking place in an Orthodox minefield, dotted with halakhic and political sensitivities. But before we delve into the details, we should begin with what is often overlooked in arguments about changes to rituals and prayers: the aesthetics, shape, and feeling of religious worship.

Thinking back, upon first entering the Shira Hadasha synagogue I was struck not by the notion or layout of the partnership *minyan*, but by a sensory experience. Specifically, the sound. It was late afternoon on Yom Kippur and a woman I didn't know was reciting from the book of Jonah during the Minḥa services. What struck me most was that the voice reverberating through the synagogue was *feminine* and high-pitched, utterly different from the vocal range I was used to in synagogue. The story about the prophet Jonah and the giant fish was familiar, and the female cantor perfectly hit all the right cantillation notes, but I, as a man and as someone who grew up in a traditional synagogue, was hearing it all in unfamiliar tones. The sounds and sights and even smells of synagogue are framed in our minds and so novelty is the gateway to disagreement about rituals and prayers and female leadership in general.

Around a year and a half before she was ordained and invited to be the rabbi of an Orthodox congregation in Chicago, Rabbanit Leah Sarna was a student at Yeshivat Maharat in New York. We met at a gathering, and she explained why the wider Orthodox public was finding it difficult to accept women as religious leaders. Her explanation, I believe, equally applies to the question of women as cantors. "Most people can't quite explain why they feel uncomfortable with women in rabbinic roles," she said, "and I think it's got something to do with the fact that we women have high-pitched voices, and we don't have beards, and we just don't look like rabbis. And people have an emotional connection to the rabbinic aesthetic. That's why men who are ordained as rabbis grow long beards and wear white shirts. There's a certain aesthetic – that's what rabbis look like. Synagogues also have their own aesthetic. You wouldn't want to see a picture of a comic-book hero on the curtain covering the ark. These principles lend dignity to what we're doing and also connect us to past generations. It's part of what we love. The Orthodox love old stuff." This is especially true with respect to synagogues.[1]

Examples of the cracking of male hegemony over prayer and ritual, within the confines of halakha, could fill a whole book. This is a dynamic and dramatic transformation, which includes women reciting the *Sheva Berakhot* at weddings, coming to synagogue with their own "four species" on Sukkot, reciting the Mourner's Kaddish, and even wearing a tallit and tefillin, although this is still peripheral in the Orthodox world. To tell the full story, we would have to explore changes around the Shabbat dinner table and describe homes where women have begun saying the blessing over the challah and joining the *zimmun*, an invitation, traditionally requiring three men, to begin the Grace After Meals. This has all materialized practically out of thin air in Orthodox society, in both Israel and abroad, and though these changes may seem minor, they represent a significant challenge for members of the community who cling to what might seem like a trivial wish – for their religious life to be a carbon copy of what they knew as children.

But for now, let's focus on the synagogue, the beating heart of religious life, because what goes on inside, even at the margins, affects the center. Orthodox society is riven with countless arguments about principle. There are debates about faith and opinions and the Torah and modernity – but nothing illustrates the social tensions quite like

---

1.   Another example of the centrality of form is the ostracization of Rabbi Adin (Even-Israel) Steinsaltz by Haredi rabbis in the 1980s. There were several reasons for challenging him, but one cardinal reason was his monumental project to translate the Babylonian Talmud from Aramaic into Modern Hebrew. The Haredim rejected this undertaking and Rabbi Steinsaltz's commentaries, but decades after he launched his project, the Schottenstein Edition of the Babylonian Talmud was published, doing exactly the same thing: rendering the Aramaic text into Modern Hebrew. This rival translation became extremely popular, including in the Haredi communities, and nobody resisted it. What was the difference? First, Haredi rabbis had gotten used to the idea and given it approval, but the Schottenstein Talmud had something else in its favor: pagination. While the Steinsaltz Talmud changed the very distinctive layout of the pages of the Talmud – one of the main charges against it – the Schottenstein Talmud transposed its modern commentaries on the traditional layout in the classic Vilna style. The form was no less important than the content.

synagogue quarrels. If members of a national-religious congregation were to declare that they were embracing biblical criticism and did not believe that the Torah was dictated, word for word, by God, they would more likely induce a few upturned noses than a rupture. But if they were to demand that women be able to read from the Torah or be cantors, a rupture would be in the offing.

The changing status quo for women in synagogues is manifesting itself in many intricate ways, each of which serves to define the congregation's identity along the religious spectrum. In many mainstream Religious Zionist synagogues, even some on the national-Haredi flank, it is normal to see women dancing with Torah scrolls on Simḥat Torah, just like men, and reading the book of Esther out loud in separate women's services on the holiday of Purim. In communities that are considered more audacious, women read from the Torah every week on Shabbat, albeit still in a separate women's service. In some synagogues, women deliver sermons from the pulpit; in more conservative communities, this might happen at the end of the service rather than in the middle. Some schools, even Orthodox ones, hold women-only prayers, where women might avoid reading from the Torah but do read the *haftara*, the additional reading from Prophets. There are many possible models, and congregations are designing their own favored format from a long menu of options.[2]

Modern Orthodoxy is also home to a more radical form of prayer that has put down roots in the community – a *minyan* that is defined as halakhic and yet allows women to lead prayers or serve as cantors, at least for part of the service, and to read from the Torah in front of an audience of both men and women, albeit separated by a *meḥitza*. This closed world is generally hidden from the view of most Israeli Jews – Haredi

---

2. In May 2022, the Pelech school, a leading high school in Jerusalem, inaugurated its new synagogue. It appears to be the first synagogue in the world to have been built solely for women. There is a *bima* and an ark but no sign of a partition, as no men are expected to attend. Significantly, though, in design and in essence, it treats the girls and their teachers as a community, a prayer quorum. That said, the school rabbi, Rabbanit Ayelet Segal, ruled that the girls would read from the synagogue's Torah scrolls, but without a blessing, so as not to cross a halakhic line.

and secular, Reform and Conservative – but marks a critical fault line within the national-religious world.

In Israel, such services are normally called "egalitarian," but Orthodox Jews in the United States would more commonly recognize them as "partnership *minyanim*" and that's the term I'll use here. Most partnership *minyanim* take the halakhic position that women can lead only parts of the service – excluding the prayers that are narrowly defined in Jewish law as requiring a *minyan*, a quorum of ten men. These sections include the *Kedusha* prayers and Kaddish. So what's left? Women in partnership *minyanim* will quite often lead *Kabbalat Shabbat* on a Friday night, the recitation of *Pesukei DeZimra* (the opening section of the Shaḥarit morning service, comprised mostly of verses from Psalms), and prayers that have traditionally also been led by boys under the age of thirteen.

Some partnership *minyanim* go for full, undifferentiated equality: whatever a man can do, so can a woman. This format is much more similar to the norm in Reform and Conservative congregations, although men and women are still generally separated by a partition. But most of these services define themselves as partnership *minyanim*, rather than fully egalitarian. This model is also known as the "Shira Hadasha model," named after the Jerusalem synagogue that made the initial breakthrough and sparked a global movement, in Israel, Britain, Australia, and the United States.

This new movement includes regular services across Israel: in Shoham, Petach Tikva, Lod, Zichron Yaakov, Mazkeret Batya, Kfar Saba, Kfar Adumim, Modiin, and more, and of course several congregations in Jerusalem. There are six partnership *minyanim* in the settlement bloc of Gush Etzion, half of them in Efrat. Besides the roughly thirty partnership *minyanim* that were active in Israel in 2019 (according to a convention of partnership *minyanim* held that year in Jerusalem), the website of the Jewish Orthodox Feminist Alliance in the United States counts forty outside of Israel. Most of these congregations meet only for Shabbat services, and some meet only once every few weeks. Orthodox partnership *minyanim* have a considerable presence on North American university campuses. Nevertheless, despite their proliferation, they still represent a tiny minority of synagogues.

The partnership *minyanim* are not identical, but they share two main anchors: they all have a *meḥitza* separating the men and women, and they all keep to the traditional liturgy. These are important identity markers. The *meḥitza* might be a symbolic or relatively low partition, separating two equal spaces, located at the same level (whereas many traditional Orthodox synagogues have a women's gallery, or an opaque partition separating a large men's section from a small women's section at the side or the back). The insistence on a *meḥitza* is not just a matter of halakha, but a socio-political statement. It acts as a symbolic buffer between them and the Reform and Conservative movements. The insistence on the traditional *siddur* (prayer book), redacted in the sixth and seventh centuries, plays a similar role. Partnership *minyanim*, even outside Israel, pray in Hebrew and do not omit key sections like non-Orthodox denominations.[3] Some congregations add short new prayers – for women denied a divorce, or expectant mothers, or IDF recruits – but as a rule, they neither skip nor rewrite the language of the prayers. The decision to maintain the ancient liturgy and the *meḥitza* has a firm halakhic and traditional grounding, and it also helps these partnership *minyanim* remain part of the broader communities from which they came.

---

3.   Over the past two hundred years, the non-Orthodox movements have published several versions of the prayer book, at different periods and in different places. Some were printed in the local language – English, German, and so forth – rather than in Hebrew, the holy tongue, as in traditional synagogues. The prayer books also tended to omit prayers for the resumption of the Temple sacrifices, and later sought to strengthen the universalist themes and obscure the particularistic Jewish themes. Reform (and some Conservative) prayer books therefore scrapped a verse from the *Aleinu* prayer that said that other religions "worship vanity and emptiness." Another section, recited after the *Shema*, which describes God's vengeance against Egypt, was elided from Reform prayer books and marked as optional in Conservative prayer books. The progressive prayer books also minimize gender inequality as much as possible, so in the ancient *Amida* prayer, some editions added to "Blessed are You, Lord, Shield of Abraham" also "who remembers Sarah." Both the Reform and Conservative movements made various additions, including modern poems and prayers and especially Zionist motifs: the Reform movement in Israel decided that on Israel Independence Day, their synagogues would read out the Declaration of Independence using the traditional biblical cantillation marks, so it would sound just like the recitation of a Torah portion.

Additionally, though its impact has by no means been uniform in nature, the Covid pandemic has affected the community's synagogues. During the summer of 2020, I traveled widely among houses of prayer, visiting established synagogues and ad hoc *minyanim* on street corners and balconies and within courtyards. Every house of prayer had its own unique story. Some sprang up out of nowhere, some grew, some dwindled and collapsed. The variables – the size of the community, the devotion of its worshipers, its geographic location, the congregants' median age – are vast. But one common trend, which however is not overarching, is that the local neighborhood *minyan* was strengthened while the established *minyanim*, of the sort that have salaried positions, suffered. The same was true of out-of-the-way synagogues, which are often dependent on congregants coming from afar to attend a specific sort of service. This was true of the partnership *minyanim*, too. At times, the congregants simply didn't come.

But there were also trends in the opposite direction. For example, at a street *minyan* in the Old Katamon neighborhood of Jerusalem, Rabbanit Hannah Hashkes, a graduate of the Midreshet Lindenbaum program, found herself delivering the Shabbat sermon every week. The community consisted of religious Jews spanning the spectrum from conservative to liberal, and in ordinary times, many of them would have resisted the notion of a weekly *devar Torah* given to the entire community by a woman, but Covid seemed to ease the opposition.

Dr. Tamar Meir, from the largely religious suburb of Givat Shmuel in central Israel, said that her neighborhood's "balcony *minyan*," during the height of the Covid outbreak, made her realize the extent to which she did not miss her usual place behind the *meḥitza*.

"As opposed to my husband and sons," she said, "I missed the synagogue a little less, and for me it was an extraordinary experience to pray with my sons for the first time in my life. It just so happened that my youngest son was called up to sing *Anim Zemirot*, for his first time ever, from the balcony, and he belted it out, really roaring, and I stood beside him. After raising five boys, I now, for the first time, stood beside my son when he sang *Anim Zemirot* and I hugged him immediately afterwards. It was mind-blowing."

Meir is the head of the Kulana women's beit midrash and throughout her professional life she has been more deeply invested in the study hall than the synagogue, and though Covid was for her a "formative experience," as she put it, she has not opted to shift course and begin praying in a partnership *minyan*. But it has, she said, shed light on questions that were lurking sleepily beneath the surface for years.

The global revolution began in south Jerusalem at two points that were twenty-two years and just under a mile apart: the Kehillat Yedidya Synagogue, founded in 1980, and Shira Hadasha, the first partnership *minyan*, founded in 2002. The two congregations have much in common. Some of their members are native-born Israelis, but American-born Jews who immigrated to Israel are by far more dominant. Both synagogues produced groups of women who placed a special emphasis on the nature of the prayers and the melodies, on making the synagogue a powerful community center, and on feminism.

These two trailblazing synagogues sit at either end of Baka, a once-Arab neighborhood, pre-1948, that was mostly populated by Jewish immigrants from the Arab world in the 1950s and 1960s and then was totally transformed decades later. Baka gradually became more Ashkenazi and anglophone; the cost of living skyrocketed. In time, the neighborhood and its environs became host to a liberal religious community. Kol HaNeshama, a Reform synagogue, was founded in Baka in the 1980s. The residents who frequented the old synagogues were replaced. South Jerusalem became a home for Orthodox women's seminaries, study programs for religious and secular Israelis alike, and the mixed religious-secular Keshet school.

Kehillat Yedidya and Shira Hadasha, both Orthodox synagogues, pioneered a new kind of service – one that initially only their members deemed appropriate, but which soon, after a long incubation period, burst out of the south Jerusalem bubble.

Kehillat Yedidya is not a partnership synagogue but introduced to Israeli religious society several innovations that have since become the archetype for Orthodox partnership *minyanim*. Unlike the synagogues of old, where the women's section is a tiny space at the back or side of the hall or in a separate gallery, the men's and women's sections in Kehillat Yedidya are on the same plane and of an equal size, separated by a low and non-opaque *meḥitza* down the middle. The architecture, common in the United States as well, became the gold standard for partnership *minyanim* ever since.[4]

No less important was the remodeling of the prayer service. During the reading of the Torah at Kehillat Yedidya, women who wished to do so went to a separate hall, where they held a women-only Torah reading, inspired by the women's "prayer groups" that had previously only taken off in Orthodox Jewish communities in the United States. After the congregation acquired a permanent synagogue building, this arrangement was retained. In the main synagogue hall, women assume certain roles, such as parading the Torah scroll through the women's section, but the main roles – those of the cantor and people who read from the Torah – are reserved for men. A separate but quite spacious hall on the ground floor hosts an alternative partnership *minyan*, led by women.

Twenty-two years after Kehillat Yedidya was founded, a small group of men and women sat in Tova Hartman's living room in Baka and decided to establish a synagogue the likes of which the Orthodox world had never known. Women would read from the Torah, not just in a side room, but in front of everybody. They would deliver sermons and be full partners in leading the services. They would perform every role that could be halakhically justified. The *bima*, the central stage, would be in the center, and the *meḥitza* would separate the equally sized men's and women's sections straight down the middle. The synagogue would not enshrine *full* gender equality, but it would be shaped by its members as they went along, and women would not have to watch from the gallery – they would be active partners.

It was Shira Hadasha that first designed the partnership *minyan*, both the format and its halakhic underpinning, and decided that it would be the only service in the community, in the main hall – not as an alternative offering in the basement. It picked up on Kehillat Yedidya's precedent and took a huge stride forward; a decade later, it was undeniable that it had sparked a revolution. But what was the story behind

---

4.   Rabbi Avi Weiss from New York told me that his synagogue, The Bayit, where the services do not follow the partnership model but adhere much more closely to the traditional Orthodox format, was the first to divide the hall into two equal areas, on the same level, with the *bima* exactly in the middle.

these partnership and egalitarian *minyanim*, what was the idea behind them, and how did the founders justify this innovation under halakha?

Every member of Shira Hadasha's founding core, who sat in Hartman's living room, arrived with a different background. Some were native-born Israelis, some were immigrants; some were old, some were young; but they all shared a frustration with the exclusion of women from traditional synagogue services. In the years before Shira Hadasha was founded, some of those present had chosen to celebrate bat mitzvas in private ad hoc family services, with borrowed Torah scrolls, so that their daughters could read from the Torah just like a boy at his bar mitzva.

Tova Hartman had done the same for her daughter, but now she wanted to make this arrangement permanent. She had spoken with several liberal-minded rabbis and congregations in south Jerusalem, hoping to persuade them to let women's voices be heard in prayer services. "Nobody was interested, and then I felt, if I didn't make the change, it wouldn't happen," she recalled. "My daughter was in twelfth grade and I said, before she finishes high school, I want her to feel obligated to come to synagogue on Shabbat for *Pesukei DeZimra* because she would be counted as a member of the quorum. I knew that change was necessary. I spoke to a few people, and we said, 'We're starting.'"

Nevertheless, Hartman emphasizes, Shira Hadasha was not founded as a "*shtiebel* that allows women to be called to the Torah": it would not be a small, informal affair founded for the purpose of handing out jobs and fancy titles to women, but would be part of a broader Jewish feminist worldview that she calls "cultural." She says that if her only purpose had been to allow women to read from the Torah, "I would have had no problem going to the Reform movement, but Reform and also Conservative Jews have never built a religious feminist congregation; they simply adopted liberal feminism wholesale. I believed deep down that Shira Hadasha's promise should be a joint prayer service that takes the human element into account. Do I think it's a success that there are partnership *minyanim* everywhere nowadays? No, that's not the point. When you join our *minyan*, your family must also sign up as being willing to host someone who has nowhere to go, who's a total stranger to you, for a Shabbat meal after the service. For me, feminism and religious feminism mean bringing what women have to offer, what they've done all these years, to the front and center of religious life: serving food to the poor, taking care of people. For me, feminism was about shifting what women represent and have represented from the private to the public spheres. Leading a religious life means you don't sit down to eat if anyone's left out. You just don't. As an overstatement – I wanted the synagogue to be a messy, chaotic place, where people could always come knowing they would always leave with someone. They'd never leave alone. Synagogue-goers who ask God to look upon them must look at everyone else, because that's the meaning of a prayerful community. People at the synagogue understood this. For me, that's feminism – to honor other lifestyles. I know how to learn Torah, but we were a group of people who wanted to create a new concept of a religious community."

These avant-garde *minyanim* were influenced by non-Orthodox egalitarian congregations in the United States, but from the perspective of the development of Orthodox feminism, they might look like a historical tangent. Jewish religious feminism emerged in women's seminaries, so it might have seemed more natural for it to develop in the direction of scholarship, halakha, and rabbinic studies, not to switch course and focus on prayer. Moreover, some of the female trailblazers in the world of religious scholarship and leadership want no part in partnership *minyanim*.[5]

---

5. The most prominent voice in this regard is Rachelle Fraenkel, whose recitation of the Mourner's Kaddish at her son's funeral made a huge public impression, concerning the role of women in public prayer and bereavement customs. But the line that Fraenkel crossed was a soft one, from the formal perspective of Jewish law, and it elicited little reactionary criticism. Like other prominent female halakhic authorities, Fraenkel is far from the philosophy of partnership synagogues and said that in hindsight, she never had any intention of becoming a feminist icon. It is doubtful whether Fraenkel, who devoted her life to the study hall, planned to become a religious leader who would change many people's minds about the synagogue.

On a personal note: Few of my dispatches have made as big an impact, or elicited as much emotion, as my report on Rachelle Fraenkel's Kaddish. Many women told me they saw Fraenkel as a role model, but a common complaint I heard, ironically from more conservative quarters, was that I should not have turned her Kaddish into a "news item" because there was nothing particularly novel about it, from a halakhic perspective. But I think this focus on the formalities of halakha allowed

This pivot, from the study hall to the synagogue, might be confusing for anyone used to conceiving of Jewish religious feminism as a movement that undermines religious commitments, even if not overtly, and is distant from religious intensity. Truth be told, this conception is not always ungrounded. Many religious feminist women, just like many religious men from the liberal flanks of Judaism, tended to channel their Jewish energies to academic research and activism in Jewish renewal movements. These are two modern (and non-God-centered) ways of exalting the values of Yavne – the city where Jewish life was rebuilt around scholarship after the destruction of the Temple – over those of Jerusalem, with its focus on ritual. But it turns out that there are many Jewish women who want to stake a claim to the parcel of Jewish life that revolves around worship and ritual: the Judaism of Jerusalem, in its modern form. Why is this happening? Why is it worship that they want now?

One possibility is that religion and ritual are hardwired into the human brain, a more powerful default mode than any fleeting ideology.[6] Vered Noam, a professor at Tel Aviv University and winner of the Israel Prize in Talmud, has a more precise answer, which specifically addresses the modern age: the increasing dissonance between what goes on inside

---

these critics to dodge the question of the aesthetic and cultural novelty of seeing a woman recite Kaddish – a novelty that may be no less powerful, and will probably be even more powerful, than any ideological or theoretical novelties. Even today, this is a change that would not be accepted by most religious communities, and in many places where it has been accepted, Rachelle Fraenkel's Kaddish made a critical contribution. The report on *Haaretz*'s English-language website attracted a record readership, for the time, and provoked a flood of comments – on the *Haaretz* website, on Facebook, on Twitter, and in synagogue newspapers and on other platforms. See: Yair Ettinger, "When Rachelle Fraenkel Recited the Kaddish, the Chief Rabbi Said 'Amen,'" *Haaretz*, July 2, 2014, available at https://www.haaretz.com/.premium-the-chief-rabbi-said-amen-1.5254214.

6. I found a literary expression of this mindset in the fictional character of Professor Andrew Cohen, the hero of Ruby Namdar's novel *The Ruined House* (English translation published by HarperPerennial, 2018). Cohen, whose Jewish identity is almost completely erased, is a postmodernist lecturer in comparative culture studies in New York, who at the pinnacle of his career is swept away by a series of frightening visions, as the descendant of an ancient priestly family, of animal sacrifices in the Temple of Jerusalem two thousand years earlier. His religious consciousness, a force he is totally ignorant of, lashes out and subdues him, mentally and physically.

the synagogue and what goes on beyond its walls. Noam became a leading advocate of equality in synagogues when she argued that Judaism loses its authenticity when religious Jews are willing to accept all sorts of double standards inside synagogue, where women are voiceless, while outside the synagogue, in the home and in their professional roles, they most certainly do have a voice. In an influential article published in 2013, Noam criticized her own society, "in which the tensions between its declared value system and the reality surrounding it and the natural spiritual inclinations of its members, have led it on a difficult path of denial, disregard, and strong repression – of both the external and the internal reality. This repression leads to duplicity, compartmentalization, deceit, double standards, and the construction of wall upon wall and partition upon partition – all honestly and truly in the name of heaven. The first ones to be crushed beneath these walls are the women, who in their very being, to their detriment, represent the fault line between the two worlds."[7]

Noam fought to have a partnership *minyan* established in her community, in Kfar Adumim, despite the opposition of the local rabbi. One year after she published her article in *Makor Rishon*, she organized a public conference in which the different sides were invited to voice their opinions about the inclusion of women in synagogues. It was there that she formulated her criticism as a question of religious fervor: "Our synagogues are sick. Let's be honest, they're wilting. Weekday prayers are a drab affair for a small group of weary men, and Shabbat is largely about flicking through the synagogue newspapers, maybe a little bit of gossip and conversation. Is what's happening there really what we'd like to have happen? Is anything real happening there? Anything spiritual? Is there a feeling of closeness to God? Is there a feeling of worshiping the Divine? The first step toward healing our synagogues is to try to imbue them with a new purpose, and that will only happen when everyone in the community is a partner. . . . Women won't just bring communal

---

7.   Vered Noam, "Beyond the Inner *Meḥitza*," *Makor Rishon*, January 13, 2013. Reproduced in Yair Ettinger, "Is Orthodox Judaism on the Verge of a Historic Schism?" *Haaretz*, July 27, 2015, available at https://www.haaretz.com/jewish/. premium-is-orthodox-judaism-on-the-verge-of-a-historic-schism-1.5379629.

authenticity, they'll also bring tremendous religious energy. If you've never seen a woman called up to the Torah, you've never seen a truly religious experience in your life. I say so also from personal experience. It's a Mount Sinai experience. It's standing at the foot of Mount Sinai. Doesn't matter where it happens – in women's readings, on Simḥat Torah, in partnership *minyanim*, in a service like this or like that. It's an unparalleled experience. Anyone who has watched it from the side or experienced it herself knows exactly what I'm talking about."

Noam was not the only woman who fought for the establishment of a partnership *minyan* in her community. In the sleepy commuter town of Shoham, a fierce argument raged after the "Nachat Ruach" partnership *minyan* was established in defiance of the municipal chief rabbi, David Stav. In a class that he gave one Shabbat for members of all of Shoham's synagogues, Rabbi Stav expressed sympathy for women's frustration with the traditional prayer service but put his foot down: the women and men praying in the partnership *minyan* were violating halakha and traditional Jewish jurisprudence.

So what do the many hundreds of Orthodox Jews who regularly pray in partnership *minyanim* rely on? In 2001, a US-born Jerusalem resident by the name of Mendel Shapiro published a comprehensive halakhic paper on this matter in the English-language religious journal, *Edah*. Shapiro had a religious education and was ordained as a rabbi but worked as a lawyer. He approached the question armed only with halakhic tools, but as an observant family man he had a pressing need for an answer: his daughter was about to turn twelve, and the family had a dilemma – whether to celebrate her bat mitzva by having her read from the Torah in front of a mixed congregation of men and women. Shapiro was not the first to analyze this question, but his paper was especially thorough and sparked a major debate.[8]

The article was quickly translated to Hebrew and played a role, one year later, in the founding of Shira Hadasha. "Thinking back, it was a formative halakhic ruling, mainly because of his halakhic integrity,

---

8. Mendel Shapiro, "Qeri'at ha-Tora by Women: A Halakhic Analysis," *The Edah Journal* 1, no. 2 (2001), available at http://www.edah.org/backend/JournalArticle/1_2_sha-piro.pdf.

making honest use of both halakhic and modern sources," recalls Tova Hartman. "But even in real time, many of the people who joined Shira Hadasha were aware of his article and had read it, and it was important for them. Personally, when we founded Shira Hadasha, I didn't need his paper, I had made up my mind in a different way, but I knew it existed and its halakhic language and halakhic discourse was of tremendous significance."

In rabbinic literature, women, unlike men, are not obligated to pray in a quorum, and certainly not to lead prayers in a quorum or read from the Torah. The halakhic debate, therefore, is about whether women are *permitted* to lead communal prayers if they so wish, not whether they are *obligated*. This is an important distinction, because even if women may perform such roles, without any positive obligation to do so, the next question is whether such activities are of halakhic benefit or value. Only if the answer to this question is yes can one argue, in the framework of halakhic logic, that a woman may *lehotzi yedei ḥova,* or help a man fulfill his halakhic obligation..

The halakhic debate over the contours of a quorum or *minyan* began in the Talmud and preoccupied the medieval sages, but only in the late twentieth century (some forty years after the issue was debated by the Conservative movement in the United States, which ruled that there were no limitations on women reading from the Torah) did Orthodox rabbis revisit the ancient texts and interpret them in the context of the dilemmas of contemporary religious communities. The modern polemic emerged sporadically, in particular in English-language religious journals. Interestingly, some of the most prominent writers in English were new immigrants to Israel from the anglophone world.

One basic concept in the halakhic debate over whether women may read from the Torah is *kevod hatzibur* – "congregational dignity." It is a meta-halakhic principle: a fundamental value from which other laws are derived, invoked both by permissive rabbis who wish to abolish prohibitions and restrictive ones who wish to add more. The Babylonian Talmud says as follows: "All people count toward the quorum of seven readers, even a minor and even a woman. However, the Sages said that a woman should not read the Torah, out of respect for the congregation."[9]

The starting point for the debate is the Torah reading on Shabbat in synagogue. The weekly portion is divided into seven sections, and each section is preceded by a blessing. Seven members of the congregation are invited to recite the blessing out loud in front of everyone; sometimes they also read the Torah portion, or the *baal koreh* might read it in their name. The Talmud's position, basing itself on an earlier source from the mishnaic period, is that there is no halakhic obstacle to having women read from the Torah and recite the blessing. But the Sages proposed that they should not exercise this right, out of respect for the congregation. The deed was deemed socially improper.

The more lenient arbiters of halakhic law argue that "congregational dignity" is by definition a flexible social norm; and since in the modern day, women not only study Talmud but also serve as doctors, company directors, and political leaders, there is no impediment to women reading from the Torah in synagogue. More hardline rabbis argue, however, that "respect for the congregation" has a rigid definition, and that traditionally rabbis only ever used this passage from the Babylonian Talmud to allow women to read from the Torah in exceptional cases in which there were no literate men in the community – a situation that does not really exist in the modern Jewish world.

There are other, tangential halakhic questions. The Torah is not read like prose but chanted, using traditional melodies and cantillation marks; this brings up the matter of women's singing and its allegedly inherent immodesty, as depicted in the talmudic refrain *kol be'isha erva*: "The voice of a woman is nakedness." Does this restriction not exclude women from reading the Torah? Moreover, since women are not obligated to recite the blessing, would this not be considered *berakha levatala*, a blessing recited in vain? There are also concerns about letting women lead services in communities that shun women's leadership in general. But the thrust of the debate pivots around the question

---

9. Babylonian Talmud, Megilla 23a, available from the Sefaria Library at Sefaria.org.

of whether letting women read from the Torah is "disrespectful" to the congregation at large.

Mendel Shapiro argued in his landmark paper that women were permitted to recite the blessing over the Torah when it was read by a man, and even to read from the Torah themselves, if the congregation did not consider this "disrespectful," given the change in women's social status. The principle of *kevod hatzibur*, he argued, only prevented women from reading from the Torah if they are considered to belong to a lower social class than the male members of the congregation.

Among Shapiro's notable adversaries were Aryeh and Dov Frimer, two brothers. Like Shapiro, they too had immigrated to Israel from the United States and were officially rabbis but worked in other fields – as a chemist and lawyer respectively. Like Shapiro, they too fought their halakhic battles in public and in English. Writing in the Rabbinical Council of America's journal in the late 1990s, they argued, based on halakhic sources, that *kevod hatzibur* is an immutable principle.[10] They later listed all the halakhic restrictions barring women from reading from the Torah or reciting the blessing over it, adding to *kevod hatzibur* concerns that it exposed men to "sexual distractions" and that inviting those who were not obligated to read from the Torah to do so belittled the commandment itself. They took their cue, in part, from Rabbi Yehuda Herzl Henkin, who wrote that although there existed a theoretical possibility for women to read from the Torah, it should not be actualized because of "accepted custom."

The debate was largely driven by private individuals who felt passionate about the subject, not by professional rabbis. The exceptions were Rabbi Prof. Daniel Sperber, who in 2007 published *The Path of Halakha: Women Reading the Torah* (Hebrew), specifically about this question. Rabbi Sperber is an Israel Prize laureate and an emeritus professor of Talmud, who served as president of Bar-Ilan University's Institute for Advanced Torah Studies. When the annals of the internal conflicts in Orthodox Judaism are written, he will surely merit a chapter of his own. Rabbi Sperber has personally ordained women as Orthodox rabbis in

---

10. See, for example, Aryeh Frimer and Dov Frimer, "Women's Prayer Services –Theory and Practice: PART 1: THEORY," *Tradition: A Journal of Orthodox Jewish Thought*, 31, no. 2 (Winter 1998): 5–118.

Israel and the United States and is a halakhic authority for partnership *minyanim* in Tel Aviv and New York. He publicly supported homosexuals and lesbians who sought inclusion in religious communities, including his filmmaker daughter Avigail, who in 2005 founded Bat-Kol – A Religious Lesbian Organization. In 2018, he established a private rabbinic court, which dissolved a marriage in a particularly thorny case of a woman, Tzvia Gorodetsky, who had spent twenty-three years trying unsuccessfully to obtain a divorce through Israel's state-run rabbinic courts.

Sperber lent his reputation and credentials to the cause and officially permitted women to read from the Torah. But he also took a more radical step and introduced another halakhic concept to the discussion: besides *kevod hatzibur*, he insisted that the debate take account of *kevod haberiyot* – human dignity, or more literally, respect for the creations. In Sperber's analysis, not only do social norms change, but in the case of women's Torah reading, the meta-halakhic principle of respecting the community clashes with another meta-principle of respecting individuals and does not, by definition, trump it.

"Nowadays," he wrote, "in communities that agree on a need for change within the normative framework of halakha, where a failure to change would cause pain and sorrow for an important section of the community, the principle of *kevod haberiyot* trumps the dubious principle of *kevod hatzibur*." Additionally: "It seems obvious that *kevod haberiyot*, individual human dignity, must trump *kevod hatzibur*, especially when the public's dignity is not truly at stake, as it might have been in antiquity and the Middle Ages."

In Sperber's view, the desire of religious women to reach ever-ascending levels of prayer and religious experience, and to delve deeper into Torah studies, are not "merely" cultural and social concerns. Rather, they count for something in halakhic deliberations because they fall under the rubric of *naḥat ruaḥ* – spiritual satisfaction: a talmudic principle that allows women to act upon their thirst for greater spiritual involvement than otherwise afforded them by halakha.[11]

---

11. See Babylonian Talmud, Ḥagiga 16b, where the rabbis explain that one reason why women were permitted to perform a certain Temple custom that they were not

In time, there was an accretion of halakhic rulings permitting women to read from the Torah. The halakhic debate on the subject is multi-layered and labyrinthine, and we have only scraped the surface, but consider two salient arguments, one from each side of the debate. Aryeh and Dov Frimer wrote: "But we do have misgivings about those who would enact women's *aliyyot* [reciting the blessing over the Torah, or reading it out loud] in practice, and hastily undo more than two millennia of halakhic precedent, simply because a publication or two has appeared on the subject. As this article demonstrates, the subject of women's role in *keriat haTorah* involves very complicated halakhic issues – which require extensive in-depth analysis. Considering the novelty of this innovation, religious integrity and sensitivity requires the patience of allowing the halakhic discourse of *shakla vetarya* (give and take) to run its course – leading to the formation of a consensus – before acting on such a significant departure from normative halakha and tradition. Modern Orthodoxy should welcome diversity and flexibility, but any innovations must be halakhically well founded and solidly based. It often takes time before a final determination can be reached as to whether or not a suggested innovation meets these standards. But that is no justification for haste. Indeed, the past decade has seen an ever-growing number of recognized halakhic scholars and authorities who firmly reject the halakhic acceptability of women's *aliyyot*."[12]

In other words, for Religious Zionist women, the time had not yet come.

Rabbi Sperber, however, took the contrary view: "A new generation is arising, of women who yearn for the Torah and ritual observance. They have invested years studying Torah for its own sake, without any financial benefit, out of a sense of devotion and dedication to their spiritual goals. They wish to rise to higher levels of spiritually by toiling in the study of Torah and delving deeply in their prayers. They marry graduates of Religious Zionist yeshivas, who are also immersed in the world of Torah. They are beginning to coalesce into young new

---

required to perform was "in order to please the women."

12. Aryeh Frimer and Dov Frimer, "Women, 'Keri'at ha-Torah,' and 'Aliyyot,'" *Tradition: A Journal of Orthodox Jewish Thought*, 46, no. 4 (Winter 2013): 120.

communities, full of joy and song, intense prayer and spirituality. And when they wish to design their houses of prayer and imbue them with a special character of joyous observance and piety, they do everything as a team, with a sense of common purpose. More active participation by these women in prayer services will not injure public dignity in the least. Must we reject such pearls in our midst and push them toward other, alien movements and frameworks? Should we not thank God that we have such communities?"[13]

Most egalitarian and partnership *minyanim*, such as that of Mechon Hadar in New York, define themselves as "halakhic" – that is, as bound by Jewish tradition and jurisprudence and grounded in the sources of Jewish law. This is essential to how they define themselves, more so than the socio-political label of "Orthodox." But what does it mean to be "halakhic"? Here, the debate appears to veer from a narrow technical discussion of what is allowed and what is forbidden to the broader question of the doctrine of halakhic rulings and the nature of halakhic thought in general. How much leeway should modern rabbis have to pick

---

13. The role of women is not the only source of contention in contemporary Orthodox synagogues. In recent years, Modern Orthodox yeshivas and synagogues in Israel and in the Diaspora, including in the mainstream, have developed a custom of festive prayers in synagogue using musical instruments on the first of every Jewish month or national holidays, such as Israeli Independence Day and Jerusalem Day. The *Hallel* prayer, recited on such festive occasions, is full of wonderful melodies, and members of these congregations were delighted to have a chance to revitalize it with musical instruments, which are not a standard feature in Orthodox synagogues, certainly not on Shabbat and during Jewish holidays, when it is forbidden to play them. Synagogues have also started holding *Seliḥot* services using musical instruments during the month of Elul and the Ten Days of Awe. A coalition of national-Haredi rabbis is resisting this new trend, among them Rabbi Yaakov Ariel, formerly the chief rabbi of Ramat Gan, and Rabbi Shlomo Aviner from the Har Hamor movement. Without getting into the reasoning of the more conservative rabbis, their prohibitions failed to stamp out the new phenomenon but only served to sharpen the distinction between the national-Haredi camp and the Religious Zionist mainstream, including but not limited to the liberal flank. Joining the trend were high school yeshivas and Hesder yeshivas, whose rabbis embraced the novelty of introducing musical instruments into the synagogue.

and choose from halakhic sources and select that which best addresses the problem at hand?

The debate over the status of women in synagogues, for example, is not driven by a "dry" halakhic analysis so much as a set of social and ideological preferences: the pull and tug of conservatism and progressivism. As can be seen from arguments about politically loaded topics such as the status of women, the dry halakhic considerations are weighted with secondary considerations, such as the conservatives' perpetual fear of a slippery slope. In other words, the "pure" halakhic questions are viewed through a lens of religious identity and politics.

This conflation is clear from the criticism of partnership *minyanim*. Rabbi Yehoshua Shapira, head of the Ramat Gan Yeshiva, was one of the first to try to place partnership *minyanim* "beyond the bounds" of the community at large, smearing them as "neo-Reform."[14] He argued that this movement would eventually splinter off from the Religious Zionist mainstream. Shortly after the Israeli journalist Kobi Nachshoni scooped a recording of his remarks on the news site *Ynet*, Rabbi Shapira clarified his thinking in a message to students at his yeshiva, which was published on its website: "Sometimes we need to say it clearly: is Shira Hadasha loyal to halakha or not? A synagogue has emerged in our midst that is unfaithful to halakha ... [but] their actions are less important than the breach in the fence, the fracturing of religious consensus about halakha and our connection to it."

Unlike Rabbi Shapira, who favors a secession, other opponents of partnership *minyanim* spoke of the possibility of a schism with trepidation, but still blamed the partnership *minyanim* for pushing their luck, or rather, trying to have their cake and eat it too. Rabbanit Chana Henkin, a pioneer of women's halakha and Talmud studies, said of partnership *minyanim* that "halakha does not treat men and women equally, and whoever avoids this reality in one place will run into it elsewhere. That's what concerns me about Shira Hadasha and the egalitarian *minyanim* .... I'm concerned about what tomorrow will bring for people who are enthusiastic about tearing down a particular wall, because at some

---

14. Kobi Nachshoni, "The Hardali Attack: 'A Reform Movement Is Springing Up in Our Midst,'" *Ynet*, July 5, 2009 [Hebrew].

point the community will hit a wall it can't tear down. I'm concerned for the future of a community that keeps trying to repeatedly push the envelope and finally the envelope can't be pushed any further."[15]

Among the founders and members of the partnership *minyanim* are many graduates of the Religious Kibbutz Movement's yeshiva, students of Rabbi Aviya Hacohen, but like many rabbis (even liberal ones), he personally avoids these services: "The egalitarian *minyanim*, with intolerable nonchalance and absent-mindedness, divided the Jewish people and built synagogues that not all Orthodox Jews can pray in. How can you create a rift like that? It's something that simply isn't done."[16]

The list of rabbis who oppose women's active participation in the synagogue is long and it includes voices from most sections of the religious spectrum. Some see a schism around the corner, precisely because so many of the members of the rapidly growing partnership *minyanim* are the flesh and blood of the Religious Zionist community. Some believe that the schism has already happened. Two denominations, two kinds of synagogue, two different models of prayer. But as the mainstream rabbis try to slam on the brakes, Prof. Tamar Ross, one of the pioneers of the wave of religious feminism, told me: "The train has left the station. The rabbis can throw stones at the windows and shout, '*Shabbes! Shabbes!*'"

The partnership *minyanim* started in Israel but draw more fire in the United States. There are many reasons for this, many related to the more institutionalized nature and defensive posture of Orthodox Judaism outside Israel, but for our purposes one practical reason suffices: most Orthodox communities outside of Israel are small, and the establishment of a rival service risks peeling off a significant proportion of a congregation's members. In a neighborhood of Jerusalem, the creation of a new *minyan* might cause a commotion or supply some good gossip. But in a suburb of Washington or London, or an American university campus

---

15. Cited in Yael Freidson, "Religious Feminism? You Can't Ignore a Thousand Years of Jurisprudence," *Makor Rishon*, March 12, 2015 [Hebrew].
16. Ariel Horowitz, "The Openness Hurts," *Makor Rishon*, May 9, 2014 [Hebrew].

with few Jewish students in the first place, a new Orthodox *minyan* will have an impact on everybody.

Leah Sarna, who would later be ordained as a rabbi at Maharat, told me that her childhood community in the Boston suburb of Newton used to have a women's *minyan*, which met every few weeks, under the auspices of the main congregation. But the establishment of a partnership *minyan*, Yedid Nefesh, caused problems. It does not hold services every Shabbat, but when it does, the main synagogue empties out – a challenge that the congregation is still struggling to cope with. She describes similar scenes in the large Modern Orthodox communities of Silver Spring, Maryland, and Skokie, Illinois.

The same was true of the Orthodox *minyan* at her alma mater, Yale, where some of the students used to pray at the regular Orthodox synagogue. "The question of the tension surrounding a partnership *minyan* depends on the campus," she explains. "On some campuses, those who would never go to a partnership *minyan* complain about those who do, because it deprives them of lots of members. And it's really not obvious that there should be two Orthodox services. Because when I was at Yale, we had to work really hard for there to be two parallel *minyanim*. It caused a lot of tension, especially at the beginning. If you don't have twenty men showing up to two prayer services, what do you do? There's no *minyan*. The members of the regular Orthodox *minyanim* grumbled, and felt like 'We're serious; they're just playing around.' One of the things that those at the partnership *minyanim* needed to get across right at the get-go was: We aren't here to fool around, and our service is no less an expression of values than yours. We represent values in a way you never will. This matters to us, and if we're no longer there – well, that would require us to compromise."

Partnership *minyanim* have upended Jewish communities not just in Israel and the United States, but also Britain. Rabbi Chaim Kanterowitz of Borehamwood and Elstree Synagogue, in a town outside London with a large Jewish community, sent a detailed letter to members of his congregation in November 2016. He explained that partnership *minyanim* were "a breach of Jewish law" and that it was forbidden to "attend, lead, or partake" in them. He also announced that men who led prayers in the partnership *minyan* in the neighborhood would henceforth be barred from leading High Holy Day services in his own congregation.[17]

The possibility of a split into two distinct religious denominations, each with different customs of prayer, and the prospect that other Orthodox Jews might refuse to enter their synagogues or partake in their children's synagogue-based celebrations, is a matter that has concerned and continues to concern many members of partnership *minyanim*. At the same time, many of them, especially members of the founding "wilderness generation" of these alternative services, feel that they have already paid a personal price for following through on their religious convictions.

Dr. Chana Kehat, the former head of the feminist religious organization Kolech, was one of the founders of the women-only *minyan* Shirat Rivka in the settlement of Neve Daniel in Gush Etzion. She has said on several occasions that she was hounded out of her community by the polemic around the *minyan*, forced to find a new place to live with her family. Dr. Gili Zivan, a Jewish studies lecturer, describes her efforts to set up a *minyan* that would meet once a month or two, to pray in the style of Shira Hadasha, in her religious kibbutz, Saad, which is not considered conservative: "Living in a small Religious Zionist community, I was quickly labeled …. I was no longer Gili but 'that crazy woman,' 'that feminist' (in this context, not a compliment), and 'the leftist.'… Some people stopped coming to my classes, boycotted my articles, prejudged everything I did or said. I walked along paths I'd taken hundreds of times before, feeling that ever since 'coming out of the closet,' I was seen as the biggest threat to the rabbinic establishment since the early days of the Reform movement in Germany."[18]

Several years after these reports, so much has changed. The membership of these *minyanim* has grown, virtually all coming from the

---

17. Simon Rocker, "United Synagogue Rabbi Defends Restrictions on Partnership Minyan Leaders," *The Jewish Chronicle*, November 18, 2016, available at https://www.thejc.com/news/uk-news/united-synagogue-rabbi-defends-restrictions-on-partnership-minyan-leaders-1.55051.

18. Gili Zivan, "The Anatomy of Religious Feminist Change in One Small Community," *De'ot* 55 (December 2011–February 2012) [Hebrew].

Religious Zionist community.[19] A minority, surely, but still an increasingly self-confident one, not least thanks to social media, which has allowed members of disparate partnership *minyanim* to see themselves no longer as fringe elements but as parts of a larger movement. "We are a fringe movement, but even ideological movements on the margins have a big influence on the mainstream," says Rabbi Mishael Zion, the founder of the Klausner partnership *minyan* in Jerusalem.[20]

But at what point will the margins stop influencing the mainstream? Will girls who are currently in first or second grade and sing *Anim Zemirot* in synagogue feel comfortable in more traditional synagogues, where women are hardly seen and never heard? Will the partnership *minyanim* continue striving for full equality, and find ways to abolish the remaining restrictions and count women toward a quorum of ten and allow them to lead the Shaḥarit prayer? Will they become completely egalitarian, drifting further away from the Orthodox mothership? Will those who insist on praying just like their parents and grandparents agree to step foot in partnership synagogues, if they view them as a grave breach of Jewish law?

Family events have already become fraught. What should traditional Orthodox Jews do if invited to a bat mitzva where the girl will read from the Torah, if they consider this to be a violation of Jewish law? Much of the pressure rests on the shoulders of twelve-year-old girls: Should they read from the Torah or celebrate in a more traditional fashion? What should they do if their classmates are split between two rival models of bat mitzva? One girl, who prays in a partnership synagogue and studies at an ordinary state-run religious school in Jerusalem, recalls that when she invited her school friends to hear her reading from the Torah in synagogue, she was bullied and called what in Israel is sometimes used as an epithet: "Reform." And there is also the flip side of the coin: What should a girl do if she does not want to read from

---

19. In 2021 the religious-feminist organization Kolech held in the city of Modiin its first ever cantor's course for religious women.
20. Yehuda Schlesinger, "Feminism Speaks with God," *Israel Hayom*, July 26, 2018 [Hebrew].

the Torah for her bat mitzva but comes under peer pressure from her classmates to do so?

Will Orthodox Jewish society in Israel find a way to accommodate these differences and complexities, or will the new synagogues force everyone to pick an ideological side, overpowering the Religious Zionists' strong tribalism? Nobody knows what the future holds, of course, but what's clear is that it will be decided in the synagogue. And truly there is nowhere more suitable.

Chapter VI

The Rabbi and the Professor – Two Streams of Conservatism

The genesis of Orthodox Jewish feminism is in the study hall; only later did it reach the synagogue.

The teaching of the largely Aramaic-language Talmud to women and girls sparked the revolution of religious feminism. Its impact has been so powerful that it is hard to remember how radical the notion once was of women, mostly in the United States, studying the texts that are the central body of work that male yeshiva students have slaved over and basked in for over a thousand years. But this all happened fairly recently, in the 1970s and 1980s, and at first it utterly horrified many rabbis and religious educators. In time, however, the resistance melted away, and Talmud study by women reached the point where it was no longer considered a fringe phenomenon. Across Orthodox institutions in the United States and Israel's state-run religious schools, women and girls commonly study Talmud. The education system has changed.

This happened thanks to the first generation of religious feminists. The third and second generations are shifting the center of gravity from the study hall to the synagogue. Much of the Orthodox mainstream has already embraced some of the changes explored in the previous chapter, but will this process transform houses of prayer as dramatically as houses of study? Nowadays, the dividing line between the two big camps runs just to the right of the partnership *minyanim*. But what does the future hold?

I came across answers to these questions in two conversations, at different points in time, with two people who have watched the Orthodox Jewish world change before their eyes, not merely as observers but as active players.

The first is Rabbi Yaakov Medan, the head of Yeshivat Har Etzion, who represents more or less the golden mean of Religious Zionism and is in touch with most of its factions – a position that he managed to maintain even during the fractious year of Bennett's rule and even while voicing support for that government's conversion and *kashrut* reforms. He is proud of being one of the first rabbis to introduce the custom of women dancing with Torah scrolls on Simḥat Torah and he is supportive of female leadership. On the other hand, he is a firm opponent of egalitarian prayer. He talks to religious homosexuals but does not always tell them what they want to hear. In 2003, he and Prof. Ruth Gavison published a charter that they hoped would bridge the religious-secular divide and settle arguments about Shabbat, *kashrut*, personal status laws, conversion, and more. This document is popularly hailed nowadays as a successful attempt to forge consensus, but it failed to overcome political opposition and was left to gather dust.

The second conversation I had was with Tamar Ross, a professor of Jewish philosophy at Bar-Ilan University. In her book on feminism and Orthodoxy, *Expanding the Palace of Torah*, Ross argues that the demand for changes to prayer services was rooted in this Orthodox women's scholarship revolution: "What was unique in the learning revolution instituted by Modern Orthodox women in the following decade was not simply the level of literacy they sought, but also its subject matter and institutional setting."[1]

I quoted Ross in a report on upheavals in the Orthodox world,[2] and the most surprising reaction I received was from Mordechai Willig, a senior American rabbi who straddles the line between Modern Orthodoxy and Haredi Orthodoxy. Willig is a congregational rabbi in New York and a faculty member at Yeshiva University. In a blog post, he called for nothing less than a full reevaluation of women's Talmud study. Quoting Ross, he wrote that the moment women had started studying the Talmud with the support of several *gedolim* (major rabbis – apparently a reference to Rabbi Joseph B. Soloveitchik), "an egalitarian attitude has colored some women's study of Talmud and led them to embrace and advocate egalitarian ideas and practices which are unacceptable to those very *gedolim*."[3]

Ross traces the roots of the religious feminist revolution to the 1970s. Medan goes even further back and points to the year 1920 as the ground zero of Orthodox Jewish feminism.

"I trace it much further back, to the debate about female suffrage, when Rav Kook ruled against women voting," he explains. "If you ask me, obviously I'm in favor of women having the vote and getting elected, but I can see the problem with the fact that such a serious man – and who was more serious than Rabbi Avraham Yitzhak HaKohen Kook? – was against it, and that female suffrage ultimately proved more powerful than him and largely disqualified him from being the oracle of the modern age … and made him the oracle of Religious Zionism. The affair pushed Rav Kook aside, but more importantly made it clear that equality was more powerful than him and his philosophy. You can see why from my perspective, as a disciple of Rav Kook, this was an extremely

---

1. Tamar Ross, *Expanding the Palace of Torah: Orthodoxy and Feminism* (Waltham, MA: Brandeis University Press, 2004), 72.
2. Yair Ettinger, "Is Orthodox Judaism on the Verge of a Historic Schism?" *Haaretz*, July 27, 2015, available at https://www.haaretz.com/jewish/.premium-is-orthodox-judaism-on-the-verge-of-a-historic-schism-1.5379629.
3. Rabbi Mordechai Willig, "Trampled Laws," *TorahWeb.org*, August 6, 2015, available at https://www.torahweb.org/torah/2015/parsha/rwil_ekev.html.

difficult moment. That's where I identify the turning point – that's when this trend, of equality for women, became something that couldn't be stopped at the synagogue door."

It looks like Rav Kook was wrong on an important point. A century later, what do you do as a rabbi to avoid making similar mistakes? The egalitarian cause has a clear demand: change can and must come to the synagogue.

"I really am in a very precarious situation, and I pray to the Holy One, blessed be He, that I won't make mistakes. In my view, equality is a positive and important development. It's also the world that God placed us in. The whole movement toward equality, including for women, is good and healthy. It's not the only important trend, but I accept it. You must remember that the entire mission of the Torah is to understand what to do with positive trends. Even the *Mishkan* [the portable wilderness sanctuary that was intended to provide access to God via worship] had restrictions. The whole objective of the Torah is to take a positive trend and know how to limit it, to balance it. There's a connection between the Torah and the world, and what it demands of us is to know how to limit, what to limit, how to balance things out. That's what I pray for every day, not to make mistakes."

How do you analyze the contemporary debate within Orthodox Jewry? Is a split unavoidable?

"Roughly at the same point in Jewish history, there was a dispute between the Sadducees and the Pharisees, which ended with a split, and another between Beit Shammai and Beit Hillel [the two dominant schools of thought in the Mishna], which didn't end with a split. The disagreements between Beit Shammai and Beit Hillel were no less significant than the Sadducee-Pharisee dispute. Where do I draw the line between them? On the question of common grounds. I agree, today's disputes are immense, I don't want to sound naive or overly optimistic. I can only say one thing. There's definitely an attempt here to come to terms with the change. There have already been attempts to grapple with the question of what will be stronger – the forces of difference or the forces of commonality? I say something else: no matter how extreme the language you use to describe the divisive factors, that still doesn't mean there's a schism. Obviously, I don't want the Religious Zionist community to split in two, and I'm not trying to persuade anyone in an egalitarian *minyan* to cleave off. I want our commonality to triumph.

"Some people see how the egalitarian *minyanim* pray and ask why they don't just become Conservative, but I don't draw the borderline where they do. The border isn't decided by the question of whether women wear *kippot* and recite *Pesukei DeZimra* [i.e., whether they serve as cantors in the opening section of the prayer service, a relatively acceptable novelty from a halakhic perspective]. The border is set by a different question, namely: Do we believe in the Torah that was brought down from heaven by Moses on Mount Sinai, that it binds us, and that the prophets spoke truth? In other words, do we believe in Maimonides' thirteen articles of faith? Conservative Jews don't. I've sat down with them in the shared conversion school [a state-sponsored umbrella institution that allows progressive movements to play a role in the conversion process], and I can tell you they don't believe in this. But the moment someone accepts Maimonides' thirteen articles of faith, I won't get into an argument about the exact nature of their faith, because in principle, they have faith. So in such a scenario, even if we're talking about a woman who recites *Pesukei DeZimra* or even reads from the Torah, in my mind that doesn't cross the line into Conservative Judaism.

"I'm talking about faith in the God-given, binding Torah; I feel this is a strong anchor, and the argument is all within the family, and then, after that – yes, I agree we have a problem. But that's where I draw the line, not about what women do inside a synagogue."

And what do you think is the problem that most needs to be spoken about on the basis of this common ground?
"There haven't been many times in my life when I decided to 'close the Talmud' [i.e., to pivot from studying to public activity]. During the Oslo Accords, I went on a hunger strike, I went to lead demonstrations in the street, I got clubbed, I was arrested, and that's when I noticed that the news stations had stopped reporting what happened to settlers in traffic accidents over the Green Line [i.e., in the West Bank], and didn't even report on terror attacks. I said, I'm closing the Talmud [temporarily to

engage in public activity]. After the assassination of Prime Minister Yitzhak Rabin…I decided to put down the Talmud and rediscover the common ground between observant and non-observant Jews. That's when I was practically stoned by religious society. But I was on a mission, and I didn't look left or right.

"Do you know what I think justifies pausing Talmud studies, nowadays? It's got to do with single-sex couples, with gender-reassignment surgeries, with efforts to change the status of women – no longer mothers, just parents. Sometimes the Hebrew language struggles to find the words. The threat to the Jewish family, as far as I'm concerned, is a threat to the existence of the Jewish people. I don't need to tell you what's going on in Europe and the disintegration of the family there. It's said that the Spanish people will no longer exist in fifty years' time."

What does that have to do with the dilemmas in synagogues?

"All the questions you're raising are interconnected. We're caught between two values here, and there's no way I can say one's white and the other's black, one's good, one's evil. Only in *Grimm's Fairy Tales* is there good and evil. I'm referring to two values that I'm paying attention to, and I'm studying them both. One is the value of equality for women, that's a very important value, and the other is the value of preserving tradition as my grandfather knew it, and his grandfather before him. These are two values that should be nurtured, and I'm the last person who'd tell you that there isn't a contradiction. I'm not the kind of person who tries to harmonize everything, in the spirit of 'these and these are the words of the living God' [Babylonian Talmud, Eiruvin 13b]. I'm not there. These values are in conflict with each other, and we have to live in the space between them and figure out the right balance. They're both important, they both matter, and they're both connected to the value of the Jewish family. I need to find a way that manages to navigate between these competing values, to find a way for each to accommodate the other so that we can find common ground between these two values."

Give me an example.

"Take the simplest problem in halakha: adding women to a *zimmun*. In the framework of a family, from a halakhic perspective, it's a green light all the way – no problem. Personally I don't do this; do you know why? Because my grandfather didn't. There are some things I do that my grandfather didn't. The Judaism that I inhabit has become thoroughly modern in the world outside the synagogue and remained conservative inside it. I want to keep this conservative spirit alive inside the synagogue, but not fanatically. People ask me whether women should be given a Torah scroll, and I say *yes*, and our yeshiva was in fact one of the first to do so for the Simhat Torah service. They say, 'Maybe the women are impure [i.e., have not visited a ritual bath after their period], they're not allowed to touch a Torah scroll,' but this is nonsense. I try to constantly keep both values in mind…. Women want to study Torah? Great. To be spiritual leaders? Excellent. Just keep it as close as possible to my grandfather's synagogue, and I can live with it."

So the debate here isn't about halakha at all, but about conservatism.

"What does halakha say about women reading from the Torah? It's allowed, [as the Talmud says] '*hakol olin*' [all are eligible]. So yes, the question isn't about halakha, it's something else. It's about the trajectory, which way is the community going? I can show you endless examples of rabbis who have prayed in improvised synagogues without a *mehitza*, next to women, despite the prohibition. It happens every day. But the basic question isn't about halakha. The basic question is about where you're leading the community, how much weight do you attach to whatever's been handed down the generations. Compared to other denominations."

In what sense do you think that if a boy sees his mother or sister serving as a cantor or reading from the Torah, that damages the Jewish family?

"It disrupts something, but I wouldn't say this disruption or concern for the child is an impassable red line for me. What is an impassable red line is to declare total victory for equality for women over Jewish tradition, and I can't accept this one-sided decision. A female cantor in a synagogue, and I'm not talking about reciting *Pesukei DeZimra* or something intermediate, goes against halakha, but besides going against halakha, it also flatly contradicts Jewish tradition and ultimately damages the family…."

This is a trend that I totally oppose. Totally. Even if it stays within the confines of the *Shulḥan Arukh*. Although this matter is in a gray area, if it is an attempt to declare victory for the admittedly very important value of equality for women against generations of Jewish tradition, if it's a bid for total victory, I think that crosses a line."

Nevertheless, you regard women and men who pray with female cantors as Orthodox?

"I don't like to use the word 'Orthodox,' I speak in terms of Jews who want to follow halakha, that's the right term. I have worked on joint efforts for years with Reform and Conservative Jews; I embrace them, so to an even greater extent I try to find the common denominator in my own community. You must understand, there's nothing milquetoast in my ideological battle against them, it's a fiery-fiery affair."

The current climate is compelling Rabbi Medan to grapple with new questions. The younger generation is more democratic, and many of the new spiritual trends are pushing back against the rabbis and the prevailing order. The Judaism that he inherited from his grandfather is just one of the victims of the age. According to Prof. Tamar Ross: "What you're seeing today is a slow, creeping movement in a direction that was set long ago. The era began with the gradual collapse of what I'd call people's modernist conceptions. Sources of authority are being eroded; there's greater mobility between communities; people are calling into question whether there's a single, exclusive, absolute truth, and other factors are throwing everything into disarray. I also think that the division of Judaism into denominations, even in Israel, not to mention abroad, is not as true as in the past. New constellations are popping up.

"On the one hand, the boundaries between the Conservative movement and Modern Orthodoxy are being blurred. On the other, although the distinction between Modern Orthodoxy and Haredi Orthodoxy in Israel is becoming more acute, here too there's a certain overlap at the edges, which reminds me of the period in which I moved to Israel in the 1950s. Back then, in my parents' apartment block, there were good neighborly relations between families from the Religious Zionist, Haredi, and secular communities. The children knew each other, played together outside, and even went to after-school activities together. At the time, I couldn't really say I had a clear-cut belonging to any particular sector. Afterwards, we saw a shift to compartmentalization and a sharpening of the symbolic borders between communities, but nowadays, we're starting to see breaches in these conventional identities.

"In short, on the one hand there's a shift to radicalization, but on the other, there's also a slight turn in new directions. The center-ground is fraying. In my book, I point to transformations that began with the Orthodox women's learning revolution, and from there they're spilling over into new modes of leadership, new halakhic and theological interpretations, and so much more."

Is it a revolution?

"It's a revolution, but since it's happening inside the Orthodox world, it's being fought with rhetoric that tries to emphasize continuity."

What caused the classic national-religious ideology to crumble beyond the bubble of Jerusalem?

"The disillusionment with the Gaza Disengagement on the one hand and with the peace process on the other led to the political empowerment of new actors. It's also a counterreaction, a statement of despair with the right-wing ideology of both Rabbis Kook, father and son. During the Disengagement, people spoke of the need to make their peace with the redemption as an incremental process, but something snapped, and something new is growing out of those fractures. This new reality is battering the old leadership and its absolute truths. Besides, we're also seeing an expression of all sorts of processes that define the transition from the modern age, and its rigid ideological definitions, to a softer, more tolerant postmodern world, and recognition of a heterogeneous social reality where people have diverse spiritual and cultural needs. Mass media is also contributing its share. Nowadays we live in a small global village, and whatever happens in Jerusalem resonates in the periphery, and vice versa."

Why the insistence on remaining part of the Orthodox camp? Isn't it all just a matter of semantics?

"It's first of all a matter of identity. The people steering this revolution feel inextricably connected to Orthodox Judaism in every respect – in terms of their lifestyle, ideology, values, social contacts. It's in their souls. This label, 'Orthodox,' also carries the connotation of authenticity, and people are looking for authenticity. The non-Orthodox solutions are based on concessions, whereas the safeguarding of the traditional rules of the game – that's something that has meaning for religious Jews. So when the more innovative elements make an effort to align themselves with the conventional, formal demands of halakha, they're insisting on their right to be counted as among the faithful successors of that tradition.

"On the other hand, I think that a lot of the anger against these new movements stems from the fact that they're coming from the grassroots, and that's something you can't easily ignore nowadays. There's a battle here over the borders of authority and control, at a time when the hegemony of the religious establishment is crumbling. There's the Chief Rabbinate, which nobody respects. Even in the Haredi world, there are no rabbis whose rulings are considered binding on everyone. There's a leadership vacuum, and that lack of a response is awakening local initiatives. It's a process that traditionalist people frown upon, because that's just not how it's done, but I don't think their demand to wind the clocks back can be easily satisfied. Modern people place a premium on their freedom of choice, and when there's no enforcement mechanism from a Sanhedrin or local community, the whole decision-making process becomes more autonomous and democratic. One obvious example is the establishment of all the services known as partnership or egalitarian *minyanim*.

"Similarly with other issues, Modern Orthodox individuals prize their ability to make independent decisions. In our neighborhood synagogue, which is far from being a revolutionary bastion, there's no rabbi. Whenever a question arises, the members of the congregation seek advice from relevant scholars and experts, but at the end of the day, the congregation makes the call. Rabbis don't have the same status as they used to, they have a role but it's less binding. In an age of the democratization of knowledge, it's not so easy to have a cult around 'great rabbis.' Moreover, if we're talking ideology, it's quite easy nowadays to guess what any particular rabbi will rule on a given issue, so absolute submission to rabbinic authority is losing its meaning.

"In this context, the women's revolution is the single most important thing that's happened to Modern Orthodox Judaism in our generation. This revolution shines a new light on the whole halakhic system. It's a more feminine perspective, which is by definition new, because it represents a group that had always been sidelined, whose voice was previously unheard. This group has insights of its own, not just about 'women's issues' but the world in general, including the role and place of halakha within it, the nature of God and His relationship with His creations... and so forth. There's also a huge new religious literature emerging from women, which is meant to fill the void of women's history, and also to add female perspectives to the stories of the Torah, which were written from a manifestly male perspective.

"When the feminist psychologist Carol Gilligan studied at Harvard and set out to write her doctorate on women's conceptions of morality, her starting point was research by her supervisor, who tried to map out human beings' moral development along an accepted scale. In this metric, the most basic stage is when children understand that if they're not 'good,' they'll be punished; and the most elevated stage is when a child does something 'good' because that's just the right thing to do. Using this scale, girls were thought to be stuck at a much lower level of moral development than boys, but Gilligan argued that this was a distorted way of looking at things. It's like putting kids from poor neighborhoods through a psychometric test that evaluates them using the same metric as for kids from wealthier neighborhoods, but the criteria and definitions of knowledge do not overlap.

"The same goes for halakhic questions. Women assess halakhic considerations differently. Not just the bottom line, but also at the stage of distinguishing what's relevant from what's not, and in reading the reality that these considerations are applied to. Similarly, in the field of religious rituals, a new form of worship is emerging, which is more personal, based less on a hierarchy of honorariums. Women tend to give a more personal touch to rituals. How do you celebrate a bar mitzva? How do you celebrate a bat mitzva? What's the significance of prayer? The female yardstick is having an impact on all sorts of fields nowadays."

Chapter VII

Mikdashnikim: The Temple Mount Faithful

"Revolutionary movements in Judaism have always been one step ahead of the rabbis. Rabbis are naturally conservative. They'll always say *no*. Take Rav Kook's halakhic ruling against female suffrage. He couldn't even conceive of such a possibility, and even a century ago, Rav Kook was a paragon of open-mindedness. Don't forget, it's a different generation. Once, a rabbi could tell you, 'That's what's written.' Nowadays, anyone can go to Google. You can't tell people Maimonides says you're not allowed to ascend the Temple Mount, when he says you are. There's unlimited information, you can't pull the wool over people's eyes. There's diversity. You can't just say, 'Judaism is like this.' Let me show you that Judaism is also like that."

The speaker: Yehudah Glick, a Temple Mount activist and, at the time of our conversation in the summer of 2017, a member of Knesset for the ruling Likud Party. Glick is active in several aspects of Orthodox Jewish life, but on one particular matter he has always been one step ahead of the rabbis: the Temple Mount. He and a handful of fellow activists have managed to shift the political agenda of the Israeli right, creating a radical halakhic movement that galvanized large swaths of Israeli society, including eminent rabbis.

Although all major Haredi rabbis have ruled that Jews are forbidden from entering the sacred ground of the Temple Mount, and although the Chief Rabbinate has unswervingly concurred, Glick and his colleagues have managed to make pilgrimages to the Temple Mount seem perfectly legitimate in the eyes of many halakhically committed, Orthodox Jews.

In late December 2017, on the morning after Hannuka, Rabbi Eliezer Melamed,[1] the rabbi of the West Bank settlement of Har Bracha, ascended the Temple Mount. Before arriving on the scene, he purified himself in a *mikve* (a ritual bath), slipped on a pair of cloth shoes (rather than leather), and undertook other preparations to comply with Judaism's stringent rules for entering this holy site. He had done his legal homework, spending years explaining why Jewish law permitted entry to the Temple Mount, contrary to the views of most rabbis. As a *rosh yeshiva* and regular columnist for the national-religious weekly *BeSheva*, Melamed had already authorized his students and his many readers to do what the most illustrious Religious Zionist rabbis, including Rabbi

---

1. Melamed offers a stunning example of a sea change within Religious Zionism. The son of the national-Haredi leader Rabbi Zalman Melamed, he was, early in his career, when the issue at stake was the sanctity of the Land of Israel, a hawk. He called on his disciples to refuse a direct order to uproot settlements. Then-Defense Minister Ehud Barak, in response, barred his yeshiva from taking part in the Hesder track. Fast forward a decade, now that the matter of settlements is hardly on the political agenda, and Melamed is being embraced by Jewish progressives and accused of spreading "lies" by the likes of Sephardic Chief Rabbi Yitzhak Yosef. The reasons for this shift include his moderate stance on female-led Jewish prayer at the plaza adjacent to the *Kotel*, his willingness to speak at a forum along with the French Reform Rabbi Delphine Horvilleur, and among several other marriage-related decisions, his ruling regarding conversion, in which he asserted that a convert need only adopt a "traditional" lifestyle and not commit fully to a life of halakhic observance as a predetermined condition for the validity of an Orthodox conversion. This shift, which led to calls of boycott in 2022 from leading conservative rabbis Dov Lior and Zvi Thau, is due, in part, to the fact that we have entered the post-Land of Israel era, in which the vast majority of the Religious Zionist community supports the settlements, but is divided, primarily, by its stance vis-à-vis the rabbinate.

Zvi Yehuda Kook and former chief rabbi Avraham Shapira, had explicitly proscribed. All that remained was for him to openly visit the Temple Mount himself (he had already made a visit years earlier, when he was still relatively unknown).

Melamed's pilgrimage grabbed headlines on Religious Zionist news sites. "Sources in the Temple Mount movements say that over the past several years, Rabbi Melamed has become very close to the process of return to the Temple Mount," reported the national-religious news site *Srugim*. "Various pressures" had forced him to postpone his visit, but "today Rabbi Melamed was seen on the Temple Mount to the surprise of people who go there regularly, having entered discreetly and modestly without being recognized by police at the site." The spokesman of a coalition of Temple Mount movements hailed the decision: "The redemption of the Mount and the return of the Temple received a big boost today from the ascent of Rabbi Melamed."[2]

Melamed added another data point to a growing tally of Jews visiting the Temple Mount. According to activist groups, 2018 marked a new record, with some 36,000 visits by Jews to the holy esplanade. This figure represents a more than sixfold jump over a decade: in 2009, the number of Jews who walked through Mughrabi Gate – the only authorized entrance to the site for Jews, accessed through a rickety bridge from the Western Wall Plaza – stood at 5,658. Almost every year since, the Temple Mount movements have celebrated a new record. In the summer of 2019, on Tisha B'Av – the traditional anniversary of the destruction of the two Jewish temples – 1,729 Jews visited during the few hours when the Temple Mount was opened to Jews. On Jerusalem Day, as in recent years, Temple Mount activists celebrated another "historic record." They frequently gush that there have never been so many Jews on the Temple Mount "since the destruction," and that's no exaggeration.

These numbers reflect a growing sector of Orthodox Jews in Israel who have shifted the direction of their prayers: no longer merely turning east, toward Jerusalem, but now gazing up at a more focused spot, up above the Western Wall, where the Temple itself once stood. When

---

2   Zvi Shaiman, "For the First Time in Twenty Years, Rabbi Melamed Ascends the Temple Mount," *Srugim*, December 21, 2017 [Hebrew].

they utter the words "May our eyes behold Your return to Zion in mercy," they are no longer speaking in the abstract. They have run out of patience, bid good riddance to piecemeal progress toward redemption. They are no longer willing to make do with substitutes such as the Western Wall, the last standing relic of the Temple, just because the actual site of the ancient holy place is off-limits as an Islamic house of prayer, the Al-Aqsa Mosque and the Dome of the Rock.

In a poll published in the *Makor Rishon* newspaper in 2014, a solid majority of 75 percent of Religious Zionists expressed support for visiting the Temple Mount. The results showed, however, that the national-religious community is split into two groups of equal size: those who personally intend to visit the Temple Mount, and those who do not. Asked, "Have you already visited the Temple Mount, or do you intend to do so in the future?," 36 percent replied that they had not visited before but intended to do so; some 15 percent of respondents had visited in the past and intended to do so again in the future. Taken together, more than half.

Given that visiting the Temple Mount used to be considered the preserve of a radical and eccentric minority, the data represents a meteoric success for Temple Mount advocacy groups within the Religious Zionist community. Party to the achievement are also those who do not themselves visit the site. Religious schools and yeshivas have added content on the Temple sacrifices and holy vessels to their curricula. The Temple Institute, which is making the instruments needed for worship in the Third Temple of its imagination, attracts enormous domestic tourism, mostly from Religious Zionist Israelis. Even from those who are not directly involved, there is plenty of hands-off support. Since 2012, *Makor Rishon* has published a weekly column by the journalist Arnon Segal, dedicated to encouraging Jews to visit the Temple Mount for a host of political and halakhic reasons. In one such column, spread across a full page, Segal used flowcharts to explain to his readers "how to burn the red heifer" – a rare calf that used to be slaughtered and burned by the Temple priests as part of a purification ritual, and the rediscovery of which, according to tradition, is to herald the messianic age.[3]

---

3. Arnon Segal, "Ashes for Generations: For How Many Impure People Will One Red Heifer Be Enough?" *Makor Rishon*, August 11, 2019 [Hebrew].

The Temple Mount loyalists, or "*mikdashnikim*," are a diverse lot. They are split into dozens of groups, from mass organizations to relatively minor factions. Some prioritize displays of strength, accentuating Israeli sovereignty at the site, even though the government of Israel, shortly after seizing control of the area during the 1967 war, surrendered its administration to the Waqf, an Islamic religious agency overseen by Jordan. Others wish to pray there – an act of worship that is forbidden to Jews – or simply to visit. Some go much farther and want to move toward the construction of the Third Temple, training themselves in the intricacies of its rituals and animal sacrifices. What will happen to the two Islamic sites on the Temple Mount, which Muslims around the world flock to and revere? Some Temple Mount activists hope to destroy them, plain and simple. Others, such as Yehudah Glick, dream of a "house of prayer for all peoples," as Isaiah prophesies, a utopia of interreligious harmony radiating out from the Mount.

This is above all a national story, with international ramifications. In Israel, the movement has managed to soften the stance of the authorities and forced the police to exercise some flexibility – all within the confines of the historical status quo governing the site and its restricted access to Jews. The change was mostly brought about by political lobbying by Temple Mount activist groups, drawing support from Religious Zionist politicians and secular ministers and lawmakers from the Likud Party. But the domestic political context is compounded by a much wider geopolitical picture. Two major explosions of Palestinian violence – the Second Intifada of 2000–2005, and the wave of attacks in 2015–2016 as well as the conflagration in Gaza in the spring of 2021 – were linked to Arab rhetoric about resisting Israel's presence at the Temple Mount.

Yet the growing prominence of the Temple Mount is also the story of a halakhic revolution. What was once considered a grave prohibition punishable by *karet*, a physical or spiritual extirpation handed down from the heavens, is now deemed perfectly permissible by tens of thousands of Religious Zionists and hundreds of rabbis. In halakhic terms, the transformation happened practically overnight – a mere fifteen years, in which nothing physically changed on the Temple Mount, and its political and diplomatic status remained static. The only change was in the eyes of the beholders, the members of the Religious Zionist community itself. To be sure, not everyone's attitudes have shifted. Many religious Israelis are still trying to hold back the tide, which places the Temple Mount – yes, it too – quite firmly on the spectrum of religious disputes that divide the national-religious community.

What linkage is there between the Temple Mount and the other religious disputes rocking Israel's Orthodox Jewish society? Unlike arguments over the role of women in the synagogue, for example, the polemic over the Temple Mount does not seem to be tearing the national-religious community apart. The *mikdashnikim*'s opponents are mostly keen to avoid direct confrontation; they are not smeared as "Reform," and they are seen, even by their national-religious adversaries, as loyal to the rabbis and the Land of Israel – and therefore as legitimate. Nevertheless, the story of the Temple Mount activists is an indispensable component of any discussion of religiosity and division in the contemporary Orthodox world.

The debate over the Temple Mount, much like other religious disputes discussed here, spans the whole national-religious community, and only it (as distinct from Haredi society, where the consensus against visiting the Temple Mount is practically hermetic). It is a political argument with clear sociological dimensions, but it also has religious elements that touch on the core of many religious Israelis' identity.

This is a new polemic. For decades, it was nowhere on the radar or at most flickering along its outermost edges, until it suddenly burst onto the national-religious center stage. Just like religious feminism, Temple Mount activism is a major spiritual trend, which is challenging the religious mainstream and demanding flexibility and adaptability from a world that is supposed to be traditional, conservative, and rigid. It is outflanking the religious mainstream from the right.

Consider another similarity between the respective anti-rabbinic revolts waged by liberal communities and the Temple Mount activists. Like the debate about the role of women in the synagogue or the army, the Temple Mount activists emerged as a grassroots movement: a coalition that championed a single issue and captured the imagination of the masses. Thanks to activists, including former lawmaker Yehudah Glick and *Makor Rishon* columnist Arnon Segal, the tally of Jewish visits to the Temple Mount has skyrocketed. They worked in tandem with the hugely influential free newsletters distributed in synagogues on Shabbat and on social media, where clips of events on the Temple Mount are widely shared. Together, they placed the Temple Mount at the forefront of the Religious Zionist community's agenda.

In the fall of 2015, Segal argued in a column that "Israel's submissive conduct on the Temple Mount can no longer be swept under the carpet, as it has been over the past forty-five years." As he put it, "In an age in which surreal videos are uploaded daily onto YouTube and Facebook, in which Jews are arrested for praying on the Temple Mount, or conversely, in which antisemitic Islamic frenzy is seen on the site, there is no chance of sticking to the policy of turning the Temple Mount into Israel's interior courtyard, which is neither visited nor seen."[4]

Segal is demanding that Jews be given the full right to pray on the Temple Mount, and it seems clear that this demand is acceptable to much of Israel's national-religious society. Dozens of prominent rabbis have led by example in visiting the Temple Mount, and their backing has given the movement a tailwind – but the fact of the matter is that many of them hitched a ride on a train that was already in motion. In other words, the Temple Mount provides additional proof of the privatization of rabbinic authority, even on matters of religious law.

The erosion of the halakhic status quo upon the Temple Mount – which places this episode within the wider metamorphosis gripping religious society – has only served to further undermine the status of the Chief Rabbinate of Israel, as it strictly forbids visiting the site. As with other hot button issues in recent years, the rabbinate has found itself on the losing side, with vast swaths of religious society openly disobeying its ruling. But on this issue their defiance is especially jarring. Those ascending to the Temple Mount are from the most conservative flank of religious society. They ought to be the rabbinate's natural supporters. Moreover, the flouting of the rabbinate's ban also attests to the community's diminishing respect for stately comportment. By visiting the Temple Mount, the masses are asserting their refusal to accept these

---

4. Arnon Segal, "If Netanyahu Loses Power, It'll Be Because of the Temple Mount," *Makor Rishon*, October 11, 2019 [Hebrew].

decorous and diplomatically convenient rabbinic rulings, which, in so far as the Temple Mount is concerned, have come as welcome news indeed for the heads of state. This is nothing less than a revolt, albeit focused, against the Chief Rabbinate of Israel and the government of Israel; its joint stance, ever since 1967, is seen by many right-wing religious youth as nothing short of defeatist.

The Temple Mount activist Yossi Peli said in an interview to the website *Kipa* in 2016: "There is a deep understanding in the [national-religious] public that we need to articulate a complete, proactive vision, not just to fight defensive wars. It's also a matter of generational change: there's a new generation that isn't content with the fact that we have a state and understands that we have to make meaningful strides forward.... In order for genuine change to happen in this field, there has to be fundamental change in our basic assumptions. Halakha says that the preferable way to build the [Third] Temple is by a king – in modern terms, that means first we have to build an enlightened leadership, one that sees the Temple as one of its main objectives."[5] Stately conduct, then, ends at the gate to the Temple Mount.

There is another point of confluence between the halakhic debates on the left and the right. The cause of Jewish prayer rights on the Temple Mount uses a discourse of civil rights that is very similar to the one used by feminists campaigning for prayer rights at the Western Wall and those seeking to immerse themselves in ritual baths without state-appointed supervision. Additionally, and rather ironically, there is a certain halakhic symmetry between the religious demands of Orthodox feminists and those of the Temple Mount activists: prayer on the Temple Mount, like egalitarian prayer, might not be explicitly forbidden in Jewish law, but since there is no halakhic duty involved, the act is considered to have zero halakhic value. While both movements fervently advocate for renewal, their critics (at least from within the Haredi camp) insist that they are not driven by "purely" religious motives and have imported alien and secular values (whether nationalist or religious) into the world of religion.

---

5.   "Rabbi Yossi Peli to *Kipa*, on the Temple Movement: There's a New Generation That Isn't Content with Having a State," *Kipa*, August 3, 2016 [Hebrew].

But besides these reasons, the debate over the Temple Mount is pertinent because both the liberals and the *mikdashnikim* are agents of change. They are departing from conventional practice and defying generations of Jewish legal tradition. The campaign for Jewish prayer rights on the Temple Mount is associated with the national-Haredi, conservative flank of the Religious Zionist world – the side that largely opposes Orthodox feminism. But it too is defying halakhic rulings by major rabbis, including Rav Kook the elder and former chief rabbis Mordechai Eliyahu and Avraham Shapira, who were all steadfast in their opposition to setting foot upon the Temple Mount. And although many Temple Mount activists speak of these rabbis with sacred reverence, on this particular issue they defer to other, less illustrious rabbis to justify their endeavors.

What is really driving the masses thronging to the Temple Mount? Religion and politics have always gone hand in hand when it comes to the Temple Mount, ever since the 1980s and the Jewish Underground's plot to blow up the Muslim sites to the Islamic Movement's near-annual "Al-Aqsa-Is-in-Danger" fests starting in the late 1990s. Dr. Tomer Persico, a theologist, argues that the Jewish Temple Mount movements not only made a radical departure from Rabbi Zvi Yehuda Kook's vision of redemption as a piecemeal process; they are also demanding the effective secularization of a holy space. The increasing visits by Religious Zionists to the Temple Mount, he writes, amount to an "active revolt against the halakhic tradition," while for sections of national-religious society "ethnonationalism is replacing their respect for state authority and, moreover, their halakhic sensibilities."[6] He also senses that Temple Mount activists are reinterpreting the idea of sacred space: instead of steering clear of this holy site, retreating from it in awe, Religious Zionists are determined to accentuate their ownership over it. In Persico's view, the Temple Mount activists' deepest motives are not connected to religious worship per se but to questions of sovereignty and control.[7]

---

6. Tomer Persico, "Why Does Everyone Suddenly Want to Ascend the Temple Mount?" *Haaretz*, November 14, 2014 [Hebrew].
7. Tomer Persico, "The Temple Mount and the Nationalization of Holiness," *Makor Rishon*, December 22, 2017 [Hebrew].

One surprising supporter of Persico's academic interpretation is Rabbi Shlomo Aviner, one of the most prominent opponents of Temple Mount activism. He contends that the side that supports visiting the Temple Mount is motivated by an urge to conquer, rather than a quest for sanctity.[8] But this criticism, which attacks the activists' motives for breaching the halakhic status quo, is highly reminiscent of the conservative criticism of Orthodox feminism, which is said to reflect a "political agenda" rather than true religious sentiment.[9]

Yet for everything that Orthodox feminists and Temple Mount activists have in common, there is much that divides them. The Temple Mount movement, dominated by far-right groups, represents a clear attempt by sections of the national-religious community to cut themselves off from Israeli society and defy the establishment, while the declared objective of liberal Orthodoxy is the inclusion of formerly excluded groups. Religious feminism is bringing Judaism closer to modern life; Temple Mount activism underscores, proudly, that which separates it from modernity.

The Temple Mount movement is fighting on two fronts, against both the political and halakhic status quo. Immediately after the 1967 Six Day War, when Israel captured the Old City of Jerusalem from the Jordanians, the Israeli government decided to permit Jews to visit the Temple Mount but not to pray there – a decision that remains in force. This resolution was, and remains, largely consistent with the position of the Chief Rabbinate of Israel. In fact, the prohibition on Jewish visits to the Temple Mount was a point of rare consensus among rabbis – anti-Zionists, Haredim, and Religious Zionists alike – long before 1948, even before the establishment of the Yishuv in the nineteenth century, and it has remained so after 1967.

---

8. Shlomo Aviner, "Ascend the Temple Mount? It's Not Time Yet," *NRG.co.il*, February 25, 2014 [Hebrew].

9. When I interviewed Chief Rabbi David Lau in 2014, he said of women who wish to study Talmud that "when it comes to objectives that are not solely about moving closer to God, but sometimes also have external agendas behind them, that definitely bothers me. There's an outside influence, and I still want to keep the shape of the Jewish people like it used to be."

Religion and politics are still in lockstep regarding the question of the Temple Mount, but there is no ignoring the halakhic debate at the core of it. The halakhic prohibition on Jews ascending to the Temple Mount is rooted in the site's inimitable sanctity as the place on which two Jewish temples are believed to have stood. After the Romans destroyed the Second Temple in 70 CE, Jews could no longer meet the ritual standards for stepping foot on such a holy site, not least because of various rules about physical impurity that cannot be overcome in the present day. The prohibition on entering the Temple Mount, in such a state of ritual impurity, is considered punishable by *karet* – a penalty reserved for some of the most grievous crimes.

But is this a blanket prohibition on any and all visits to the esplanade on which the mosques now stand? This is not a question just for rabbis, but for archaeologists, because the answer hinges on where exactly the temples stood and how they were arranged internally. Only with this information can we know the exact location of the Holy of Holies – the area that was always off-limits to all but the High Priest, who could only enter in a state of ritual purity and only on Yom Kippur and when the Temple was operational – and other sections of the holy site, which were open to those who had undergone a more straightforward purification process in a ritual bath.

These details were of no concern to most rabbis throughout history, because visiting the Temple Mount was a purely hypothetical possibility; for most of the period of Ottoman rule, Jews were forbidden from entering the site anyway. The main historical point of reference for Temple Mount activists is a letter by Maimonides, the great Sephardic Jewish medieval scholar, who wrote that he had visited Jerusalem and "entered the great and holy house and I prayed in it."

Yet even once the question had real-world implications, the rabbis preferred to dodge it, because if they got the answer wrong, those entering the Temple Mount could face the punishment of *karet*. The uncertainty about the precise location and boundaries of the different wings of the Temple deterred them, and even once the Temple Mount was mapped out in great detail, they feared that authorizing entry would encourage those who lacked the necessary knowledge, and that, in turn, could lead to grave transgressions of religious law. The rabbinic reluctance, stretched over the course of several centuries, led to the emergence of the Western Wall as an alternative prayer site; after all, as the space adjacent to the Temple's retaining wall, it was obviously not on sacred ground.

Almost all rabbis, both before 1948 and after 1967, forbade entry to the Temple Mount. Prior to the establishment of the State of Israel, Rabbi Avraham Yitzhak HaKohen Kook wrote a succinct summary of the prohibition, beseeching: "Dear brothers who approach our holy city of Jerusalem ... from near and far, please observe the strict prohibition on entering the site of the Temple and the Temple Mount." His son Rabbi Zvi Yehuda, the spiritual doyen of the Religious Zionist elite, took the same approach after the conquest of Jerusalem in the Six Day War in 1967,[10] as did Israeli chief rabbis Isser Yehuda Unterman, Yitzhak Nissim, and Ovadia Yosef, and the two enduringly influential leading Religious Zionist rabbis, Avraham Shapira and Mordechai Eliyahu, who favored building a synagogue in a corner of the Temple Mount but forbade Jews from entering the site in its present configuration. The strongest advocate of Jewish prayer on the Temple Mount after 1967 was Rabbi Shlomo Goren, but he refrained from taking an official position during his tenure as chief rabbi, and only in the 1990s, one year before his death, did he publish his book analyzing the halakhic aspects of entering the Temple Mount.

But by the nineties and even more so during the early years of the next millennium, the questions, which required the expertise of a rabbi and an archaeologist, were being asked with greater urgency, battering the ironclad prohibition on entering the Temple Mount and sparking a revolution.

What triggered this change?

The erosion of the prohibition can be traced through the evolving attitudes of Religious Zionist rabbis. Years before Rabbi Melamed's

---

10. In 2018, after the Temple Mount loyalists claimed that Rabbi Zvi Yehuda Kook had indeed permitted Jewish visits to the Temple Mount, the news site *Srugim* published an old recording in which the rabbi said explicitly that it was forbidden to visit the site. Aryeh Yoeli, "Listen: Rabbi Zvi Yehuda Kook in His Own Voice, Opposing Visits to the Temple Mount," *Srugim.co.il*, February 6, 2018 [Hebrew].

visit in 2017, Rabbi Shlomo Goren was the only chief rabbi of Israel who openly opposed the so-called "status quo" at the site and the decision to return the keys to the Muslim Waqf in 1967. Rabbi Yisrael Ariel founded the Temple Institute in the 1980s. In 1996, the Rabbinical Council of Yesha, a coalition of Israeli settlement rabbis, published a letter authorizing visits to the site. Rabbi Haim Druckman, Rabbi Avraham Zuckerman, and Rabbi Zephaniah Drori added their approval in 2007, a year that seems to have been the turning point, when dozens of rabbis started visiting the Temple Mount. Rabbi Yuval Cherlow, who staked out a liberal position against more conservative colleagues on many other issues, added his support and visited the site – an illustration of just how broad the new halakhic consensus on the issue had suddenly become.

Yet on the other side of the barricades, the resistance is no less fierce. Chief Rabbi Yitzhak Yosef said in 2014 that "fourth-rate rabbis must not defy the greatest rabbis of the generation." The Haredi daily *Yated Ne'eman*, which decried Jewish visitors to the Temple Mount as a corrupting influence, wrote after Tisha B'Av in 2017: "These rule breakers have insolently and shamelessly committed a terrible transgression, ignoring the Torah and halakha and entering the Temple Mount, desecrating the site of the Temple, while making the wider public sin, as some try to create a discourse and convince others that there is no prohibition on entering the Temple Mount at all, despite the unequivocal and forthright instructions of the greatest rabbis of every generation." Rabbis from Yeshivat Har Hamor have joined the ranks of the resistance, reaffirming the traditional policy of the Chief Rabbinate in a series of public letters; Rabbi Shlomo Aviner also added his voice to the chorus.

But however important and influential the debate among the rabbis, it was the Temple Mount activists themselves who played the decisive role in forcing the matter onto the agenda, cultivating a favorable climate of public opinion, and ultimately transforming the status quo. They did not hide in the shadows but thrust themselves into the spotlights, catalyzing both halakhic and political change.

The Israeli religious right's attraction to the Temple Mount can also be explained as a function of Israel's security situation. The Jewish Underground plotted to blow up the Al-Aqsa Mosque and the Dome of the Rock in the early 1980s. More than a decade later, on the backdrop of the Oslo Accords and in an act of protest against the Israeli government and its state symbols, several rabbis, in 1996, authored a ruling permitting Jews to ascend to the site. Sarina Chen, whose book *Speedily in Our Days* describes the transformations of Religious Zionist attitudes toward the Temple Mount, argues that this desire for access intensified during the Second Intifada, when Jews were almost entirely forbidden from entering the site.

These were not the only milestones that rallied Temple Mount activists to action. Ahead of the 2005 Gaza Disengagement, an association known as "El Har Hamor" launched a novel activity: on the eve of every new Jewish month a large group gathered in the Old City and marched around the Temple Mount and stopped at every gate – Jews, as noted, are forbidden from entering through all but one – and recited Psalms. This circumvented both the police ban on prayer at the site and the halakhic prohibition on stepping foot on grounds that may once have been the Holy of Holies. Many Jews who had avoided entering the Temple Mount because of the halakhic proscription found an outlet for their religious energies by encircling it instead. During the lead-up to the Disengagement, this initiative, which began with a few dozen participants, attracted thousands of religious youth every month.

Nadav Shragai, an Israeli journalist and Temple Mount expert, observed teens affiliated with Kach – an illegal far-right party – dancing in circles and singing their own variation of a popular Jewish melody. The original lyrics say, "The Temple will be rebuilt!" but these extremist youth added: "And the mosque will be blown up." Yossi Peli, one of the founders of the initiative to encircle the gates, told Shragai that the teens singing about burning Al-Aqsa was "a random provocation, a fringe phenomenon." In his view, encircling the Temple Mount was a way for thousands of Israelis "to express their yearning and longing for the Temple, without breaking the law."[11]

This activity intensified in the days leading up to the Disengagement and in its immediate aftermath, and it was then that the man who did more to force the Temple Mount into the center of the Religious

---

11. Nadav Shragai, "Speedily, in Our Days," *Haaretz*, October 9, 2004 [Hebrew].

Zionist conversation, certainly more than any rabbi, burst onto the scene.

Yehudah Glick had been an official in Israel's Ministry of Immigration and Absorption, but once the Israeli government approved the Gaza Disengagement plan, some six months before its execution, he became the first public servant to resign in protest. He decided to devote his time to the Temple Mount, became the director general of the Temple Institute, and soon founded the Temple Mount Heritage Foundation. The cause of the Temple Mount, as reflected in his later career developments, had finally shifted out of the eccentric fringes and into the heart of the national-religious consensus. In October 2014, outside the Begin Heritage Center in Jerusalem, a Palestinian assassin on a motorbike pulled up alongside him, accused him of being "an enemy of Al-Aqsa," and opened fire. He was gravely wounded. The assassination attempt shocked the Israeli public and first brought Glick and his activism to a wider audience. The reporter Ilana Dayan followed him for a special report on her flagship investigative show, *Uvda*. Glick was a member of the ruling Likud Party and announced that he would run in its primaries. He was ranked too low on the party list to win a Knesset seat, but in May 2016, after former defense minister Moshe Ya'alon resigned, Glick was sworn in as his replacement. The poster boy of the Temple Mount loyalists brought the cause into the heart of the Israeli parliament.

How does Glick conceive of the connection between the Disengagement and the Temple Mount movement? "We had a few crises in the Religious Zionist community," he told me. "In the Babylonian Talmud, Tractate Berakhot, it says that when the houses of righteous people are destroyed, it's a tragedy for a slave and his master alike. If God doesn't have a house, then our houses are also destroyed. Look, I was also there during the evacuation of Yamit [the largest Israeli settlement in the Sinai Peninsula, evacuated in 1982 as part of the Israeli-Egyptian Peace Treaty], which didn't cause such a huge trauma. The eviction from Gush Katif caused a crisis. Yamit was a settlement that had only existed for seven years, it was seen as something for immigrants from America and Russia, it didn't catch on. Gush Katif had the finest people in the world. Simple people. It wasn't Ofra [a well-off, ideological settlement], it was Netivot [a poor town]. Good, good people. They built an economy.

Developed factories, agriculture. You tell yourself, my God, how could this have happened? These were people who always spoke about love, about love conquering all. You wonder, God Almighty, are these the people you're messing with? I think it caused such a profound crisis and people looked for something else to latch onto, and the Temple Mount was there. One more thing – I have no doubt that people feel that the settlements are a fait accompli, so they're asking what's next? The youth want also to break boundaries."

Haviva Pedaya, a scholar of culture and Judaism, investigated the theological underpinnings of Religious Zionists' attraction to the Temple Mount after the eviction of the settlements in the Gaza Strip. She concluded that the Disengagement was a breaking point that shattered Religious Zionists' confidence that the State of Israel was an instrument of the Redemption and directly boosted the symbolic capital of the Temple Mount. In other words, the Temple Mount helped to reaffirm the faith of those questioning how the redemptive process, which was supposed to be irreversible, could have taken a step back with the demolition of Jewish communities in the Gaza Strip. The pivot toward the Temple Mount was supposed to prove, both inwardly and outwardly, that the Redemption had not been dealt a lethal blow in Gush Katif, and that it could be given a fresh burst of momentum. Moreover, argued Pedaya, the campaign for the Temple Mount "became a kind of religious ritual. In other words, rather than the religious ritual that is no longer practiced on the Temple Mount, the struggle for it has become the ritual in its place."

Avishay Ben Haim, an Israeli journalist, believes that the cause of the Temple Mount is overshadowing the whole settlement enterprise. Writing on Facebook, he called Glick "enemy number one of the Land of Israel." For the Temple Mount activists, he wrote, "the national, Zionist, all-Israeli cause of love for the Land of Israel has been pushed aside and replaced with a religious clarion call, which most of the nation cannot connect to, namely the aspiration to return to animal sacrifices on the Temple Mount…. Glick and Co. have managed to completely push the ideal of settling the Land of Israel out of the Israeli public conversation." Curiously, Gershon Salomon, the leader of a tiny movement called the "Temple Mount Faithful," has never been called an enemy of the settlers.

For decades, the group attracted mostly fringe elements, far from the sociological and ideological fabric of the Religious Zionists in the pre-Disengagement era.

Visits to the Temple Mount, which became commonplace by the mid-2010s, were not the only manifestation of Religious Zionists' growing interest in the site. No less theatrical were the staged reenactments of Temple sacrifices.

On Passover Eve in 2017, Temple Mount activists held their sixth annual rehearsal of the ancient Passover sacrifice, performed by barefoot priests in white robes, using spray-painted gold replica Temple vessels, and joined by a group of rabbis calling themselves "the Sanhedrin." Of all the Temple Mount advocacy groups, the one behind the annual Passover sacrifice is by far the most zealous, at the fringes of the religious right. That year, it claimed a tangible victory: it secured police approval to hold the ceremony in the heart of the Jewish Quarter of the Old City of Jerusalem, just a few hundred yards from the Temple Mount. At the climactic moment, in the plaza facing the Hurva Synagogue, a lamb was slaughtered offstage, skinned, carried onto the improvised altar, and roasted in a wood-fire oven. Hundreds of men, women, and children watched, transfixed – a much larger audience than the year before, which had already broken the previous year's record. In 2018, the reenactment was allowed to inch even closer to the Temple Mount, to the archaeological site at the southeast corner of the base.

The Passover sacrifice reenactment has become an annual ritual, but so has another stranger, more fanatical, and more dangerous activity. In the hours before the Passover Seder, Jewish men and teens try to steal past the police officers in the Old City and into the Temple Mount, sneaking in one by one or breaking into a sprint together, clutching live kids – young goats that they intend to slaughter. Is this really their plan? To date, none of these would-be infiltrators has managed to reach "touchdown" on the Temple Mount before being caught by the police.

These events are organized by a far-right group known as Chozrim LaHar – "Returning to the Mount." Yehudah Glick seemed to fit into its messianic zeal when he proclaimed from the stage of the sacrifice reenactment one Passover: "God Almighty, Your people are gathering here to say: we want to enter into a covenant with You, let us sing how much we miss You, how much we want to feel Your divine presence inside us!" But in many respects, Glick was the odd one out. Although he had done more than anyone to make the Temple Mount a consensus issue in the national-religious world, many Temple Mount activists insist that he is neither their leader nor their spokesman. At that particular event, one of the *kohanim* behind Glick on the stage muttered in disgust that he was the "envoy of the left." It is easy to understand the hostility toward the relatively soft-spoken Glick in a movement with young members who sing about blowing up the Al-Aqsa Mosque and wear t-shirts reading "Kahane Was Right" – a reference to the late rabbi Meir Kahane and his extremist agenda. Many of them see themselves as disciples of Yitzchak Ginsburgh, a far-right, Chabad-influenced rabbi on the anti-state fringes of the Religious Zionist movement.

Glick is an odd bird among them. In fact, both the Israeli left and right have a hard time figuring him out. He is a man steeped in the neo-Hasidism of Yeshivat Otniel, who believes that the Temple Mount is the only place on earth where a genuine Israeli-Palestinian peace can be forged. And that the Al-Aqsa Mosque will ultimately remain standing.

Glick's exceptionalism is not just a product of his staunch belief in the possibility of religious utopia radiating out from one of the most fraught spots on earth, a belief that many right-wing Israelis consider alien, but also of his religious pluralism. He is not dogmatic. He could have easily been the poster boy of the liberal Orthodox avant-garde, the face of the campaign to privatize the rabbinate's authority. Besides Jewish prayer rights on the Temple Mount, Glick also supports promoting women in spiritual leadership roles and halakhic egalitarian services. He is not a fan of Reform Judaism, but he utterly rejects the widespread support among Religious Zionists for excommunicating it; he wants to limit the powers of the Chief Rabbinate; and he demonstrated outside the rabbinic courts to protest the retroactive nullification of Jewish conversions. As one who views Jewish prayer on the Temple Mount as a question of freedom of expression and civil rights, Glick believes that the Women of the Wall should be allowed to pray at the Western Wall Plaza as their conscience dictates, wearing *tallitot* and reading from Torah scrolls.[12]

"I believe, I truly believe, that the Holy One, blessed be He, has decided that the world needs to march in a more feminist direction, and the same goes for the Temple Mount," he tells me. "It comes from a religious place. In terms of the Temple Mount, the pushback serves me, just as it serves every new movement in Judaism. Imagine the Hasidic world without the *Mitnagdim* [the scholarly opposition to the mystical Hasidim in eighteenth-century Lithuania]. Without them, Hasidism would have fizzled out. Rabbi Levi Yitzchak of Berditchev put God on trial, he used some harsh rhetoric. Nowadays, religious feminism needs an opposition, and so do I. When I visit the Temple Mount, I need rabbis to tell me: Listen, we're against all this. That's how I know I'm standing my ground, but there's also someone checking on me. Look, 30–40 years ago, only a handful of rabbis supported visiting the Temple Mount, maybe two or three, and they were considered crazy. Somehow, the Holy One, blessed be He, moved the Temple Mount into the center of the national-religious conversation."

Was that move made possible through a certain Temple Mount activist named Yehudah Glick?

"The Holy One, blessed be He, always has His emissaries."

---

12. Pnina Peli, a prominent Orthodox feminist activist in the 1970s, was a member of the Temple Mount Faithful group led by Gershon Salomon, but it is hard to say that such isolated cases attested to a broader trend.

Chapter VIII

Halakha and Inclusion

One Saturday morning in June 2009, a Kiddush was held in a public park in the center of an avenue in the old north of Tel Aviv. A few dozen men, women, and children walked there, under a blazing sun, after the Shabbat prayer services. Some brought food and refreshments, others pushed strollers with babies or held their *tallitot* in velvet bags. They had come to raise a toast to two female members of the congregation who had married in a private ceremony a few days earlier – a ceremony recognized by neither the Chief Rabbinate nor the Interior Ministry. The atmosphere was festive but tinged with unease.

In virtually every Orthodox synagogue in the world, no matter how liberal, the idea of celebrating a gay or lesbian wedding is unthinkable, and anyone who dares to assert otherwise would be put abruptly in their place. At this synagogue, where the spirit was generally open-minded, the Kiddush went ahead – but not without friction. Some congregants sought to celebrate the nuptials; others took the more traditional view that it was inappropriate, certainly in a synagogue, to celebrate that which is forbidden by the Torah.

The secession came in a matter of months. The congregants who participated in the Kiddush that Shabbat joined others in walking out of the congregation to found Yachad, the first Orthodox congregation in Israel and maybe the world that was not just gay-friendly but that celebrated religious LGBTQ couples no less openly than straight couples. Short of a traditional marriage service, with *ḥuppa* and *kiddushin*, Yachad was as inclusive as could possibly be.

Chana and Aviad Friedman, two of the most senior members of the original congregation, assumed the leadership of Yachad, whose members include gay and straight couples alike. Dr. Chana Friedman, a native of Jerusalem, was studying at the time for a women's equivalent to rabbinic ordination, which she later obtained, at Beit Morasha. She is currently a member of Beit Hillel, an organization of male and female rabbis, and is the principal, as noted earlier, of the Tel Aviv branch of Pelech, a liberal Orthodox girls' school. Friedman has said on several occasions that meeting and getting to know religious gay men and women in Tel Aviv shaped her mindset as a halakhic authority. Friedman is a progressive: she wants Orthodox communities to not just accept gay men and women but to find halakhic ways to allow them to live as couples. Halakha, she says, must take the high road in confronting the challenge of homosexuality.

The question of the place of LGBTQ individuals in Orthodox Jewish society is broad and dynamic. It marks another fault line between religious red lines and the demand for equality. It's true that here, as with many of the other hot button issues described in this book, the majority of Orthodox Jews are bystanders in this battle. But the two poles are so far apart that it is hard to see how they might ever be reconciled. One side, citing Leviticus, cries, "Abomination!" Sometimes it adds, "Perverts!" as Rabbi Yigal Levinstein famously said at the Eli pre-military academy. The other side, no less religious, considers halakha binding but protests this offensive rhetoric and regards any manifestation of homophobia as an affront to its core values, including its religious values. The dispute over LGBTQ individuals, like other debates that touch at the heart of halakha, involves sensitive questions about the place of halakha in the modern world and perhaps also about the meaning of religious life.

As in the debate over the place of women in the synagogue, in the polemic over LGBTQ individuals, the rival sides insist that the language and spirit of halakha favors them. And as in the debate over women, the most explosive point is not the demand for halakha to evolve, but the mere existence of the conversation about rights, self-determination, and identity for unorthodox minorities in Orthodox society. The debate is not about scrapping red lines but about whether they are red at all.

This debate also touches on additional "others" denied equality by the Torah and the two millennia of rabbinic literature. Equality is a supreme Western value, and although it was not born Jewish, it has become so for a whole generation of Western Jews. Recent years have seen a vibrant halakhic and social debate about the place of physically and mentally disabled individuals in the synagogue, including those who suffer from a mental-health disorder that, in principle, exempts them from halakhic obligations. There is also a debate about ideological "others," with whom relationships raise all sorts of social and political questions – secular, Reform, and Conservative Jews, and non-Jews as well. There is particular interest in "others" who do not fit into traditional family structures: unmarried men of certain ages and divorcees who live alone, by choice or not; single women who conceive using sperm donations; and of course, homosexuals, lesbians, bisexuals, and transgender individuals.

The question of homosexuality is no less difficult for Orthodox society than the question of women. Perhaps more so. The unequivocal biblical prohibition on male homosexual intercourse forms the basis of a fierce clash with modern values. As Leviticus 18:21 commands: "Do not lie with a male as one lies with a woman; it is abomination." This prohibition does not distinguish between homosexual one-night stands and stable, loving relationships. But in the modern age, homosexuality is not just a sexual act, but an identity, a community, and a lifestyle, and it often finds expression in long-term relationships and shared parenting. What, if anything, does halakha say about this relatively new conception of sexuality? And what does it say about people who hold both identities – both gay and religious? And at what point will the "others" be satisfied with their level of equality, recognition, and acceptance? And are there other core issues in halakha that demand reexamination?

Since the phrase "religious homosexual" was until recently seen as an oxymoron, it was rare to encounter such an individual. Over the years, homosexuals in conservative societies, especially in observant Jewish communities, chose one of two options: to live in the closet, or to walk out of both the closet and religious society at once. The demand by Jewish homosexuals and lesbians to be part of religious life and society, whether or not they were raised religious, contains the implicit and not entirely obvious assumption that such an arrangement is possible and desirable.

This demand landed like a stun grenade in the middle of the halakhic debate. In the aftermath of its introduction, there were two opposing positions. One relies on the letter of the halakhic law: the homosexual act is strictly forbidden in the Torah and therefore it has no place among a God-fearing, Torah-abiding community. The other takes a more modernist approach, by which sexual orientation is generally innate and God-given and therefore, for the sake of the homosexuals among us, we must grapple halakhically with the issue.

The relatively new demand by religious gay men and women to brandish both identities simultaneously is a demand for some radical answers from halakha. Fully accepting such individuals would require interpretive acrobatics, far beyond the conventional contours of Jewish law. Dr. Micah Goodman, a leading Israeli philosopher and educator, once told me that liberal Orthodoxy differs from its conservative form in that it "recognizes that some people's basic identity clashes with halakha, but they're still bound by it. You can't think about halakha the same way after the gay issue comes up. Something's changed." If halakha turns into a "problem," can Orthodox Jews still consider it fully binding?

The existence of out-and-proud gay men and women, who are observant Jews and wish to be active members of Orthodox society, is yesterday's news. It became old news in the blink of an eye. When director Sandi Simcha DuBowski's documentary *Trembling Before G-d*, about the lives and dilemmas of homosexual Orthodox Jews, was released in 2001, it caused a storm in American Orthodox society. Tremors of these internal quarrels soon reached Israel, especially after *Keep Not Silent*, a documentary about Orthodox lesbians, directed by Ilil Alexander, was released in 2004, and after director Chaim Elbaum's short film *And Thou Shalt Love*, about a yeshiva student who tries to suppress his sexuality, came out in 2007.[1] But only in 2010, when a gay character first appeared in the popular Israeli drama *Srugim*, did it dawn on everyone in Israel that Orthodox homosexuals, and all the associated dilemmas, were here to stay and that the issue had to be addressed.

The religious gay community has traveled a long road, albeit quickly, between the emergence of the first discreet support groups for oppressed and deeply closeted homosexuals in the 1980s to the open conversation that began in the 2000s. As with questions over the role of women in religious leadership roles and a host of other moral issues, society was ripe for change before its leaders. At first, religious homosexuals set up closed study and support groups, and later they started a dialogue with the outside world – with their families, their friends, and the intra-community media. Social networks played a key role.

This open dialogue started in the United States and, after an incubation of a few years, reached Israel.[2] The bottom-up forces did the trick. In an article for *Maariv* at the dawn of the millennium, reporter Vered Kellner published a series of lengthy quotes from religious gay men and women. Ziv, one of Kellner's interviewees, later wrote in a religious LGBTQ internet forum: "I hope every religious gay man and lesbian reads this article, to know they're not alone and that the Holy One, blessed be He, loves them, and He's with them in all their distress, in all the suffering, in all the pain. They mustn't think for a second that the Holy One, blessed be He, has abandoned them."

Two years later, the right-wing weekly *Makor Rishon* published a piece that was considered groundbreaking at the time, in which

---

1. Also in this list was psychologist Irit Koren's book *Altering the Closet: Stories of Religious Gays and Lesbians* (Yediot Books, 2003) [Hebrew].
2. Rabbi Steven Greenberg from Boston is still considered the go-to person for religious homosexuals, even outside the United States, because he was the first Orthodox rabbi to come out of the closet and has written extensively about the issue and offered ongoing support. He wrote a halakhic paper in 1993 on the subject, at first anonymously and later in an extended version under his own name. Steven Greenberg, *Wrestling with God and Men: Homosexuality in the Jewish Tradition* (Wisconsin: University of Wisconsin Press, 2005).

an anonymous writer explained that as a religious homosexual, he intended to avoid the planned Gay Pride Parade in Jerusalem: "Many people remain ignorant of the immense difficulty of living as a religious homosexual, because it's too difficult to describe. You need only imagine a single day in the life of such a person, who spends every day praying and begging God to relieve him of his sexual orientation and falls asleep while making one final, futile request, as his tears dry – and the next morning when he wakes up, the first thing he knows about himself, even before reciting *Modeh Ani*, is that the quality whose name he dares not speak is still part of him and will follow him around wherever he goes – to synagogue, to yeshiva, to work, to prayers, to boarding school, to the religious men's beach, and the *mikve*. Living this reality day in day out is as close to torture as hell itself. In any case, after many exhausting years, I was forced to make my peace with my sexual orientation before I fell apart, and I told myself quietly: *That's it. I'm a religious homosexual.*"[3] The anonymous writer later stepped out of the shadows: Ze'ev Schweidel, a criminologist, who started writing in his own name after his public coming-out.

Around the same time, new organizations started popping up, such as the religious lesbians' group Bat-Kol (founded in 2005), and the religious homosexuals' organizations Hod (founded in 2008) and Havruta, which was founded as a Jerusalem-based support group and soon became the largest religious Jewish LGBTQ group in Israel. They initiated a dialogue with a small group of rabbis and halakhic experts: Rabbi Prof. Daniel Sperber, whose daughter Avigail, as noted earlier, founded Bat-Kol; Dr. Chana Friedman; and Rabbi Benny Lau, who had already engaged with the issue publicly and privately before doing a joint newspaper interview with his gay brother, the independent Conservative rabbi Amichai Lau-Lavie. Joining them were Rabbi Yuval Cherlow, a yeshiva dean and one of the heads of the Tzohar rabbinic organization; Prof. Tova Hartman; Rabbi Yaakov Medan; Malka Puterkovsky;

---

3.   "The Cry of the Brothers Who Won't March," *Makor Rishon*, July 14, 2006 [Hebrew]. The piece was originally published under the pen name "Yair Dror." Schweidel later revealed that he had been asked to use a pseudonym. He had already published an article under his real name, exploring halakhic positions on homosexuality.

and more. Each came with a different message and approach, but the fact that they were even having this conversation was nothing short of sensational.

For the participants at the Havruta conference in 2009, the event was a dream come true and a huge step forward for religious Jewish homosexuals. By the end of the evening, many of them felt for the first time in their lives that the inescapable clash between their two identities – as gay and observant Jews – would not necessarily condemn them to exile. But even before the event started, a minor event had a transformational impact on two men in the room: Rabbi Yaakov Medan and one of his former students, Eyal Amir.

Amir had been an outstanding student at Har Etzion, the yeshiva that Rabbi Medan headed. Even after leaving the yeshiva, he remained in close touch with Rabbi Medan but he never told him what he had told several other rabbis. Only now, in the run-up to the conference, did Rabbi Medan realize that the openly gay man with whom he would be sharing a stage was his former pupil. As the hall filled up, the neon lights flooded the room. In the corner, in clear view of the crowd, Rabbi Medan gave Amir a fatherly embrace.

"I told him I was terribly embarrassed, and he told me that he'd only come on my account," Amir described later.

"I only found out about him three weeks ago," Rabbi Medan added, "and he's the reason I decided to come. He's my own flesh and blood. I decided I had to give him support. It was a very difficult, but genuine moment. I only came because I understood that his problem is my problem, that I'm absolutely not off the hook, that I must offer him an outstretched hand, and do everything I can do for him."

The mere fact of Rabbi Medan's participation at this event attested to the rapid transformation that the gay religious community had undergone, from being a closely kept secret to an issue that could, in certain circumstances, be discussed. Medan is a mainstream figure, a Torah authority accepted by conservative sections of society, and rabbis who knew of his intention to attend the event tried to dissuade him. But he decided to show up. For nearly the whole evening, he used the rabbis' favored euphemism – "those of the opposite orientation" – but by the end, he managed to say the word explicitly: "The best friend of the gay man [*homo*, in Hebrew] is the Holy One, blessed be He," he told the audience.

Why did the LGBTQ issue not appear on the Orthodox Jewish radar until so very recently? The timing, of course, is connected to the evolution of Western culture and the achievements of the international LGBTQ struggle. The State of Israel, where marriage for Jews is authorized solely by the Chief Rabbinate, does not recognize gay or lesbian weddings, and on some issues, it still lags behind other Western states, but it has experienced far-reaching changes thanks to Supreme Court rulings, army changes of protocol, and a largely supportive public. Same-sex unions are recognized for the purposes of tax and inheritance law. Tel Aviv is an international capital of gay tourism and pride parades are a regular fixture there and in other cities, including Haifa, Beersheba, and Jerusalem.

Israel is not free from homophobic incidents, and the worst was the murder of Shira Banki at the Jerusalem Pride Parade in 2015 (alongside the attack that killed two and injured eleven at the Bar-Noar gay center in Tel Aviv in 2009 – a case that still remains unsolved), but the ineluctable trend is in the direction of growing inclusivity, which is also trickling into religious society.

Homosexuality is undergoing a process of normalization in Israel's national-religious society. The biblical prohibition on sodomy has not been repealed and Religious Zionism has not suddenly embraced queer culture. But there is a growing awareness, and a growing understanding, of the human experiences of gay men and women. The taboo on discussing the issue has fizzled away, both in the national-religious media and even in the weekly free newspapers handed out in synagogue – and it doesn't matter whether they choose to rebuke the morality of gay culture or print nuanced human interest stories or express human empathy. This normalization is keenly felt in the Religious Zionist street and within its cohesive army platoons, in the corporate open spaces, and especially on Facebook and Twitter. The result: fewer religious men and women who are able, as they were years ago, to deny the very existence of homosexual inclinations.

Faced with this development, national-Haredi rabbis fervently believe that their role is to protest more loudly, advocate more strongly for what they regard as "normal" and "healthy" behavior, and encourage skepticism about the scientific consensus. These rabbis and their associated organizations are standing guard all along the watchtower against the normalization of homosexuality, both in the IDF and civilian life.

In the blink of an eye, the defense of heterosexuality has become a supreme value for the conservative flank of Religious Zionist society. Israelis who had never heard of the Har Hamor milieu gained their first glimpse of it when they saw billboards and online videos defending "normality" as part of a campaign by Noam – a far-right party that today has representation in the Knesset within the Religious Zionism Party and which pushes for what it calls "normalcy" rather than normalization. "That's it, we can't remain silent," the party wrote on its website. "Someone is trying to re-engineer us, to change every concept, to blur every value, to erase the family, to confuse our children about gender identity, to privatize conversion and cause the Jewish people to assimilate, to weaken the army and suppress the value of victory, and to turn Shabbat into a regular weekday and the Western Wall into a circus."

Ahead of the Pride Parade in 2019, the national-Haredi group Chazon ("Vision") erected billboards around Israel, reading "Father + Mother = Family" and "The Courage to Be Normal." The campaign also involved online videos, which accused the LGBTQ community of terrorism, no less. Several influential rabbis, including Zephaniah Drori, Dov Lior, Zvi Thau, and Shmuel Eliyahu, exhorted the public to join the protest, which until just a few years earlier had been associated with the far-right extremist group Lehava. They urged the public to trumpet "the Jewish people's voice of normality."

But rather than attesting to a shift toward extremism, the rabbis' participation in the protest movement was proof of their marginality. The rabbis were trying to resuscitate a protest that had long since been orphaned, abandoned by its original parents – the leadership of the most zealous Haredi sects, who had decided several years earlier to let the gay pride parade pass unprotested. Their reason was internal: the issue was so explosive from a Haredi educational perspective that they preferred not to touch it with a ten-foot pole. The absence of the Haredim turned the Jerusalem Pride Parade into a contest between the LGBTQ community's strongest supporters and most virulent detractors in the

Religious Zionist community. Both groups set out to demonstrate, and to demonstrate their strength.

From day one, the Jerusalem Pride Parade attracted religious Jews, including both openly gay participants and straight allies. Year by year, *kippot* have become a more regular sight on the heads of a minority of demonstrators, waving placards with variations of "Thou Shalt Love" and occasionally bursting into dance routines straight out of the yeshiva repertoire and singing verses from liturgy. Unlike the religious groups protesting homosexuality, these ones are protesting homophobia, specifically from conservatives in their own community. The Jerusalem Pride Parade has become a Religious Zionist derby, a clash of two home teams.

The opening bell rang in 2016, when Rabbi Yigal Levinstein, the dean of a conservative pre-military academy in the West Bank settlement of Eli, gave what became widely known as his "perverts speech." His intention was to inform the conservative Religious Zionist (and nearly all-male) audience at a conference about what he saw as disturbing developments in the Israeli army, his most grievous allegation being that the IDF's education system was promoting messages of pluralism and inclusion. Levinstein's implicit premise was that this represented a threat to national security. He used his speech to assail Brig.-Gen. Avner Paz-Tzuk, the commander of the IDF Education Corps. "He sees value in teaching soldiers to accept the other in the context of individual rights and accepting difference, and the perverts are of course the number one cause here."

Levinstein believed that his provocative rhetoric would expose and stop these transformations in the IDF, but what he revealed in practice was a profound change in Israeli society, and specifically religious society, in attitudes toward homosexuality, as well as toward him and his ilk. In fact, he not only revealed the change; he catalyzed it.

Levinstein and his acolytes were roundly rebuked. Dozens of rabbis defended him, publishing open letters in the national-religious press, but he spurred hundreds of straight Orthodox men and women to join the Jerusalem Pride Parade in protest (against him) and in solidarity (with the LGBTQ community). Several rabbis and female halakhic leaders also joined the chorus against him, including Benny Lau,

Yaakov Medan, Rachelle Fraenkel, and Malka Puterkovsky. Suddenly it became clear: there was an opposition to Levinstein, and it was religiously observant. Naftali Bennett, then the chairman of the Jewish Home Party and a man with his finger on the Religious Zionist pulse, responded by saying, "His remarks are unacceptable to me, and this is not the way of Religious Zionism." It is hard to remember when the leader of a religious nationalist party had ever so publicly clashed with a major national-religious rabbi.

One year earlier, in the wake of the murder of sixteen-year-old Shira Banki at the Jerusalem Pride Parade, Education Minister Naftali Bennett met with LGBTQ leaders and promised to increase the budget of IGY, an Israeli gay pride youth movement. Bennett also came out in support of his spokeswoman, immediately after her sexual orientation as a lesbian was made public. "Anyone who thinks I ought to discriminate on the basis of someone's sexual orientation, gender, or skin color will encounter a total refusal from me," he tweeted. "Beloved is everyone – everyone – created in the image of God." Bennett was hardly the LGBTQ community's biggest cheerleader in the Knesset, but his statement had an impact, especially on the political discourse in the national-religious community.

There is no reason to think that those who must reconcile their identities as gay and religious are, in this day and age, going to be spared the agony and plight of coming out. Anti-gay statements are still heard everywhere and plastered on billboards, but religious homosexuals and lesbians now have religious figures they can look up to, from the gay American Orthodox rabbi Steven Greenberg, to Rabbi Prof. Daniel Sperber, Rabbi Benny Lau, and dozens of openly gay, religious public personalities. Social media is changing the rules of the game, far from the reach of rabbis and educators. In 2017, tens of thousands of Israelis watched a video clip of a man proposing to his boyfriend – both were wearing *kippot* – at a concert by Ivri Lider, an openly gay Israeli artist. Another viral video, from early 2018, was filmed at the wedding of another gay religious couple under the *ḥuppa*, the wedding canopy. The mother of one of the grooms, wearing a modest dress and full head covering, touched many hearts when she said: "I have accepted Chaim [my son] as he is, with love, even though I dreamed of something else."

True to the finest of Jewish tradition, even the gay religious community was not immune from factionalism. There are currently two main gay religious movements: one conservative and one liberal. In 2011, several members of Havruta split off to form a breakaway gay religious organization, Kamoha ("Just Like You"). Its founder, who chose to use a pseudonym, argued that Havruta was too halakhically permissive – "Reform," even – because it failed to take a clear stance on gay sex. He built a more stringently halakhic Orthodox group, many of whose members are still closeted and struggling with the dissonance between homosexuality as a legitimate sexual orientation and homosexual intercourse as a prohibited act. The organization hosts Shabbat getaways for its members, all in a thoroughly religious atmosphere, with lectures, social activities, three traditional meals, and Shabbat songs. One of these weekend getaways took place in Hebron, home to a staunchly conservative settler nucleus. Unlike Havruta, Kamoha is not opposed to conversion therapy – treatment that can supposedly "cure" a person's sexual orientation. It also supports a matchmaking service that pairs up religious gay men and women so that they can have ostensibly traditional, heterosexual families together.

Over on the other, liberal side of Religious Zionist society, family life looks completely different, with gay and lesbian couples whose children, raised in religious communities, are already reaching bar mitzva age. According to Aviad Friedman, one of the founders of Yachad in Tel Aviv, twenty-two babies were born into the congregation in 2015 – half of them with two fathers or two mothers.

The Reform and Conservative movements have already addressed most of the dilemmas related to LGBTQ issues, in a series of official and unofficial decisions.[4] Haredi rabbis generally ignore the issue, as does their

---

4. The Reform movement abolished the prohibition on sodomy by arguing that the relevant passage in Leviticus only refers to prostitution and idolatrous sexual cults. The Conservative movement spent years conducting a rigorous halakhic debate and came to various contradictory conclusions about homosexuality, before finally swinging the door open to LGBTQ people. Nowadays every Conservative rabbinic college and practically every Conservative congregation in the world treats LGBTQ individuals equally, and it is not rare to find Conservative rabbis who will conduct

flock, apart from the vocal – and in and of itself anomalous – protests against the Jerusalem Pride Parade.[5] The late Rabbi Moshe Feinstein, one of the towering Jewish religious authorities in the United States, was a rare example of a Haredi rabbi who addressed the halakhic implications of homosexuality directly in an answer to a man who admitted that he had failed to overcome his inclinations. Rabbi Feinstein dismissed the idea that men might actually be sexually attracted to other men. "The desire for homosexual relations is against natural lust and even the wicked do not have a desire for it itself. Rather their entire desire for it is only because it is something prohibited and the *yetzer hara* seduces them to rebel against the will of God." He assumed that such unnatural sexual acts, which are strictly forbidden, must be rooted in a rebellious impulse – a desire to enrage God.

The fundamental religious question in this debate is whether homosexuality is an innate or acquired trait, a matter of choice or not. Rabbi Feinstein is probably the most senior halakhic authority to have dared to touch the issue, but in the twentieth century the Conservative

---

same-sex religious weddings. Some members walked out of these movements in protest at their resolutions on the matter, including Rabbi Joel Roth in the United States and Rabba Einat Ramon in Israel, who headed the Schechter Rabbinical Seminary (the Conservative college in Jerusalem) and defected to liberal Orthodoxy. She explained her reasons for the switch in an essay titled "Why I Left the Conservative Movement" in the *De'ot* journal in mid-2016. The differences between these movements and the contours of the Orthodox discussion are immense. Note that Orthodox Judaism, unlike the progressive movements, has no supreme rabbinic councils or rabbinic courts accepted by everyone, which might dictate policy or articulate a comprehensive vision.

5. In 2007, masses of Haredi demonstrators took to the streets at the behest of their rabbis, chiefly Rabbi Yosef Shalom Elyashiv and Rabbi Ovadia Yosef, to protest the upcoming Jerusalem Pride Parade. "Every Jew who wishes to honor our sacred Torah and honor Jerusalem, the holy city, must protest this abomination," they said. After that summer, the Haredi leadership understood that their protest had not only failed to stop the march but had inadvertently exposed the rank-and-file to a whole new world of content about homosexuality. The Haredi mainstream dropped its active resistance. The protest fizzled out into rhetorical opposition, such as when Jerusalem Chief Rabbi Shlomo Amar called the LGBTQ community a "cult of abomination" in an interview with Yehudah Schlezinger of *Israel Hayom*, November 17, 2016.

movement in the United States, and in its wake Modern Orthodox and Religious Zionist rabbis, subjected the question of homosexuality to comprehensive halakhic scrutiny. Two main approaches emerged, which differ first and foremost in their terminology: while liberal rabbis use terms such as "LGBTQ," "gay," "lesbian," and "same-sex," the more conservative rabbis stuck with the coinage "opposite orientation." This term implies that even if homosexuality is something one is born with, one can still choose to control it. That it is a kind of weakness that one succumbs to, a debility that can be "cured."

The most high-profile advocate of the latter approach is Rabbi Shlomo Aviner, who founded an organization that offers so-called conversion therapy, including workshops with titles like "Journey into Masculinity" led by psychologists and rabbis. In an article for one synagogue newspaper, Rabbi Aviner wrote of the dilemmas facing religious homosexuals that "this prattle is nothing new but a well-known problem.... Every human being on earth has urges ... and his role is to overcome them."

Careful not to say the h-word itself, Aviner wrote: "There is no such thing as a religious 'hom...' The definition of religious is someone who observes [Jewish law as codified in the *Shulḥan Arukh*], and this is against the *Shulḥan Arukh*. It suits the ancient pagan culture, which still echoes widely in Western culture.... Obviously every Jew should be accepted with love and warmth, but love is not legitimacy. Even perverts merit our love, and the Sages explain that even a prisoner on death row is covered by the commandment to love thy neighbor. And precisely because we love them, we want to help them eliminate and overcome their urges, so they can marry and live natural, normal, happy lives. It's not true that escaping this condition is damaging. It's all lies, to legitimize something bad.... They can all, without exception, be cured in a relatively short time."

Rabbi Aviner was one of the first figures in the Torani conservative flank of the national-religious world to write about homosexuality. Many of his colleagues thought that it did not befit a public response. But in time, many other voices joined the fray, including Rabbi Zvi Thau, the co-founder and president of Yeshivat Har Hamor.[6] In March 2017, his

---

6. Rabbi Yehoshua Shapira, the dean of the Ramat Gan Hesder yeshiva, wrote in the *Olam Katan* synagogue newspaper in August 2010: "Many people nowadays wish to

students printed and disseminated booklets with a transcript of a conversation with him several months earlier, during a time of crisis between Religious Zionist rabbis and the Israeli military. For Thau's disciples, this was an emergency, and their mission was to recruit the national-religious mainstream against LGBTQ-friendly reforms in the IDF.

Rabbi Thau called homosexuality "the ugliest perversion, which uproots family life and damages fertility rates, and violates the first principle of human existence.... Academics and the media have managed to 'purify' this stain by speaking of the need to 'accept the other,' saying everyone is free to live as he pleases and families do not conform to a single template – changes that trickled down over time and made people look at and speak about this phenomenon differently, accepting it as something natural. Nowadays, anyone who begs to differ is passé, treated as primitive and out of order. But besides the matter itself, it is also a challenge to normalcy – to the possibility of defining a certain range of behavior as normal and whatever lies beyond it as abnormal." The editors of the booklet censored a comment by Rabbi Thau, which had already been published on the website *Srugim*, in which he asserted

---

tame the intellectually primitive 'sons of darkness' and cleanse the scourge through various 'studies' and pseudo-scientific statements nurtured by a rotten culture that wants to resurrect the world of abominations of Egypt and Canaan. Thankfully we have a divine point of purity, which has already spoken unambiguously and settled this whole debate with an acerbic term – *abomination*." Speaking of "a phenomenon that it is hard to believe anyone will justify," he added, "I won't beat around the bush, there are some difficult cases and nobody can say that there is a direct path to a perfect solution for everyone. Nevertheless, I have personally met at least one or two people who have managed to change their [sexual] orientation and build faithful Jewish families." There was a flood of similar reactions after Rabbi Levinstein's "perverts speech." Rabbi Yehoshua Weitzman, the head of a Hesder yeshiva in Maalot, quoted to his students a well-known dictum by Rabbi Kook about what he called "the evil inclination." Rabbi Weitzman said: "Rabbi Kook believes, and so do I, that this defect can be fixed. Giving this legitimacy and turning it into something natural and correct erodes the general motivation to fix it.... Whoever, God forbid, has such an inclination must believe that it can be fixed ... and he is not exempt from having to marry a woman. He is obligated to do so and it is essential to put this on the table, that a man has no option but to marry a woman. There are no other solutions." Quoted on the website of Kamoha, July 27, 2016.

that homosexuals "play around with their anuses all day, so the whole house stinks, and that's how they raise children."[7]

Besides assuming that sexual orientation is a matter of choice, hardline rabbis tend to focus on the homosexual act, rather than the homosexuals. Yehoshua Gurtler, a gay lawyer and one of the co-founders of Yachad in Tel Aviv, addressed this point at a joint conference hosted by Havruta and Bat-Kol, in front of a mixed gay and straight audience, including several rabbis: "I want to propose to the religious world that we have a conversation about homosexuality without mentioning sex. The prohibition on sodomy is a commandment that is between man and God. We don't have to discuss that here. That's the personal responsibility of every Jewish man and woman, between them and their Creator. I want to talk about other commandments: *Love thy neighbor as thyself*, a commandment between an individual and his fellow human being; *You shall not hate your kinsfolk in your heart*, another commandment between an individual and his fellow human being. These commandments are the responsibility of the community. The discourse about homosexuality, lesbianism, and transgenderism doesn't have to start with sodomy. The question of what homosexuals do in bed or what lesbians do behind closed doors is the last question that should be asked in the Jewish conversation about homosexuality." He added: "Let's not confuse the sexual act with sexual identity and sexual orientation…. We *kippa*-wearers were all taught the value of humility. As I see it, sitting around the table and talking about anal sex and oral sex and masturbation and erections is not modest. There are more important things to talk about than what happens in the bed I share with my partner."

Furthermore, he went on: "I've never been to a synagogue where someone stands at the door and asks: *Has your wife been to the mikve this month? Has yours? Madam, have you been?* It doesn't happen. When people are invited to recite the blessing over the Torah, nobody dares ask them whether they observe the laws of *nidda* at home. Some commandments are between man and his Creator, and there's a reason why – let the community discuss communal affairs, all the more so when talking

---

7. Zvi Shaiman, "Rabbi Thau: The IDF Chief of Staff and Head of the Manpower Directorate Are Behaving Like a Junta," *Srugim*, December 11, 2016 [Hebrew].

about commandments that involve such sensitivities as the ones we're discussing tonight."

Gurtler's wish, and that of so many other Orthodox Jewish homosexuals, has come true – at least partially. The national-Haredi dogma, that homosexuality is "curable" and effectively made up, is losing its grip on swaths of religious society. "Jewish law and the religious community are under incessant assault, from without and within, by a demand to void of all content, or even eradicate, the verses and laws that treat sodomy as a sin," warned the editor of the *BeSheva* religious weekly, Emmanuel Shilo. "Many in the religious community, and even some of our rabbis, are buckling under this moral and public pressure."

But is this only a matter of public pressure? Naftali Bennett's successor as chairman of the Jewish Home Party, Rabbi Rafi Peretz, admitted in an interview to Dana Weiss on Israel's Channel 12 in July 2019 that as a rabbi he had referred young gay men to "conversion therapy" to try to make them heterosexual. "It's possible, I myself have done it," said Peretz, Israel's then-education minister. But just a few days later, after a huge public outcry, Peretz quickly backtracked. He wrote a letter to the country's teachers, many of whom were outraged by his comments: "I have never suggested conversion therapy, which I utterly oppose. I know that conversion therapy is wrong." This sudden U-turn by a rabbi and educator of Peretz's stature betrayed more than a concession to public pressure. The conservative flank of Religious Zionism is increasingly befuddled by this reality, struggling to reconcile it with the prohibitions in the Torah.

Indeed, the "assault" that Emmanuel Shilo referred to is keenly felt by the conservative quarters of national-religious society. In March 2019 the free newspaper *Olam Katan*, tens of thousands of copies of which are distributed in synagogues every Shabbat, published a letter by an anonymous homosexual yeshiva student, under the headline: "Closet Within a Closet." The man complained that in his society, "whoever puts his foot down to fight for his principles and adhere with all his might to the possibility of living a life that conforms with his personal values and the laws of the Torah finds himself silenced and paralyzed." He demanded that his rabbi, whose name was not published, accept difference. "I'm not asking for legitimacy, only empathy," he wrote. The platform that this newspaper gave an anonymous yeshiva student to write about his sexual orientation was a novelty (although he wrote that he still wanted to build a family with a woman), but it did not herald an abandonment of its editorial position. Two weeks earlier, the publication had also given a platform to the head of the Chazon organization, which ran the billboard campaign that preached that a "father + mother = family."

The reactions and counterreactions prove that the LGBTQ issue has touched all quarters of national-religious society, to varying extents, but who can articulate any sort of consensus? How inclusive should Orthodox Jewish society be toward religious LGBTQ individuals and groups? The most eminent rabbi to rise to the challenge was Aharon Lichtenstein, a leading Modern Orthodox rabbi, who earlier in life had studied under Rabbi Soloveitchik and gained a PhD from Harvard in English Literature. He stated in 2012, around three years before his passing, that homosexuals and lesbians should not be excluded or rebuked any more than other "sinners," such as Jews who violate Shabbat. Many other rabbis, including from the religious mainstream and even the conservative camp, in Israel and abroad, followed suit and adopted this view.

Among the first rabbis to address the extent of Orthodox society's inclusion of LGBTQ individuals were: Rabbi Yuval Cherlow, dean of the Hesder yeshiva in Orot Shaul, and Rabbi Chaim Rapoport, a member of the British chief rabbi's advisory council (or "rabbinic cabinet") and a medical ethics expert. Rapoport published a book on Judaism and homosexuality from an Orthodox perspective. Cherlow was one of the first to initiate a dialogue on halakha with individuals and groups from the religious LGBTQ community. He has also addressed the subject in a Q&A format on the internet and in articles.

The two rabbis reasoned that LGBTQ individuals should be accepted in religious society despite the Torah's prohibition on gay sex. Blaming religious homosexuals for their sexual orientation, they argued, was a grave violation of another halakhic prohibition – the public humiliation of one's fellow man. The novelty of this approach was to clearly recognize the existence of sexual orientation and the acute distress of religious individuals who are so inclined. The rabbis did not give a green light for homosexual relationships, and certainly not for homosexual intercourse, but they argued that religious society's severe judgmental-ism toward homosexuals, as opposed to other "sinners," was unfair.

This position was initially considered groundbreaking, but other rabbis soon jumped on the bandwagon. In 2016, before the scandal around Rabbi Levinstein's "perverts speech," dozens of Religious Zion-ist rabbis affiliated with Beit Hillel urged their communities to be toler-ant of homosexuals. "Although forbidden sexual relations must not be permitted, there is room for leniency in society's inclusion and accep-tance of them [homosexuals]," they wrote in a halakhic legal opinion. The rabbis ruled that gay people could lead prayers in synagogue "and fulfill the obligation of the public and serve in all communal roles."

This document, written over the space of several months in dia-logue with representatives of the gay religious Havruta organization, was presented at an event in Raanana, attended by the parents of Shira Banki – the sixteen-year-old girl murdered at the Jerusalem Pride Parade. The document avoided the use of terms such as "gay" or "lesbian," but rather "people with same-sex orientations."

A few months later, the Religious Kibbutz Movement, an umbrella group for many thousands of Orthodox Jews across twenty-three communities, held a landmark conference in Kibbutz Be'erot Yitzhak in central Israel and announced that it was embracing all its LGBTQ members, in the spirit of the Beit Hillel document.

The distinction between homosexual individuals and homosex-ual intercourse is beginning to gain a grip on the mainstream of Israel's Orthodox Jewish society, including its more conservative communities.[8]

---

8. Rabbi Eliezer Melamed, a prominent voice on the conservative flank of Religious Zionism and a regular columnist for *BeSheva*, who serves as the local rabbi of the settlement of Har Bracha, described homosexuality as a "disease" but acknowledged that "in our generation this phenomenon has become more widespread and we have to deal with it. Above all, we must be careful not to offend or insult anyone suffering such an inclination. Sometimes the grief, frustration, and shame that come together with this inclination are so difficult that some young people choose to end their lives, because it's so painful." He wrote, similarly to Rabbi Lichtenstein a few years earlier, that "homosexuals should not be shamed" and that "in any case, these sinners should be treated no more gravely than sinners who perform other grave violations, such as desecrating Shabbat. And just as people who desecrate Shabbat are still allowed to recite the blessing over the Torah as long as they do not do so

Nowadays, the standard rabbinic opinion seems to be one of "empathy but not legitimacy," as Rabbi Chaim Navon proposed in the aftermath of the Rabbi Levinstein affair.

But few rabbis are willing to touch halakhic questions that arise from same-sex partnerships. One of the only figures to address this issue is Rabbi Ysoscher Katz, a faculty member at Yeshivat Chovevei Torah in New York, who formulated a halakhic responsum to questions he was asked about monogamous relationships between religiously observant homosexuals. He told me that his conclusion was that religious LGBTQ individuals should enjoy a kind of religious "presumption of kosherness" – that there is no reason to presume that they are transgressing halakha – even if they live in a shared household with a partner. To his left, another lone voice is Rabbi Steven Greenberg, who wants to permit intimate homosexual relations under Jewish law and has ruled that the biblical prohibition applies to coercive sexual relations, not to egalitarian relationships between individuals of the same sex. This is a radical reinterpretation of Leviticus, although in practice there are many men and women in same-sex relationships who still regard themselves as religiously observant. Whether or not they choose to invoke Rabbi Greenberg's loophole, many of them insist that they are acting within the bounds of halakha.

Does this call for inclusion and appeasement suffice? Will LGBTQ individuals moderate their expectations and make do with letters from rabbis issuing generalized statements about limited inclusion? Will homosexuals be content with answers addressed to their social milieu rather than to themselves directly?

Dr. Chana Friedman, having already received her rabbinic ordination, posed these questions most bluntly when she was invited to speak at an event in which Beit Hillel presented its halakhic position, urging inclusion of homosexuals in religious communities. She welcomed

---

lehakhis (to spite others), people who commit this sin [of homosexual intercourse] should also be allowed to recite the blessing over the Torah, as long as they do not do so *lehakhis*. All the more so when it seems they are careful not to commit the grave sin of sodomy." Eliezer Melamed, "The Disease of This Generation and Attitudes Toward It," *BeSheva*, February 26, 2015 [Hebrew].

some parts of the decision, criticized others, and compared the status of religious homosexuals to that of people the Talmud describes as "half a slave and half free" – individuals whose legal, social, and professional status the Sages of the Mishna struggled to define.

"Our inability to look at gays and lesbians and tell them, 'We have a solution for you too, not just for the community that must embrace you,' that's a grave statement," Friedman said. "And it's not just a problem for LGBTQ individuals. I feel that it's the whole religious community's problem nowadays, because not only people with same-sex orientations feel this pain. The whole of society is looking at halakha...and sees a system that can't accommodate certain people and tells them, 'Sit to one side if you can, leave that outside the synagogue.' It's extremely problematic, it's anomalous, it's a test case that might be an outlier, but it reflects something much deeper about the nature of halakha, and that hurts me. It's not a pain for someone else, it's my pain, because this is my halakha, and it's my Torah. I don't think we can keep up the status quo, where we tell the community: You be inclusive, but to the individuals themselves we can offer no guidance."

Friedman's demand, therefore, is for halakha to provide solutions that address relationships between one gay man and another, or one lesbian woman and another. She critiques a situation in which as far as halakha is concerned, there is no difference between homosexuals who live in modest, monogamous, and God-fearing households and those whose lives are "one-night stands in bars and all that that entails."

Friedman's remarks touched on the biggest challenge of all: updating halakha. Can one truly be committed to halakha while demanding reforms on core moral issues, such as homosexuality? It is relatively easy for rabbis to foster a positive and inclusive atmosphere toward "others" in their communities, but can they and do they even want to grab the bull by the horns when it comes to major changes to halakha? What about *agunot* – women who are "chained" in broken marriages because their husbands refuse to grant them a divorce? What about converts who must lie to rabbinic courts by pretending that they are religious, because to be Jews in the Jewish state, the Chief Rabbinate expects converts to live fully observant lives – a commitment that, perhaps, not all of them sincerely wish to make? On the other hand, is Friedman's radical solution even consistent with halakha and its traditions? Does it still count as "Orthodox"?[9]

These challenges to halakha meet the reality of the religious street on countless occasions, on matters old and new, and not merely on those that relate to homosexuality. Religious men and women are marrying later, and therefore living as singles for longer; divorce is more widespread, bringing to the fore new dilemmas concerning lifestyle choices, extramarital sex, and women's freedom to bring children into the world as single mothers.

Even today, few Orthodox rabbis would openly allow a single, middle-aged woman to conceive using a sperm donation. Most rabbis do not consider artificial insemination using a foreign donor expressly forbidden (and even prefer a non-Jewish donor, thus avoiding future doubts about the infant's ancestry), but their concern is more social than halakhic. Orthodox Jewish society, as a rule, venerates the nuclear family – father, mother, children – so conservatively inclined rabbis offer older women just one hope, the realization of which may be practically

---

9. Friedman came under a massive public onslaught, including in the wake of her remarks at that conference. In 2018, when she was a candidate for running the middle school at the religious Zeitlin High School in Tel Aviv, the religious newspaper *Olam Katan* plucked quotes from her speech at Beit Hillel's gathering and ran a front-page character assassination: "Mrs. Friedman would certainly not identify as Conservative, but judging by her opinions, certainly her progressive calls for halakhic recognition of all versions of what is known as 'the new family,' we are at minimum dealing with an ideological identity that is a country mile away from Jewish tradition, certainly from the world of halakha. More specifically, her rhetoric is entirely halakhic, but her ideology is light years away from being so. The simpler elements of the worldview that Friedman propagates are the egalitarian services, including calling up women to recite the blessing over the Torah in front of everyone, but she also has no compunctions about going to extremes and calling to emulate the changes made in the Conservative movement less than a decade ago. In a panel at 'Beit Hillel,' Friedman advocated for the extreme position of 'recognizing same-sex families,' in her words, and even of finding a way to change halakhic attitudes on this matter." Beit Hillel gave Friedman its backing, but the article fueled the ongoing campaign against her at Zeitlin, which ended with the school she ran, the Tel Aviv branch of Pelech, breaking away from the main Zeitlin boys' school to its own premises in Tel Aviv.

dubious: to freeze their eggs, to be used only once they have found a suitable partner for wedlock.

Rabbinic approval is a valuable commodity for single Orthodox women wishing to conceive using sperm donations, as well as single mothers who are already raising children in religious communities and want them to integrate, despite all the hardship, as normal students in religious schools. Such legitimacy is also important for religious lesbians who wish to raise children with their partners, or alone. One of the first rabbis to accommodate single women and openly permit conception using sperm donations under certain conditions was Rabbi Cherlow. In 2007, he published a halakhic responsum on the subject, and there followed a predictable backlash. Rabbi Nachum Rabinovitch, a senior halakhic authority and the late head of the Maale Adumim Hesder yeshiva (he passed away in 2020), said at a rabbinic conference soon thereafter: "It is inconceivable to deliberately bring a fatherless child into the world. Any woman planning on willingly conceiving such a child just to satisfy her desire to be a mother – there is nothing more wicked or cruel. Such a woman is not worthy of mothering any human creature." Dr. Chana Catane, a gynecologist and well-known personality in national-Haredi quarters of society, says of women who conceive using sperm donors: "Their children are born with a kind of defect. They're fatherless. Why? What did they do wrong? Why shouldn't they be born into a standard family?"[10]

Such opinions are apparently only voiced before an audience of faithful acolytes. The conservative gatekeepers are not always successful in keeping up with change in religious society, which is reshaping its own present without them.

In October 2014, the conservative religious newspaper *BeSheva* ran a front-page story about religious singles who were *shomer negia* – who observed the religious prohibition on touching members of the opposite sex who were not their spouses. In so doing, the paper argued, these young men and women proved that despite the difficulties of refraining from physical contact as young, unmarried adults, it was still

---

10. Interview with Roy Sharon on Israel's Channel 10, as part of a series on religious women, November 2016.

possible to abide by religious law. The article was a response to report a few weeks earlier in *Makor Rishon,* citing a poll according to which 43 percent of religious youngsters flouted the ban on physical contact with members of the opposite sex. But strikingly, the men and women quoted by *BeSheva* were kept anonymous; and instead of their photos, the paper printed an illustration of two shadows. The Israeli journalist Akiva Novick blasted the feature as an own-goal for religious conservatives: "Not even a thousand sociological studies could so succinctly communicate the collapse of commitment to halakha among religious youngsters like this article," he wrote. Referring to the choice to keep the interviewees anonymous, he lambasted that this was the equivalent of the raising of an ideological white flag and added: "To think that twenty years ago, it was those who didn't avoid physical contact who guarded their anonymity and were represented by illustrations."

The question of religious singles sparked a ferocious halakhic argument when Zvi Zohar, a professor of religious law at Bar-Ilan University, published an essay in 2006 about cohabitation outside of wedlock.[11] Citing halakhic sources about the legal status of concubines, Zohar argued that there is no prohibition on extramarital sex in exclusive and religiously observant relationships – something that, according to him, was already commonplace in religious society. The paper, published in a high-quality journal, caused a sensation. Many rabbis felt compelled to respond and vigorously protest, and the argument spilled over from the pages of journals into religious news websites.

It is impossible to know how this polemic might have affected religious dating habits. These intimate questions are not decided in yeshivas or in "ask the rabbi" columns in religious newspapers, but in young religious singles' rented apartments. Some of these households are home to religious singles whose commitment to halakha is weak or nonexistent in regard to certain issues, or for certain periods of their lives. Such singles and divorcees do not expect to get their rabbis' approval, forging a new culture along the religious spectrum. This is a social story with halakhic, and perhaps also demographic implications.

---

11. Zvi Zohar, "Living Together as a Couple Without Ḥuppa and *Kiddushin,*" *Akdamot* 17 (2006) [Hebrew].

Interestingly, a decade after Zohar's article, a group of religious women already felt sufficiently comfortable in their practice to publicly petition Israel's Supreme Court (rather than a rabbinical court) to allow any woman who wished to use a public ritual bath, to do so, without being watched over and quizzed by an attendant. Ordinarily, married Orthodox Jewish women visit the *mikve* (ritual bath) once a month after their periods, to "purify" themselves before resuming sexual relations with their husbands. But among the petitioners were single women who wished to purify themselves, either in order to visit the Temple Mount or in order to have sex with their partners after their periods. They argued that the *mikve* attendants, employees of municipal religious councils, had refused to let them use the ritual baths upon discovering that they were unmarried.

And on the backdrop of this discussion it is interesting to note that religious homosexuals – who present an even more radical halakhic challenge than single heterosexual women – are clamoring for rabbinic acceptance. Rabbis are invited to conferences held by Kamoha and Havruta, and to pray at Yachad in Tel Aviv. When Rabbi Benny Lau and Rabbanit Carmit Feintuch hosted an evening of open conversation with gay men and women and their religious families at their Jerusalem synagogue in 2018, hundreds of Israelis from around the country packed the hall. That same year, Rabbi Lau also joined the wedding party – he explained that he was careful not to attend the ceremony itself – of two religious men. On the other hand, adult religious singles and divorcees see their condition as temporary, and certainly not one that calls for separate organizations or lobby groups. All they need are some private chat groups on social media, and perhaps at most some dating apps.

We have briefly discussed singles and slightly more so the challenges posed by homosexuals, but the flexibility of halakha is tested in many other fields, both private and public. Several thinkers and writers who grew up in the Religious Zionist community have proposed, for example, setting up a model of "Israeli conversion," which would require converts to study Jewish-Israeli culture rather than commit to religious observance, or forging a new form of authentically Israeli Judaism, which would offer appropriate answers for modern life.

How far will the calls for change go? How far can halakha be stretched? The immediate challenge, long before the bigger theoretical questions, is how to address personal and familial troubles: gay identity and partnerships; men who refuse to grant their "chained" wives a divorce; infertility; and tensions between halakha and medical science. Observant Jewish men and women stuck at the bottom of the halakhic and social pyramid are running out of patience with answers that leave them hanging dry, calling on them to make fateful concessions. Perhaps the biggest innovation of the current era, though, is that they are standing up tall and demanding answers.

Chapter IX

The Battle over Women in the Army

"Anyone who harms the soul of the state also harms the state itself. A girl who enlists in the IDF claiming that she wants to contribute is indeed contributing – she is contributing to the destruction of the state."

> – Rabbi Shlomo Aviner,
> *Srugim*, November 2, 2015 [Hebrew]

"The tenderness eroded by the rough and tumble of military life is…vital to the character of a daughter of Israel…. The emotional need to have our normalcy validated by secular society is tampering with our moral priorities."

> – Rabbi Azariah Ariel,
> "Women's Enlistment – Keep Away,"
> *Makor Rishon,* January 24, 2014 [Hebrew]

"The overwhelming majority of girls were strengthened [in their religiosity] during their military service and only a tiny minority were adversely affected. We have thoroughly checked the situation compared to the alternatives.... These results are excellent, in both absolute and relative terms, to our great fortune."

– Prof. Amnon Shapira,
"The Whole Truth About
Religious Women's Service in the IDF,"
Kipa, November 24, 2013 [Hebrew]

"Girls undoubtedly contribute to the army. But they also contribute to a collapse in military discipline. An atmosphere that is contrary to the IDF's goals."

– Rabbi Eitan Eisman,
"One Year in Civilian National Service
Is Better than Two in the IDF,"
Kipa, November 28, 2013 [Hebrew]

"Experience teaches us that most religious girls who go to the IDF emerge damaged. Those who go to administrative positions – their modesty and religiosity is damaged. Those who go to combat roles – they are also physically damaged, because of the stress fractures."

– Rabbi Shmuel Eliyahu,
Kipa, November 14, 2013 [Hebrew]

"I get a sense that there's a hidden mechanism that wants to 'spoil' our girls' morality, to turn them into pawns for the army's whims – and for the men serving there, God help us."

– Rabbanit Rivka Shimon,
"Why Are You Even Enlisting in the IDF?"
Kipa, February 9, 2012 [Hebrew]

"If 2,000 girls (out of 6,000 a year) were to start professional studies immediately and get married two years earlier, instead of performing national service, in 60 years there would be another 16,500 Jews in Israel."

– Rabbi Eliezer Melamed,
"Rethinking National Service,"
De'ot, July 2012 [Hebrew]

"The push to enlist girls is part of a culture war and a campaign to destroy the family."

– Rabbi Zvi Kostiner,
dean of Yeshivat Mitzpe Ramon,
in a speech to female students, January 29, 2018

"When you forcibly, I'd say even violently, rip women away from their traditional family-building role, you thrust the next generation into crisis.... This will be our demographic ruin."

– Rabbi Yaakov Medan,
Head of Yeshivat Har Etzion, May 2018

The girls at Ulpana Tzfira, a religious school in central Israel, will remember Memorial Day 2015 mainly on account of a scandal that garnered national attention. Three female soldiers, former students at this mainstream institution, were asked to leave the memorial ceremony, despite having arrived especially from their bases to honor the fallen. All three were clad in their IDF uniforms. In their account of events, the principal blasted them as a "failure" and then showed them the door. For years, the school has impressed upon the all-female student body the need to volunteer, post-graduation, for civilian national service rather than military service, and to always wear skirts rather than trousers. These three graduates – observant young women all – violated both of these norms.

Some Israelis accused the principal of intentionally humiliating the young women and saw this degrading episode as proof of religious extremism; others accused the women of being deliberately provocative. But if we take a step back, the bottom line is brought into view: these three women in uniform, IDF insignia dangling from their shoulders, were emblematic, above all else, of the faculty's weakness, or even impotence, in the face of a burgeoning independence.

Israel has mandatory military conscription for Jewish men and women but gives blanket exemptions to Haredim and to religious women. All that is required of these young women, in advance of their draft date, is to appear before IDF authorities and assert, for the record, that their faith prevents them from service. The routine is a formality. And for decades, Israeli rabbis and educators – mostly men – have tried to ensure compliance by, among other things, lambasting the idea of women's service in the IDF. They are still going strong. They accuse the Israeli military of having a negative influence: of causing religious boys, and all the more so religious girls, to lose their faith, and of damaging female soldiers' prospects of building a family after they return to civilian life. There are both moral and educational arguments, but their halakhic bottom line is explicit: women are forbidden from performing military service. This rabbinic ruling is issued as an order. Young religious women, if they wish to retain their place in religious society, are expected to make use of this exemption under Israeli law and avoid the draft.

But while the rabbis fret and fume about "the girls" and the dangers lurking for those who choose to don the uniform, a quiet, jean-skirted revolution has been underway. According to data published by the IDF in 2019, the enlistment rate for graduates of Israel's religious girls' schools has broken new records year after year. In 2008, 18.5 percent of all young women who graduated from religious schools enlisted in the IDF. By 2019 that figure had risen by 55 percent.[1]

---

1. These figures, representing a moderate but consistent rise, were published by the IDF in September 2019, correcting official data that had come out in previous years showing a series of sharp spikes in religious women's enlistment rates. The incorrect data, which was proudly trumpeted in the IDF Manpower Directorate's annual reports and later cited in the press, included not just graduates of religious state schools but other groups, such as female graduates of regular state schools, who self-identified as religiously observant. The IDF was severely criticized for publishing incorrect data. The new figures included only graduates of religious girls' schools. The updated data was based on long-term monitoring: the army counted not only women who joined the army in the year after finishing high school but in the *three* years after finishing their studies, in order to count young women who had decided to defer their service.

This pronounced shift is clear not just from the data but from the reality on the ground: the pool of religious female recruits has widened and become more diverse; religious female officers are a more common sight; more religious women are serving in intelligence and field units; and more religious high school girls are attending the army's pre-enlistment orientation days. In the upper echelons of the military, IDF Chief of Staff Lt.-Gen. Aviv Kochavi in 2021 promoted two Religious Zionist women to the rank of brigadier-general, one as the head of the appeals court and another as the head of the behavioral science department in the manpower division. But from the perspective of the rabbis and religious educators, this is only part of the story. The most dramatic change has been the profile of the female religious recruits. Unlike in the past, the IDF is attracting high-quality, if not the most high-quality, graduates of religious girls' schools. They are also more religious than they used to be. "The army has turned into an *ulpana* [a religious girls' school]," noted Rabbi Ilay Ofran of Kvutzat Yavne, who actively encourages young women to enlist in the IDF and once taught at an all-female pre-military academy.

This is the broader context for the incident at Ulpana Tzfira. Several months before the 2015 Memorial Day scandal, at a conference organized by the IDF in Tel Aviv for religious female twelfth-graders, I came across a sizable group of girls from that school. They had shown up despite it being a normal school day, and despite knowing that the faculty disapproved of their attendance. Like other religious institutions, Tzfira has barred IDF representatives from coming on campus to pitch military service. This conference, in late 2014, with stalls representing units that wanted to attract religious female recruits, was attended by 1,400 high school girls – 500 more than the year before. They packed the entrance hall and the corridors to the point that some were left outside. The following year, to meet demand, the IDF held two such events.

Why are thousands of young religious women suddenly crossing a line that they, their parents, and their older sisters were always told was inviolable? Why are self-identifying religious women daring to defy not just their religious teachers but also stark rulings made by the Chief Rabbinate of Israel and most mainstream Religious Zionist rabbis? Do they remain religious in the army? What are their bewildered rabbis and teachers overlooking as they behold the rise of this unstoppable wave?

The enlistment of religious women in the IDF is a prime example of the religious feminist revolt against rabbinic authority, but it is not necessarily a statement of liberal feminism. This rebellion by young religious women strengthens the case that the changes sweeping the Religious Zionist world are not the sole preserve of groups on the margins. The enlistment of thousands of religious women a year – over a quarter of each year's graduating class – will have consequences both for the Israeli army and for religious society in Israel.

"We hereby – after having investigated the situation – declare the enlistment of women, even single woman, in the army, in any form, to be strictly forbidden!" So proclaimed the Chief Rabbinate of Israel on February 27, 1951. The decision was signed by Israel's two chief rabbis, Isaac HaLevi Herzog (the grandfather of Israel's current president) and Ben-Zion Meir Hai Uziel, bequeathing to future generations the conceptual language in which the argument over the enlistment of religious women would be fought, and has been ever since: an unambiguous terminology of halakhic rulings, a firm statement of the prohibited and the permitted – and not the language of education and morals. It was already clear that for the rabbis, this was a first-order religious question that touched on the religious minority's relationship with the secular state, and that they believed it necessary to lend their full weight to the cause.

The Chief Rabbinate published this proclamation as the Knesset debated the Security Service Bill, which intended to include mandatory conscription for women. The IDF had already created a loophole for women on religious or conscientious grounds, but the issue returned to the agenda when legislators proposed toughening the law by requiring female draftees to undergo a medical examination and appear before a committee in order to be eligible for an exemption. The initiative triggered a political crisis. The Haredi Agudat Israel Party repudiated the bill and even stormed out of the coalition when it was passed into law. Jerusalem's Kikar HaShabbat intersection became the scene of stormy protests against women's service in any form and against any government or military oversight.

Whereas the Religious Zionist community largely accepted civilian national service as a fair alternative to the military draft, the Haredi community completely opposed the notion of letting their eighteen-year-old daughters leave the house. In the 1970s, several rabbis, including Rabbi Ovadia Yosef (the chief rabbi of Tel Aviv at the time), signed a letter forbidding women from volunteering for civilian national service, since military service for religious women was, to their mind, at the time, unthinkable. "This terrible decree, which will lead to emotional and spiritual suicide and a collapse of the foundations of modesty and the family in the people of Israel … is infinitely more difficult and dangerous for Israel than public violations of religious law, as it comes in the guise of volunteerism," they wrote.

The Chief Rabbinate of Israel took an intermediary stance between the Religious Zionists and the Haredim: it opposed military service for women, without encouraging, but also without disqualifying, civilian service. The issue rose to the fore every now and again. The 1951 ruling against women's military service was reaffirmed by subsequent generations of chief rabbis and was returned to the agenda in 2013, at the initiative of Rabbi Shmuel Eliyahu, the chief rabbi of Safed and a member of the national Chief Rabbinical Council. Eliyahu, the son of a former chief rabbi and a hardline nationalist who has issued rabbinic rulings outlawing the sale and rental of homes to Arabs citizens of Israel, a stance for which his visa to the United States was revoked (and at the same time has waged a valiant battle against sex crimes within the Religious Zionist and Haredi communities), is perhaps the most stalwart opponent of the enlistment of women – secular and religious alike. In 2018, he called upon the commander of the IDF to resign over a new directive to open up more roles to women (from all walks of life) in field units. But the matter closest to his heart has long been the future of religious girls and the cessation of female religious enlistment.

The first stage of Rabbi Eliyahu's initiative was to reaffirm the halakhic ruling of 1951. A meeting of the Chief Rabbinical Council on December 2, 2013, produced a consensus against female enlistment (as expected), but it was still a far more contentious affair than previous deliberations. In 1951, the Chief Rabbinate had vigorously opposed what it perceived as government coercion, or pressure from above; in 2013, the Chief Rabbinate felt the heat from below, from the religious community itself. Those who were supposed to meekly obey the rabbinate had stopped taking orders. The Haredi rabbis at the meeting – including Rabbi Yehuda Deri, who declared the prohibition against female enlistment to be a cardinal sin, one which a Jew must sacrifice her life before committing – were probably unaware of this difference, but Eliyahu, who convened the meeting, knew that the challenge was being made from within, from the mainstream of "his" community, and more precisely, from the young women of the community, who were making up their own minds.

Rabbi Eliyahu took aim at Aluma, a religious group that sidesteps the establishment and helps religious female high schoolers navigate the military enlistment system, even as such organizations are barred from school grounds. The organization, working in partnership with the Defense Ministry and the IDF Manpower Directorate, has been in Eliyahu's crosshairs since its founding in 2002.

"They're innocent girls, eighteen-year-olds," Eliyahu told his rabbinic colleagues. "In comes a professor and gets on stage, at a conference that invites religious girls with long dresses, and he tells them it's important to volunteer and enlist in the IDF." The academic he was alluding to was most likely Amnon Shapira, a Bible scholar and former secretary-general of the Bnei Akiva youth movement, who has emerged as a supporter of female enlistment.

Fearful for these "innocent girls," Eliyahu wanted to secure the rabbinate's backing to conduct a poll that would present a different picture from the one that Aluma has been using to make its case in religious high schools. According to a poll commissioned by Aluma, 86 percent of female religious soldiers remained just as religious or became more religious during the course of their military service. Eliyahu believed that if he could convince religious society that military service was actually causing the spiritual degeneracy of female recruits, others would be deterred. But Chief Rabbi David Lau rejected his proposal, saying that even if 80 percent of female religious soldiers became more religious during their service, that would not change the halakhic fact, as articulated in 1951, that women are strictly forbidden from undertaking "any form at all" of military service. Eliyahu was forced to make do with a reaffirmation of the prohibition on military service by women. But by then, the standing of the rabbinate in the religious community had undergone such depreciation that, as expected, it was incapable of stopping the rise of female religious enlistment. The numbers continued to climb during the following year.

One section of the national-religious community that has long rejected the Chief Rabbinate's ruling against women's military service is the Religious Kibbutz Movement. Ideologically linked to both the Mizrachi movement and the wider secular kibbutz movement, the religious kibbutzim have actively encouraged their female members to enlist since the fifties.[2] And to this day high schools in religious kibbutzim stand out in terms of the sheer numbers of women who proceed to military duty.[3] Young religious women from urban communities have over the years also signed up through Bnei Akiva's Garin Nahal program, which combines military service with agricultural work, or volunteered for the IDF Education Corps, but this was a trickle, a marginal phenomenon, rather than a movement.

Over the years, religious supporters of women's military service have marshaled various halakhic rationales for female service in the IDF, but their motives seem to have been rooted more in politics and their broader worldview, namely their desire to share in the communal burden of defense, shoulder to shoulder with their secular Zionist peers. In 1979, Dr. Yehezkel Cohen, the founder of the Ne'emanei Torah Va'Avodah movement and positioned on the moderate flank of Religious Zionist society, penned a booklet challenging the halakhic reasoning against women's service. Cohen strung together a series of halakhic opinions

---

2. The Religious Kibbutz Movement remains quite religiously open-minded, relatively speaking. For example, it reformed its education system in 2017–2018 partly out of a desire to present an alternative to the increasingly conservative direction of the state-run religious schooling system.

3. The IDF Manpower Directorate published recruitment data in 2018, including a list of the leading religious high schools, in terms of enlistment rates. Top of the table was Kibbutz Sde Eliyahu (81 percent enlistment), followed by Kibbutz Kvutzat Yavne, the Midrashiya High School for Girls (a branch of the Shalom Hartman Institute), Pelech in Jerusalem, and the Amit High School in Beersheba.

that permitted women's military service and concluded that women were religiously obligated to perform IDF service, including the duty of bearing arms – but that they should not do so in roles that might challenge their religious, cultural, and spiritual identity. He did not rule out the option of civilian national service but declared that "dodging any form of service is a desecration of God's name, since it stamps the whole community that bases its life on the worship of God with the reputation of shirking."

So what does halakha really say? The debate runs along two main axes: the question of women's duties during what Jewish law considers "obligatory wars," and another about the scope of the prohibition against wearing uniform and bearing other "male" accouterments, including weapons. Both questions have sparked lively debates and spin-off debates. Here are the arguments in brief.

Jewish law distinguishes between two kinds of wars: *milḥemet mitzva* ("obligatory war") and *milḥemet reshut* ("elective war"). The Mishna states that in the former, unlike the latter, "everyone goes [into war], even a groom from his room and a bride from her wedding canopy" (Mishna Sota 8:7). No man, and no woman, is let off the hook. Supporters of women's military service cite this text, as well as Maimonides' definition of obligatory wars as defensive campaigns against enemy assaults that pose a genuine existential threat. In a "war to assuage Israel of a persecutor," as Maimonides put it in his magisterial *Mishneh Torah*, halakha mandates emergency general conscription, including of women. Eminent Zionist rabbis, such as Zvi Yehuda Kook and Shlomo Goren, argued that the Jewish community in the Land of Israel was in a permanent mode of "obligatory war" (although they still opposed women's service). The Haredi leadership rejects this contention and also instructs young men to avoid the draft.

Opponents of women's military service argue that even if the State of Israel were on an "obligatory war footing," as a constant or intermittent reality, there is still no place for women in the army, because as the Babylonian Talmud states, "It is not the way of a woman to wage war" (Kiddushin 2b). They argue that during times of national crisis, it is enough for women to support battlefield operations from outside the army, in civilian frameworks. In 2014, Israeli Chief Rabbi Yitzhak Yosef addressed the Mishna's allusion to women's duties during obligatory wars, saying, "That doesn't literally mean women will pick up arms and fight, but that they should help the army. They can cook for them and do their laundry."

The second axis in the debate concerns the biblical prohibition that "a woman shall not wear that which pertains to a man" (Deuteronomy 22:5). The Talmud, in Tractate Nazir, picks up on this, recording: "Rabbi Eliezer ben Yaakov says: From where is it derived that a woman may not go out with weapons to war? The verse states: 'A woman shall not wear that which pertains to a man, and a man shall not put on a woman's garment' (Nazir 59a)." For those who oppose female enlistment, this statement, combined with Tractate Kiddushin's observation that "it is not the way of a woman to wage war," precludes any possibility of women's military service. At times of emergency, as Rabbi Ovadia Yosef opined, women might be allowed to carry weapons for personal defense if they live on the frontier, but military service is out of the question.

How do the liberal voices contend with this? They invoke Maimonides and other major medieval commentators, namely Jacob ben Asher and Joseph Karo, who argued that the prohibition that "a woman must not put on man's apparel" does not apply to bearing arms, only to clothes and other accessories that might serve to blur gender identity or play a sexual function of some sort.

In May 2014, when the question of military service by religious women flared up again, the Beit Hillel organization published a detailed halakhic opinion on the matter: there is, they determined, no halakhic prohibition on women's military service.[4] Beit Hillel's members include dozens of

---

4. Beit Hillel published its position paper on women's military service for women after conducting an in-depth study day for an internal panel in January 2014. The closed-door session discussed the educational and halakhic implications of integrating women into military service, and the rabbis were critical of the development. Rabbi Meir Nehorai, the chairman of Beit Hillel, said that the enlistment of religious women in the IDF was "the most explosive issue in the religious community." Rabbi Shmuel Eliyahu from Safed said, "I came here because it's important for us all to be on the same page. What is the average person to think when one group of rabbis issues one halakhic ruling and another says something else? What's he supposed to

Orthodox rabbis and, uniquely for an Orthodox rabbinic organization, female halakhic authorities and public figures. It was founded in 2012 with the aim of providing "attentive Torani leadership" and a moderate, centrist form of Judaism, hoping to be an authoritative counterweight to what it saw as religious extremism in Israel. The organization was much more daring than other rabbinic coalitions, such as Tzohar, in its willingness to take on the national-Haredi rabbis. The men and women of Beit Hillel took their cue from a different tradition and allowed women to dance with Torah scrolls on Simḥat Torah and recite Kaddish in synagogue, while staking out a nuanced position on whether women could deliver halakhic rulings, and gave their full-throated approval to proper bar mitzva ceremonies for disabled children, and yet – they were cautious not to go too far, to stretch the rope to the breaking point.

Beit Hillel's halakhic opinion on women's military service was more rigorous and comprehensive than Dr. Cohen's three and a half decades earlier, but the biggest change was the social environment in which it was published. By 2014, service in the IDF was no longer such a taboo, and rabbis and educators had no illusions about which way religious twelfth-graders were leaning. The purpose of the 2014 document was not to make military service religiously obligatory but to "provide halakhic grounding for young women who decide to perform their national service in the army." Its authors sought to explain why women who chose to enlist were not violating Jewish law, and that not only was their military service permissible, but that it could be regarded as the fulfillment of a "big and important commandment."

The document's comprehensive halakhic discussion was rooted in, among other things, Maimonides' rulings about "obligatory wars," but ended on an ambivalent note: "A woman's decision about the nature and

---

do? The girls should follow halakha, not feel they're going against halakha." Rabbi Ohad Teharlev, from Midreshet Lindenbaum in Jerusalem, said that institutions that prepared religious women for military service were "buckling under the growing numbers. Hundreds of girls want to study in these pre-military institutions and there's no space for all of them." He argued that they were "speaking a different religious language from what we're used to" and that "they are influencing and changing the army." Quoted from a summary of the closed-door proceedings on the "Young Rabbi" blog written by a Beit Hillel member.

location of her service must be examined in light of an array of halakhic and personal considerations, specifically related to the place of her service. Some sections of the military are more suitable for women's service than others; some women are better suited to military service than others; and some are better suited to civilian rather than military service."

At the end of the document, Beit Hillel's rabbis addressed the Chief Rabbinate's position, noting that despite its steadfast opposition to women's service, previous chief rabbis had shown "flexibility and fissures of permissibility" regarding the draft and at any rate, they wrote, "a profusion of discourse between the Chief Rabbinate and the institutions of the IDF was a worthy endeavor." The dialogue, "alongside a clarification of the situation, will lead to decisions that are better suited to the present reality in the army." Beit Hillel paid homage to the rabbinate's "honorable and important status," and yet, by openly defying it, the organization removed yet another brick from the wall: a hardly marginal, national-religious entity voicing its outright opposition to the dictates of the rabbinate was both a pattern that would be widened and a frontal assault on the hegemony of the institution.

If these are the voices on the Religious Zionist street, it is easy to guess what the Chief Rabbinate, which is predominantly run by Haredi rabbis, thinks of the community's prevailing sentiments. The Sephardic chief rabbi, Yitzhak Yosef, after a call by then-Finance Minister Yair Lapid to dismiss the chief rabbis from their state-funded posts, made his position clear: "Many people who aren't big Torah experts, who are half-religious, or a third-religious, or a quarter-religious, come and ask us: What do you mean girls mustn't serve in the army? Look, the Mishna says, 'Everyone goes [into war], even a groom from his room and a bride from her wedding canopy.'... Have no fear. Women, girls, must not enlist in the army, under any circumstances. That's the opinion of the greatest rabbis of the generation. Any truly great rabbi – truly great – takes this view."

The thousands of religious young women enlisting in the IDF have not waited for this ponderous religious argument to reach its conclusion. Nor has the military. The IDF, a large, cumbersome organization that nonetheless is capable of impressive learning and strategic planning, promptly invested tremendous resources to encourage observant female high school seniors to enlist. Religious girls who express an interest in military service are logged in the IDF's computer system under a unique heading, and from that point on the soldiers of Meitav, a unit within the IDF Manpower Directorate, keeps tabs on them. According to sources familiar with the recruitment process (a selection that is intentionally obscure, much like at certain US colleges), the large majority of female religious recruits are assigned to one of their top-three preferences – a totally different picture from the conscription of secular women. The moment that religious women are drafted and assigned a role, a special section of the Military Rabbinate, set up in 2012, is responsible for guiding them through their service. In the Israeli army, religious women enjoy positive discrimination.

The turning point came in 2012–2013, when the IDF Manpower Directorate discovered a human gold mine: women who were actively volunteering to enlist, having chosen to forgo their right to an exemption on religious or conscientious grounds. Unlike male religious conscripts, who demanded various special arrangements, not least related to gender segregation, religious women, at least back then, had no expectations of placing limitations on their male colleagues. The only privileges given to female religious soldiers were the right to wear a skirt (instead of trousers), time to pray in the morning, and one day-off a month for religious studies.

The most prestigious IDF units, including the signals intelligence Unit 8200, which is akin to the NSA, and even the IAF Flight School, started courting twelfth-graders in religious girls' schools. This is not just a matter of numbers; many of the girls graduating from the elite religious high schools have some of the highest matriculation scores in the country and are considered to be top caliber recruits. The IDF Intelligence Directorate appointed a full-time female officer with the rank of major to headhunt girls at religious high schools, encouraging them to volunteer and seeing to their welfare while in uniform. In 2014, the Military Intelligence Directorate reserved some two hundred positions in Unit 8200 for female religious recruits; it also parachuted others straight into field intelligence roles.

Once the IDF instituted affirmative action for religious women and made minor adjustments to accommodate their social and religious needs, the number of religious women in IDF combat units soared by 71 percent in the three years after 2013, and the number of female religious officers in compulsory service (that is, excluding the IDF's professional, career-soldier ranks) jumped by 30 percent. According to data released by the IDF Manpower Directorate in November 2015, among the top ten high schools with the highest proportion of female graduates who signed up for combat service were two religious girls' schools: one in Netivot (number 5 on the list) and another in Tiberias (number 10).

This revolution happened mostly on the watch of Brig.-Gen. Rachel Tevet-Wiesel, the Women's Affairs Advisor to the IDF Chief of Staff – a role that was created in order to provide female soldiers with a direct channel to the officer at the very top of the pyramid, enabling them to file grievances without fear of retribution from their direct commanders. She described the alliance between religious women and the army as a "win-win," telling me: "These are girls who have chosen to serve in the army. There is no problem of motivation. They have chosen to do this, that's a critical fact. They arrive with a drive to excel, with motivation and social values."

For her own part, Brig.-Gen. (res.) Tevet-Wiesel is a graduate of Ulpanat Tzfira, as are her daughters. She encouraged the IDF to rethink the place of religious women in the army and worked closely to coordinate with Aluma, the NGO that guides them through the enlistment process; the Manpower Directorate, which enlists them; and the Military Rabbinate, which accompanies them during their service.

The enlistment of religious women has required the IDF General Staff to make certain adjustments, from major questions about men and women's joint service to matters of dress and discipline. Tevet-Wiesel decided to introduce, for the first time ever, IDF field skirts for women in non-combat roles (their peers in combat roles must still wear trousers). Even before this reform, noticing the growing number of married recruits wearing headscarves, she issued an order that, she says, "caused religious girls not to like me: any married woman wishing to wear a head covering must choose between black, gray, blue, or green. Otherwise, it starts looking like a circus."

What caused so many young religious women to escape the path that their rabbis and teachers, and for the most part even their parents, had charted for them? Is it just the inducements the IDF offers or something deeper? The more conservative rabbis place the blame at the doorstep of the IDF and Aluma. It was to them that Rabbi Yigal Levinstein of Eli was likely referring when he howled, "They've driven our girls crazy!"

But to a certain extent it was the other way around: the rabbis, watching the rising numbers, were only further agitated by the army's emerging policies. In 2016, the IDF unveiled its new Joint Service Ordinance, reformulating its policy on military service by women, religious and secular alike. For the first time, the IDF decided to recruit women as combat soldiers in the armored corps and in other field units. Rabbi Thau slammed the IDF as a "junta," but even rabbis who supported the enlistment of religious women, including some who taught at women-only pre-military academies, criticized the reform. The Joint Service Ordinance, which triggered fears of a radical overhaul of the IDF's field operations, created a temporary consensus among national-religious rabbis against the army.[5] In 2022, once the army published a new set of criteria, opening new combat roles to women, including the air force's elite Unit 669, the rabbis again joined hands in protest. From all across the spectrum of Religious Zionism rabbis were united in their call to "not divide the IDF!" and warned that the desegregation would lead to "a tribal army" in which the religious youth would all cluster together in the remaining male-only units.

---

5. At first it seemed like most rabbis, liberals and conservatives alike, were united against the directive, but as the rhetoric escalated in the conservative camp, cracks began to reappear. Such was the case when Rabbi Shlomo Aviner wrote to one young man who consulted him, in a public responsum, that it would better not to enlist in the IDF at all until "the problem is fixed," meaning until national-religious soldiers are promised hermetically gender-segregated units, as is made available to Haredi soldiers. Such was also the case when Rabbi Shmuel Eliyahu urged the IDF Chief of Staff to resign over the Joint Service Ordinance. Then-Education Minister Naftali Bennett, from the national-religious Jewish Home Party, slammed Rabbi Eliyahu's remarks as "impudent" (and later apologized for doing so), and there have been so many examples of Religious Zionists voicing public criticism of venerable rabbis, such as when the *Haaretz* columnist Israel Harel called for Eliyahu to be fired from the role of chief rabbi of Safed. Note that after protests from rabbis and religious soldiers, the IDF decided after a trial period to scrap its plan to integrate women in tank units.

Rabbis affiliated with Har Hamor attacked the decision to integrate female soldiers in combat units but they were especially strident on the question of religious female soldiers. Rabbi Eliyahu said in January 2018, "There's a war here, and this war can and must be won. We're not exempt from the fighting, and you must remember: the yeshiva students are in our hands, not theirs. Girls at religious high schools – they're ours, too. We have to act on every front. Only in Israel and North Korea is there mandatory conscription for women."[6] Citing a recent newspaper report about inconsistencies in enlistment rate data, he added, "Have you seen how the IDF spokesman is lying and mocking religious people? He's making things up about the enlistment of religious women."

But the main obstacle facing the conservative camp is not merely the IDF, but a combination of the rabbis, the army, and the female draftees themselves. The rabbis remain confounded by the changing of the old order: young women, like many of their male counterparts, no longer heed the exhortations of the rabbis. Moreover, the silent majority of the national-religious public is watching this grassroots transformation with approval, unmoved by halakhic pronouncements and rabbinic declarations. The tectonic plates of religious society are shifting. It is hard to put any stock in conspiracy theories or allegations about top-down social engineering when every year thousands of young women are choosing of their own free will to serve in the IDF in defiance of their rabbis and the Chief Rabbinate. They could easily obtain an exemption but are actively choosing to step out of their controlled environment. Even in some of the most conservative West Bank settlements, places with a distinct national-Haredi character, it is not a rare sight on Sunday morning to see female soldiers in uniform returning to their bases.

On the ground, the growing presence of religious women in the IDF is familiar to anyone who has visited an army base or taken an army course or attended a military graduation ceremony and seen female soldiers in long skirts standing in formation. Even the architecture of

---

6. This is incorrect. Israel is relatively speaking a world outlier but it is joined by five or ten other countries, depending on how you qualify compulsory service; in Sweden and Norway, for example, there is a law requiring twelve months of army service for men and women alike, but in practice no one is forced to serve against their will.

military synagogues is changing. Only in the twenty-first century did the Military Rabbinate start planning women's sections in new synagogues on army bases. Till then, nobody had imagined that female soldiers or officers might wish to pray in army synagogues during their service, with the possible exception of festivals and the High Holy Days. But as soon as so many religious women started marching through the gates of the IDF's bases, wishing to pray on Shabbat and weekdays, the army's synagogues had to make the necessary accommodations.

What has happened there, in military synagogues, is instructive not only regarding the number of religious women in unform, but also the nature of the religious women in uniform.

The synagogue at the IDF Officers Training School, a feat of architecture inspired by the burning bush in Exodus, features an elevated women's gallery. It's similar to that of many old-style synagogues the world over and it was built into the original architectural design. But back then, in 2009, the architect, Eli Arnon, could not have guessed how many religious female cadets would train at the base each year or how many would frequent the new synagogue. Female officers, who completed their training at the base soon after the synagogue was opened, said that the women's gallery on Shabbat was full to the rafters, for both morning *minyanim*.

The overcrowding of the women's sections in army synagogues is a powerful symbol of the burgeoning presence of religious women in the IDF, and perhaps also a sign of things to come, when bases might have to add a third back-to-back prayer service to meet demand. Assuming the IDF meets the targets set by its Manpower Directorate and the number of female religious recruits keeps rising, how will this transformation affect the Israeli army?

Over the years, religious women who enlisted in the IDF received the backing of several notable liberal rabbis, such as Shlomo Riskin, Benny Lau, and Ohad Teharlev, the head of Midreshet Lindenbaum, which runs a program to prepare religious women for military service. When I started writing this book in 2015, I described this coterie as "a very small minority among rabbinic circles."[7] That was accurate at the time, but there has since been a sea change. Nowadays, many rabbis seem to prefer to simply avoid publicly addressing the issue. Some religious schools have even started inviting representatives of Aluma to their campuses. But the official position remains unchanged. The policy of the body that oversees Israel's Religious Zionist school system is: boys should be encouraged to enlist in the IDF through Hesder yeshivas, and girls should be directed to civilian national service.

An advocate of the official policy, which has not budged in the face of battalions of female religious soldiers voting with their feet, was elected in 2019 as chairman of the national-religious Jewish Home Party: Rabbi Rafi Peretz, a former IDF chief rabbi. Like all rabbis affiliated with Har Hamor, Peretz is an opponent of military service by religious women, although he concedes that "the moment a girl enlists in the IDF, she should receive the same moral and spiritual support as any male recruit."[8] Nevertheless, Peretz's approach was a marked shift from that of his predecessor as the chairman of the Jewish Home, Naftali Bennett. As education minister, Bennett expressed support for letting representatives from Aluma into religious girls' schools. In response, dozens of rabbis, many of whom were affiliated with Har Hamor, signed a letter in 2016 demanding that the minister "safeguard the values of religious education." Bennett provoked further outrage when he described the rising numbers of female soldiers in IDF combat roles as a "wonderful trend." This time, national-Haredi rabbis from the Chotam Forum retaliated with a caricature depicting

---

7. Yair Ettinger, "A Quiet Coup: Young Religious Women Are Flocking to the Israeli Army," *Haaretz*, November 25, 2015, available at https://www.haaretz.com/a-quiet-coup-young-religious-women-are-flocking-to-the-israeli-army-1.5402164.

8. Rabbi Peretz made this statement to the media after it was alleged, shortly after his election to the Knesset, that he had refused a spontaneous request for a conversation from young religious women who were about to enlist in the army. Responding to Kan 11, Israel's national broadcaster, Peretz said that he had no intention of snubbing the women and that as the IDF chief rabbi he had helped female religious soldiers with "moral and spiritual support."

Bennett encouraging religious girls to stream out of their *ulpanot* and jump into tanks.[9]

The draftees themselves have also been a target. The Chotam Forum and Liba Yehudit have been fundraising for social media campaigns aimed at religious high school girls. When the Chief Rabbinate's ruling against female service fell on deaf ears, these organizations pivoted to warning of the hidden dangers awaiting female recruits. One cartoon disseminated by Chotam shows a white-skinned, light-haired religious female soldier dreaming of making a meaningful contribution being thrust into a secretarial job and serving "in a raging sea of men." At one point, she is ordered to go on guard duty with a dark-skinned male soldier, who tells her, "I've got my eye on you, I rather like you." Her friend, who has opted for civilian national service, tells her that she has become "coarse," but when she tries to get out of the army, the gates are shut in her face. Another activist group published an anthology of testimonies by religious women who had served in the army; they warned of weight gain and "expressions of lesbianism."[10]

Who exactly is deterred by these warnings? Unlike with other power struggles in the Religious Zionist world, the female high school graduates volunteering for the army cannot be easily sorted into liberals and conservatives, and the bug of military service has bitten religious women from all across the country, not just urbane Jerusalemites and hands-on kibbutzniks. Shira-Mazal Peretz is a former basic training commander and a graduate of the Tzahali women's pre-military academy. She says that growing up in Afula in northern Israel, "it was considered dishonorable to serve in the army, a stigma. Nowadays people say, she dares, she's brave, she's even became more religious." When Peretz was in twelfth grade, every rabbi she met in her hometown community and at

---

9. In 2019, after the Israeli Education Ministry instituted regulations to facilitate visits by representatives of Aluma to religious girls' schools, the Chotam Forum held a protest in front of Education Minister Naftali Bennett's office, brandishing placards calling his ministry the "Re-Education Ministry." It accused the ministry of "succumbing to external pressures and promoting values that clash with our faith. Efforts to lobby religious girls to serve in the army are damaging us and the whole civilian national service system, which is our responsibility."

10. Reported by Uriah Elyakam on Kan 11, February 6, 2018.

school said that army service was forbidden. "But I admired Major Eliraz Peretz – I saw him as a model of national service," she says, referring to an Orthodox officer (no relation) in the Golani Brigade, who was killed in action in Gaza in 2010, some twelve years after his brother was killed in Lebanon. "I approached a rabbi, I told him how much I wanted to serve, and he said, 'You should probably enlist, that's your mission.'"

Speaking to religious female IDF soldiers is an easy way to dispel the popular canard that military service, in defiance of the rabbis, is an elitist or feminist phenomenon. Such conversations can also shed light on why it is so hard for rabbis to hold back the tide of female recruits. Shira-Mazal Peretz did not enlist before consulting a rabbi, but she speaks of balancing two simultaneous commitments: an adherence to a religious lifestyle that's rooted in values, and an acceptance of the yoke of a national burden. Religious female recruits are not blind to the spiritual and moral challenges inherent in military service, but unlike their rabbis, they are undeterred. This is an attitude that a cluster of religious women's pre-military academies has actively cultivated. It also mirrors a trend that many of these young women witnessed in their fathers' generation: a community-wide emphasis on military service, especially as officers, as a way of rising up through the ranks of Israeli society later on life – a trend that Prime Minister Naftali Bennett well embodies.

Rabbi Ohad Teharlev, the head of Midreshet Lindenbaum, where almost all of the female students proceed to military service, elaborated on this in an article for the religious news website *Kipa* in January 2014. "The rabbis' war against women's enlistment is futile," he wrote. "It is only natural that just as the establishment of Hesder yeshivas for boys created a model of religious observance that combined Torah study with the reality of modern Israel, through the microcosm of Israeli society known as the IDF, the same should happen for religious girls, combining intensive Torah study... with military service through tracks that are suitable for women. A new model of religious observance has emerged."

Teachers at religious high schools and yeshivas in Israel have always maintained that military service comes at a cost. Numerous Israeli men and women have ended up abandoning religious observance during their service. The IDF, according to the older generation, is the number one force behind the secularization of religious high school graduates – a fear that not only makes Haredim recoil from military service (even for men) but also serves Haredi rabbis in disparaging the national-religious way of life.

The Religious Zionist community, in an effort spearheaded by rabbis and parents, went to great lengths to ensure a lasting commitment to religion in the army, creating several frameworks in which the teens could prepare for military service along with a peer group of similarly devoted Orthodox youth and then serve alongside them. The first program was Garin Nahal, which allowed religious youth to enlist as a group, live together, and combine their military service with other volunteering activities. This was followed by the Hesder yeshiva track, which allowed young men to combine partial military service with advanced Talmud studies. Some Religious Zionist youth deferred their service to study in higher yeshivas or the pre-military academies that started popping up in the 1980s. The idea behind these programs was to try to immunize Religious Zionist youth against the supposedly adverse influence of service in a mostly secular army.

Religious women serving in the IDF had no equivalent programs until 1986, when a religious women's seminary was opened in Kibbutz Ein HaNatziv in the upper part of the Jordan Valley. It encouraged and legitimized two activities that many religious educators had long sought to deny women: advanced Torah studies and military service.

The official rhetoric backing up the ban on Talmud study and army service is always the same, halakhically speaking, but lurking behind the official language is an unofficial norm, never expressed in print, that views such programs as a kind of frivolous gap year: an unnecessary delay before going to university, learning a trade, and starting a family. Advanced Talmud studies for women – offered at the time only in a select few seminaries in Jerusalem and serving mostly American immigrants – was simply not an option for Israeli-born religious women in their early 20s.

Midreshet Ein HaNatziv initially attracted young women just after their army service, but by the late nineties, once its student body included women from all over Israel and not just the religious kibbutzim, it set up a separate track for high school graduates before enlistment. The study program, Maayan ("Spring"), was similar to another track established around the same time at Midreshet Lindenbaum in Jerusalem, in which young women studied together and then enlisted together, at first mostly within the IDF's Education Corps as NCO teachers and later into other units within the Intelligence Directorate. Nowadays, similar pre-military programs for young women exist in the settlement of Migdal Oz in Gush Etzion and elsewhere.

The diverse menu of women's religious academies now represents practically every religious subsector, from the most liberal to the most conservative. The dozen-or-so seminaries across Israel, each with a distinctive character, run special programs for young women between high school and basic training. This "gap year" has become the norm, whether before or after military service, and it has cast a light on the fissures in the old Religious Zionist social order, revealing a shifting attitude toward women during the years in which they remain unmarried, and the rapidly evolving perspectives – across all sections of religious society – on Talmud studies for women. The most recent trend has seen the establishment of such academies for women preparing to go into civilian national service; these preparatory academies, run by the conservative *yeshivot hakav*, are situated in places like Kfar Tapuach, deep in the West Bank.

This is all relevant to our inquiry because these seminaries are turning out to be a fascinating point of confluence between two or three processes that are not inherently linked: the growing appetite of women to study Talmud; the urge to leave the "safe space" of the community; and the desire for self-expression, including in religious life. Midreshet Lindenbaum, for instance, addresses all of these goals under the same roof: it readies young women for life in the military, far from the controlled environment of the community, it teaches them Talmud, and it prepares them, at a later stage in life, for roles as religious leaders.

On October 15, 2014, dozens of hikers were killed and hundreds were wounded in an avalanche in the high country of Nepal. Among the four Israeli victims was Cpt. Tamar Ariel, an F-16 navigator in the Israeli Air Force; a native of the national-religious Moshav Masuot Yitzhak, she was trekking along the Annapurna circuit with friends during a vacation from the army. Many had already heard of her by her initial, "T," but when her picture and full name were cleared for publication posthumously, and when her story was released, Tamar Ariel, who used to ride her off-road motorcycle on leave and had flown combat sorties over Gaza in Operation Protective Edge, became an icon for thousands of young Orthodox Jewish women. Besides enjoying the vaunted status of the fighter pilot, and besides smashing a glass ceiling as the first religious female navigator in Israeli history, and one of the first women in this role, Ariel had helped legitimize the idea of military service for religious women – something that had been unthinkable for the generation that came before her.

For years, it was all too easy in the Religious Zionist conversation to dismiss female soldiers as having veered from the straight and narrow. But Tamar Ariel, like many of her peers, wore a long skirt, was strictly observant, and lived and breathed the religious language she had imbibed at school. At the IAF Flight School, as a woman among a sea of male cadets, she used to consult a rabbi whenever there arose a halakhic dilemma. Many Religious Zionists also appreciated the fact that military service was not her first choice. Ariel had initially volunteered for civilian national service – the safe, "kosher" option – and only toward the end, once she felt spiritually ready, did she choose to don military fatigues and sign up for flight school.

On the eve of the ceremony in which she received her wings, Ariel said in an interview on Channel 10 that it took a lot of effort to remain religious in the army: "There were some really tough moments when you start thinking, 'My goodness, what have I done, how did I get here?'" But she seemed to have no regrets. Whenever Ariel spoke to young religious women during her service, she described her choice as a calling but stressed that she had no desire to become a symbol. And yet, despite not having launched the movement of religious female soldiers, she became its icon. After her tragic death, the Tzahali pre-military academy for religious women decided to carry her name.

The Tzahali Tamar Ariel Pre-Military Academy for Religious Girls offers high school graduates a year of advanced Torah, ethics, faith, mysticism, and women's studies. The institution opened in 2013 with thirty-nine students; the next year, the student body grew to fifty-one; by 2015–2016, there were seventy-four students across two campuses. Once a marginal and unknown entity, it became more of a household name as the resistance to it intensified. In 2018, in honor of Israel's seventieth Independence Day, over two hundred students, graduates, and educators – some in uniform – converged on the campus in the religious kibbutz of Ein Tzurim to salute religious women in the IDF. The video of the event was widely viewed on social media.

Four years earlier, in 2014, Michal Nagen, the head of Tzahali, told me: "Tzahali is the cutting edge of religious feminism, for all sorts of reasons. We dared to go one step further and told the girls, you're not going to enlist as a *garin* [a tight-knit unit]. We're going to embellish the battalions, we're not going to spread across the whole army, we're not just going to safe spaces. We're going everywhere, you're going to be the vanguard at the front of the camp – stay out front, and be religious. Be a *dossit*," she says, using the Hebrew slang term for "religious" with a hint of self-deprecation: "The rabbis ask me everywhere, in the field, 'How are these girls such *dossiyot*?' And I tell them, 'That's the whole revolution.' It used to be easy to say that the less observant girls enlisted in the army. No. The world has changed. The most pious girls are enlisting and creating change. The army is the place in the world that least respects women. You need to have fully self-aware women there, who can create change from below. Who won't agree to be objectified. Change must come from below, only self-aware women can do this, not women who are just out to equalize conditions of service. They won't succeed."

Quite naturally, the Religious Kibbutz Movement, which traditionally encouraged young women to enlist in the army, is the main organization behind Tzahali. But it is impossible to describe Nagen, who led the academy from the wings to center stage, through any institutional affiliation. She was educated at the Pelech school and served as an IDF officer in the 1980s, but she is hardly the poster child of the progressive Orthodox Judaism headquartered in Jerusalem. She lives in the West Bank settlement of Otniel, mixes in diverse political and religious circles, and represents a fusion of generations in the Religious Zionist community.

She grew up in Jerusalem, the scion of a religious and academic dynasty started by her grandfather, the philosopher Prof. Ernst Akiva Simon, a member of the far-left Brit Shalom, and continued by her father, Prof. Uriel Simon, a religious leftist and a Bible scholar of global renown.

As far as she is concerned, there is no paradox between this background and her belonging to the group of settlers who follow the late rabbi of Tekoa, Menachem Froman. They believe in peace and dialogue with the Palestinians, and their peculiar fusion of religious nationalism and peace activism sits uneasily with the Israeli public conversation, especially within the left and within the internal discourse of the settler movement. Michal's husband, Rabbi Yakov Nagen, is a New York native who teaches at Otniel's yeshiva and works on promoting interfaith dialogue.

Froman's followers took a different attitude toward women; different from the previous generation of settlers and different from liberal Orthodox feminists. Froman was deeply interested in the differences between masculinity and femininity. He once told me that in the Zohar, the seminal work of Jewish mysticism, "masculinity is water, moving top-down, and femininity is fire, moving bottom-up." The kabbalistic idea that masculinity is from above and femininity is from below is hardly in tune with the feminism of Simone de Beauvoir, but here we return to Michal Nagen, who identifies herself not as a feminist but as "post-feminist."

Nagen presents herself as "a daughter, a mother, a wife, and the head of the Tzahali pre-military academy for religious girls" – in that order. At the academy she teaches classes on faith, Hasidism, "sanctified unions," and femininity. She also speaks highly of what she sees as the essential differences between men and women. "Feminism at first said equality of rights for all, liberal feminism. Our status was equalized with that of men," she says, citing Miller v. Minister of Defense, a landmark Israeli Supreme Court ruling from 1995 that compelled the Israel Air Force to admit Alice Miller, a woman, to its flight school. "Then along came feminism and said, the culture must change. But there was another voice it overlooked. The voice of essentialist feminism. I'm an essentialist. I say: We're a Jewish-religious-feminist-essentialist academy. Women have a distinct essence, that's what the religious world believes. Precisely because the modern world allows so much choice, you as a woman must choose which roles to play and which not. But it's not 'anything goes,' you have to be careful. That's where we have to tighten the conversation and help them understand what it means to be a religious girl, an envoy, and what it means to be a religious woman."

Militarism is not an option on the essentialist menu that Nagen serves her students, although they will all proceed to wear the uniform. She opposes combat service for women. "Combat duty is for liberal feminism, which says: Anything you can do, I can do better. That's just not true. They, the boys, will be warriors. They're men. But you, a woman, came into this world and will have to bring life into this world. You will carry another life inside you, so how do you create your spiritual destiny? Not at any price. In this regard, we have to work very carefully, both to allow the horses to gallop forward but also to help them direct themselves. Our great mission is not to go overboard with the ambition to be combat soldiers. In Tzahali there is a small minority, two or four girls out of two hundred graduates, and we are with them all the way. But we also talk a great deal about how women should stay women, stay Jewish, stay with the values of the Jewish home, with the family. For me, that's critical."

So what does the Orthodox feminism of halakhic rulings and partnership *minyanim* have to do with the religious girls and their desire to serve in the military? Nagen is not so sure that these two trends are interrelated, besides the de facto privatization of rabbinic power. "In this world, you can't choose for the girls," she explains. "In general, the youth say: 'We want to choose things you tell us aren't allowed,' and we educators can't tell them what to do. The father of Cpt. Hadar Goldin [who was killed during Operation Protective Edge in the Gaza Strip in 2014] said: 'The youth want most of all to smash frameworks.' That's definitely true for our girls. They want to be there. They want to remain religious and they come to Tzahali to study Torah; like Tamar Ariel, who was driven to do this for her own reasons, they all so want to be able to explain it themselves. Give me the knowledge, and then I'll be able to do it."

It is hard to say whether Nagen's students are feminists. The story that the female recruits tell is virtually devoid of politics. If it can be said to contain feminism, then it is of an unconscious sort, unstated and unspoken. "For the religious girls, entering the army is a Zionist act," Nagen explains. "There is also a feminist element, because we as a society place our sons at the head of the camp – they are the cultural heroes. Well, you can't educate the boys in the house to run ahead and carry the nation on their shoulders and tell the girls: Ho! Be still! This notion has already entered their feminism and is connected to their inner religious identity. They say, 'Just a second, I will not stop being Orthodox.'"

To what extent is this mass enlistment of religious women a revolution? "I want it to be sanctified," Nagen says, "and only then for it to be a revolution. I agree that going to the army is a kind of revolution, and it requires girls to be much more cautious," Nagen explains. "We always tell every girl, 'Choose carefully which wall you want to come barging through. You have to be a *dossit*, you ought to be Tamar Ariel. If you want to prove it's possible, be religious.' They need to channel their energies to there, but we're at a stage in feminism in which we can't choose for them."

And in fact, despite Nagen's teachings, more and more girls from within the religious pre-military academies are choosing to serve in combat roles.

Of all the disputes rocking the Religious Zionist world, this is an example of a mass movement, waged in defiance of the rabbis, that has surpassed all expectations. Nowadays, most girls in Israel's religious education system still choose to perform civilian national service rather than military service, but the wind, it seems, is at the backs of those who embody change, while the rabbis and the older generation feel it blowing, stiffly, in their faces.

Chapter X

Halakhic Activism

The guests at Yechiel and Tamar's wedding ceremony in 2009 thought that they had come to a typical wedding between a man and a woman raised in the heart of religious society. The ceremony was officiated by a well-known *rosh yeshiva*, the band played Hasidic tunes, and all was consecrated "according to the law of Moses and Israel." The only unusual fact was that the couple, in their first joint commitment, had resolved to never step foot inside the Chief Rabbinate.

In Israel, it is only possible to register a marriage through recognized religious institutions: Jews may only marry Jews (the definition of which is carefully controlled by the Chief Rabbinate); Muslims may only marry Muslims; and Christians may only marry Christians. But before the wedding, the couple had managed to exploit a loophole: a concession granted to the Eda Haredit sect since Ottoman times, allowing it to sidestep the Chief Rabbinate and officiate its own lifecycle events. They had also signed a halakhically binding agreement of mutual respect, to avoid any complications with Israel's rabbinic courts if one day they opted to get divorced. In so doing, the couple believed, they were working to undermine the Orthodox establishment that they so deeply opposed, exercising their freedom of religion without conceding as much as an inch of their commitment to religious observance.

Yechiel and Tamar – not their real names – had chosen one of many ways to get married under Jewish law without involving the Chief Rabbinate of Israel.

"My motivation," Yechiel told me, "after many years of activism revolving around questions of religion and state, feeling that the Haredi establishment is claiming ownership over religion in Israel, is, in one way or another, to smash the monopoly and offer alternatives. I saw myself as obligated, in my personal life as well, not to do things the easy way and register to get married through the Chief Rabbinate, because I felt estranged from the institution, which is drifting ever-further away from what it was and from what I think it should be. I come from a more pluralistic background, my wife less so, and we're striking a balance. From her personal experience, she was also really supportive of not going through the rabbinate, and we made the decision together. At first we considered a private halakhic ceremony or a civil ceremony [abroad] so we could still be registered with the Interior Ministry as married, but then, in a compromise that was also a kind of protest, we decided to do things semi-officially through a private Haredi track recognized by the state."

When it comes to weddings between Jews, Israeli law grants the Chief Rabbinate the exclusive power to oversee, register, and certify the officiating rabbis. But in recent years, in a clear expression of how Judaism is being privatized in Israel, what began as a minor trickle of a few outlaws – such as Yechiel and Tamar, and other couples marrying in defiance of the law – has become a torrent. Religiously observant liberal Orthodox Jews are openly defying the exclusive authority of the State of Israel's official body responsible for halakhic matters. They are claiming that power for themselves, bypassing the rabbinate in every area under its auspices: kosher food certification, marriage, conversion, divorce, ritual baths (*mikvaot*), and burial. A report published by the Israeli Ministry of Religious Services in early 2019 revealed a drop in the number of weddings officiated by the Chief Rabbinate; among the reasons listed, besides an increase in weddings conducted by Conservative and Reform rabbis, was "a rise in the number of weddings officiated by Orthodox rabbis outside the official marriage bureaus." It spoke of "at least" four-teen Orthodox rabbis involved in officiating private weddings.[1]

In this chapter, we shall see how Orthodox Jews in Israel have fought to privatize its state-run religious services. The movement began with several lone activists, intensified with the emergence of a few small rebel groups, and in just a few years – the blink of an eye, really – gained the support of influential rabbis and became, for several months, the official policy of the Government of Israel.

The religious activists boycotting the Chief Rabbinate as an act of politi-cal protest (often in violation of the law) have different goals in mind from the rabbis who wish to find organized remedies to specific prob-lems, at least until the rabbinate evolves. But the cumulative effect of these power struggles over religion and state is to prove that the biggest threat to the Chief Rabbinate nowadays comes from within: from Israel's Orthodox citizens rather than from secular, traditionalist, Reform, or Conservative Israelis, who all harbor other gripes against it.

For decades, Religious Zionists took pride in the Chief Rabbin-ate as an indispensable institution, but in the run-up to its centenary it became a kind of political Rorschach test: a fault line in the heart of the national-religious community between those who supported its hege-mony and others who were exasperated with it and wanted alternatives. The halakhic activism of the rabbinate's detractors has much in common with Orthodox feminism, not least in highlighting the diminishing status of rabbis and the office of the Chief Rabbinate of Israel in particular as institutions possessing both national and religious value.

There have always been private means of sidestepping the rab-binate in Israel, especially in the Haredi community, and occasionally by those citizens who had no recourse to the state-run religious insti-tutions, such as those who are not officially recognized as Jewish (over 350,000 Israelis who officially belong to the Jewish nation are termed "religion-less" because, though they qualify as Jews for purposes of the

---

1. This figure first appeared in a report by Panim – The Association of Israeli Judaism Organizations, which stated that at least fourteen Orthodox rabbis had conducted at least 150 halakhic weddings outside the rabbinate in 2017.

Law of Return, which puts them on the path to immediate citizenship upon arrival, the Chief Rabbinate does not recognize them as halakhically Jewish). But over the past decade, a kind of spontaneous revolt has emerged against the rabbinic establishment, offering a non-institutionalized Judaism that invites Israelis to "go private" of their own choice. Women seek to use a *mikve*, a ritual bath, without having to answer to a Religious Council-appointed attendant; couples choose to have Jewish weddings without going through the Chief Rabbinate; and Israelis prefer to eat in restaurants with alternative kosher certificates, not issued by the rabbinate.

Yechiel and Tamar's story was published in *Haaretz* in the fall of 2011 as part of a series I wrote on "Judaism outside the rabbinate." The piece was shared widely, and for years after it was published, it continued to attract interest. Every once in a while, I receive an email from a young couple – religious or secular – asking for further details or seeking recommendations for rabbis who officiated such underground weddings.

These rabbis are defying not only the Chief Rabbinate's instructions but a law dating back to the British Mandate period, the 1919 Marriage and Divorce (Registration) Ordinance, which requires all Jews to marry through the rabbinate. As of late 2013, rabbis and couples who hold private Jewish weddings are also risking a two-year jail sentence under a law passed by the Knesset (but never enforced) to try to tackle these pirate wedding ceremonies, which have rattled the Chief Rabbinate.

But the halakhic activism continued apace. As far as these Orthodox Jews are concerned, this is a perfectly legitimate form of religious observance – in full adherence to the *Shulḥan Arukh* but without the bureaucracy and institutional middlemen. It is both another practical form of privatization and a protest against the Chief Rabbinate of Israel, which was established by the founding father of Religious Zionism, Rabbi Kook, and was, in its early years, the crown on the head of the religious community.

How did the Chief Rabbinate reach a situation in which so many Orthodox Jews have joined the radical cry to strip it of its powers – a campaign that for most of Israel's history was led by secular activists and the Reform and Conservative movements? How is it possible that as it approaches its hundred-year anniversary, the Chief Rabbinate has ceased to represent not only secular and traditionalist Israelis but even swaths of the national-religious community?

From the moment it was founded in the 1920s, and especially after the establishment of the State of Israel in 1948, the Chief Rabbinate has always hungered to be, and in fact was, much more than the official arbiter of all that is deemed kosher. Religious Zionist educators and influencers saw it as a central component of their ideology and theology. The Rabbinate was hailed as the supreme religious authority of the new Jews in their ancient homeland – a modern-day Sanhedrin that was to imbue the secular Zionist enterprise with deep spiritual renewal. The rabbinate held onto its legitimacy as the polemics surrounding it multiplied: over the question of "Who is a Jew?," the public character of Shabbat, women's military service, and so forth. Most of these controversies brought it into conflict with Israel's secular citizens. But despite its many detractors, and despite decades of criticism from judges, politicians, journalists, state comptrollers, and ordinary citizens – the Chief Rabbinate remained a non-partisan state institution, whose legitimacy in the eyes of the Religious Zionist community was unshaken.

For a while, the Chief Rabbinate was dominated by Religious Zionists, at least at the bureaucratic level, under an unwritten agreement with Israel's ruling parties – at first the left-wing Mapai, then the right-wing Likud – which prioritized political stability and were therefore happy to award Orthodox citizens a franchise with which to run the country's religious affairs. Religious Zionists were the nation's *kashrut* supervisors, and only a voice as radical as Prof. Yeshayahu Leibowitz dared to describe the rabbinate, in 1960, as an institution established by "an atheistic government for reasons of political gain," that would, inevitably, serve as "a prostitution of religion, destruction of the Torah, and desecration of God."

This picture changed in the 1980s when three Haredi parties – Shas, Degel HaTorah, and Agudat Israel – grew more powerful in Israeli governing coalitions and began to seriously influence the structure of, and appointments to, the Chief Rabbinate, the municipal religious councils, and the rabbinic courts. The rabbinate was transformed from a Religious Zionist asset to a Haredi one. This was a slow and gradual process, but in 2013 it erupted into a public power struggle – perhaps the most tempestuous and divisive in the rabbinate's history – over the election of two new chief rabbis. The election of Rabbi Yitzhak Yosef and Rabbi David Lau with the support of the Haredi parties, defeating the Religious Zionists' candidate, Rabbi David Stav, was the straw that broke the camel's back in terms of national-religious attitudes to the institution. But some Religious Zionists had long since conceded that the honeymoon was over. The recurrent clashes with the rabbinate, and the internal arguments in the Religious Zionist community between its supporters and detractors, were already a story foretold.

The Haredim see the Chief Rabbinate as a means of administering religious life in Israel in order to strengthen the state's Jewish character, and as a non-negligible source of political power and jobs. As a rule, this was also the traditional approach of Religious Zionists – except, unlike the Haredim, who control the Chief Rabbinate but defer to their own rabbis, the Religious Zionists revered the rabbinate's halakhic authority as an extension of the Jewish state.[2] For evidence of Haredi leaders' cynical exploitation of the Chief Rabbinate of Israel, consider the election of Yona Metzger as the Ashkenazic chief rabbi in 2013. The late Haredi rabbi Yosef Shalom Elyashiv promoted Metzger's candidacy not because he was a great Torah scholar but mostly because he wanted to block the Religious Zionist candidate, Rabbi Yaakov Ariel.

Metzger's election was a key stage in the institution's fall from grace, but the rabbinate had already come under intense pressure from

---

2. Modern Orthodoxy was particularly dependent on the rabbinate because its conversions were subjected to continual scrutiny. Chief Rabbi Shlomo Amar, who also served as the president of the high rabbinic court, ordered rabbinic judges and officials to rigorously interrogate Orthodox rabbis before authorizing their documents in Israel, an instruction that targeted converts but also sometimes hurt ordinary members of the community, Jews from birth, who needed confirmation of their Judaism in Israel. In effect, the Modern Orthodox found themselves in an inferior position to their Conservative and Reform peers, whose conversions conducted abroad were guaranteed to be recognized in Israel further to a Supreme Court ruling. Orthodox Jews from the Diaspora came under the auspices of the Chief Rabbinate, which occasionally doubted the validity of their conversions. This had practical ramifications because the rabbinate had no compunctions about flexing its muscles when Orthodox Jews from abroad were in need of its services.

the public, both on account of corruption and its severe, Haredi-like policies on matters of religion.

In 2017, after a police investigation and lengthy trial, Metzger was convicted of embezzlement and accepting millions of shekels in bribes during his tenure as chief rabbi, partly in exchange for forged conversion certificates. The same year, the chief rabbi of Holon, Rabbi Avraham Yosef, was convicted of exploiting his power over kosher certifications to promote his brother's financial interests. The courts also reviewed evidence of a major scandal in which police officers and civil servants, with the support of rabbis, fraudulently obtained salary raises by acquiring fabricated rabbinic ordination certificates. The case led to the conviction of another chief rabbi, the late Eliyahu Bakshi-Doron (later overturned by the Supreme Court).

These and other sagas caused many Israelis to become disenchanted with the rabbinate, and subsequent arguments touched at the core of the institution's ideology. According to halakha, for example, Jewish-owned land in Israel is supposed to lie fallow every seven years, during the agricultural Sabbatical year (*Shemitta*). In order to allow farmers to earn a living during this year, rabbis found a loophole to bypass this economically ruinous biblical prohibition: they would simply issue "sales permits" that allowed Jews to temporarily sell their fields to non-Jews every seven years in order to continue cultivating them. For years, this creative workaround was considered emblematic of the Chief Rabbinate's nature as a Zionist organization, one committed to adapting Jewish law to the realities of a modern Jewish state. But in 2007, Chief Rabbi Metzger refused, at the behest of his Haredi patrons, to issue these sales permits. In order to continue cultivating their land that year (and more importantly, to sell their produce to religious consumers), Israeli farmers had to rely on certificates from local religious councils, and even this strained form of legitimacy was only rendered possible thanks to the intervention of the Israeli Supreme Court.

Soon thereafter, the Chief Rabbinate did something truly explosive. Israel's highest rabbinic court, in a ruling authored by the Haredi justice Rabbi Avraham Sherman, a member of what is known as the "Litvak" (Lithuanian or non-Hasidic) sect, handed down a verdict that retroactively annulled thousands of conversions performed by certain state-run courts; those courts, which were relatively lenient, operated under the auspices of Rabbi Haim Druckman, a leading national-religious rabbinic figure. The ruling was rooted in halakha but was undeniably political, building on decades of fundamental disagreements between the Haredi and the Religious Zionist camps regarding the function and purpose of the Jewish state. For many Religious Zionists, the crisis thoroughly delegitimized the Chief Rabbinate. They took the episode particularly badly, both because they considered this urgent round of conversion a Zionist cause (unlike the Haredi community, which is generally suspicious of it) and because Rabbi Druckman was such a respected figure.

The election of the two chief rabbis in 2013, therefore, came at a particularly sensitive moment, when the standing of the Chief Rabbinate was already shaky and even devout Religious Zionists started doubting if it could fulfill its purpose. The rabbinate seemed increasingly to be a Haredi stronghold, and the more immersed it became in controversy, and the more tainted it became by corruption, the more Religious Zionists began to conclude that the institution might be irredeemable. Then to add fuel to the fire, the Chief Rabbinate started harassing liberal and mainstream Religious Zionist rabbis.

In the summer of 2015, for example, the Chief Rabbinate tried to oust Shlomo Riskin, the well-known chief rabbi of Efrat, who heads several pre-military academies for religious women and even ordains women. At the time, Chief Rabbi Yitzhak Yosef publicly called him "that guy from Efrat who's into all sorts of innovations, a news-maker and rabble-rouser." The pretext for the attempt to dismiss him was his advanced age, but nobody doubted that the reasons were political and the decree had to be fought, and decided, in the political arena.

Then in 2016, an exposé revealed that the municipal rabbinate in Haifa had been harassing couples who had chosen to marry through the Chief Rabbinate but with the support of Tzohar, a Religious Zionist alternative to the state institution. Channel 12's religious affairs correspondent Yair Cherki reported that the Haifa rabbinate had been effectively blacklisting these couples and barring them from marrying, citing various trumped-up reasons, such as that they were not Jewish or were born out of wedlock and therefore unable to marry. The rabbinate even started debarring Modern Orthodox rabbis in the United States and Canada who were considered excessively liberal, including Haskel Lookstein and Avi Weiss, both of whom head major congregations in New York. Religious Zionists in Israel and Modern Orthodox Jews in America thus found themselves under a concerted attack from Israel's Haredi rabbinic establishment.[3]

As the Chief Rabbinate's standing deteriorated and the tensions increased, more Religious Zionist rabbis started openly expressing their disappointment with the institution. The first heads above the parapet were those of liberal rabbis, but in time rabbis from the Religious Zionist mainstream joined their ranks. The small set of national-religious rabbis who were willing to conduct discreet private Jewish weddings when I reported on them in 2011 were joined in 2015 by an American-born rabbi from Beit Shemesh, Chuck Davidson. Unafraid of incurring the rabbinate's wrath, he openly and defiantly offered to officiate private weddings for any Jewish couple who so wished. The backdrop for his decision was the Knesset legislation to make private weddings a criminal offense punishable by two years in jail, for the officiating rabbi and the newlyweds.

Davidson gave interviews to the media, wrote long Facebook posts, and was quoted by Be Free Israel, a movement for religious pluralism, as saying: "Don't let anyone define what Judaism is. Because Judaism is our collective heritage, not that of any particular community and certainly not that of the Chief Rabbinate. The Chief Rabbinate has no monopoly on halakha, certainly not on Judaism, and I think we mustn't let them behave as if they do." Others joined the booming marriage privatization movement, and in the summer of 2018, the alternative *kashrut* agency Hashgacha Pratit started renting out marriage canopies for wedding ceremonies conducted outside the realm of the rabbinate. Its aim was to challenge the Chief Rabbinate's legal monopoly over marriage in the same way as it had done over *kashrut* supervision, as we shall see later in this chapter.

---

3. Batya Kahane-Dror, for example, an attorney who headed an organization that helped *agunot* (women trapped in marriage), tried to wage a legal battle against the prohibition on private wedding ceremonies and set up a network that openly conducted private weddings and private divorces with the support of Rabbi Avraham Dov Levin, who heads a private Haredi rabbinic court. Other rabbis have conducted low-key, unpublicized private weddings.

Nobody in the Religious Zionist community is oblivious to the chatter about privatization and the revolt against the rabbinate. It touches on the question of marriage but spans a far wider field. For evidence that the spirit of revolution has migrated from the fringes to the communal leadership, consider how in the summer of 2015, a group of eminent rabbis, including some from the heart of the religious establishment, joined forces to set up alternative conversion courts, Giyur K'Halakha, which would, among other things, convert children whose parents wanted them to undergo the process – something that Israel's state-run rabbinic courts refused to do. These children were born to parents eligible for citizenship under the Law of Return, which means that they were welcomed into the country as "olim," but were not recognized, in terms of Orthodox halakha, as Jews. The Giyur K'Halakha rabbis opined that these children – born to a Jewish father, perhaps, or a Jewish grandparent who was not their maternal grandmother – ought to be afforded, within the confines of halakha, a more lenient path to conversion. [4]

Specifically, the rabbinate's policy meant that hundreds of thousands of Israelis who identify as fully Jewish are unable to marry in Israel. The late Rabbi Nachum Rabinovitch, a founding member of the initiative and the head of Yeshivat Maale Adumim, described these new rabbinic courts as a "historic endeavor to heal the rift that emerged in Israeli society as a result of the failure to deal with the problem of the personal status of immigrants from the former Soviet Union…. Some people are trying to paint us as lenient, but truth be told, we're very strict," he said. "We're very strict about the unity and sanctity of our nation." The creation of this workaround, with the support of such mainstream figures as Rabbi Riskin and Rabbi Stav, proved that the Chief Rabbinate

---

4. When the Haredi weekly *BaKehila* covered the establishment of the private national-religious rabbinic court, it stripped Rabbi Nachum Rabinovitch – one of the leading Religious Zionist halakhic authorities – of the title "rabbi." Although Rabbi David Stav did not personally spearhead the initiative, he was depicted as having done so by his detractors, perhaps because many Haredi Israelis had long seen him as an ideological nemesis. *BaKehila* ran a picture of Rabbi Stav on its front page with a quote that the late Rabbi Ovadia Yosef said about him two years earlier when he ran for the position of chief rabbi: "He is completely impious. His friends testified to me: That man is a danger to Judaism, a danger to the rabbinate, and a danger to the Torah."

had lost sections of the national-religious center-ground. For many Religious Zionists, it also showed that the Chief Rabbinate was not as holy as it had seemed.

Every challenge to the Chief Rabbinate from Religious Zionists provoked fresh arguments, divided national-religious society, and triggered a wave of reactionary protests. Rabbis affiliated with Har Hamor formed the nucleus of the counterreaction, aimed at protecting the rabbinate's privileges. The erosion of its status led to a tantalizing role reversal as Haredi elites leapt to the defense of the Chief Rabbinate – the same state institution that they had treated with contempt in the first few decades of its existence.[5]

Dozens of rabbis, led by Dov Lior and Zvi Thau, signed a public letter supporting the Chief Rabbinate, which it called "the only center in the state for matters of conversion and for all state-related matters concerning Judaism." Protesting the establishment of private rabbinic courts, they wrote: "The Chief Rabbinate…stands at the core of our state's Jewish identity. Private conversions represent a grave affront to state interests and destabilize our country's foundations as a Jewish state. These deeds represent a de facto separation of religion and state and contradict our holy Torah, which is the sole wellspring of our Religious Zionist philosophy."

The rival sides launched an epistolary war, disseminating fiercely worded petitions signed by long lists of yeshiva heads and communal rabbis, denouncing the religious rebellion against the Chief Rabbinate.

Rabbi Druckman, the founder of the special conversion courts and one of the first casualties of this pileup on the Religious Zionist highway, sided with the establishment on this issue. "Privatization is dangerous," he said. "Thank God in the State of Israel there is a Chief Rabbinate that has everything under its authority, which guarantees that everything is run as it should be. I think that in this matter, as with *kashrut*, it's dangerous not to walk in lockstep with the Chief Rabbinate."[6]

---

5. Gidon Dokov, "Rabbi Druckman: Oppose the Chief Rabbinate? Dangerous," *Makor Rishon*, June 14, 2016 [Hebrew].
6. According to the Kashrut Fraud Prevention Law, which was historically overturned in 2021 by Religious Affairs Minister Matan Kahana, food establishments may only

But Tzohar, an organization of mainstream Religious Zionist rabbis, started drifting away from the Chief Rabbinate. It began lending its support to initiatives that undermined it: from the private conversion courts to a new *kashrut* supervision agency based on the seditious initiative of Hashgacha Pratit. Even before, Tzohar already had its own nationwide department to register rabbinate-approved marriages, which at first brought it into collision with the Religious Services Ministry but was eventually recognized in law in 2013. The organization, it seems, is trying to turn itself into a multidisciplinary Zionist alternative to the Chief Rabbinate, at least until the rabbinate evolves, and perhaps until it passes to the control of Religious Zionist rabbis who subscribe to Tzohar's more inclusive philosophy.

Unlike Tzohar, Rabbi Aaron Leibowitz's Hashgacha Pratit initiative is determined to permanently limit the oversight powers of Israel's official religious services agencies, not just to provide a temporary remedy to Haredi rule. This grassroots movement has no desire to run centralized state religious services.

Hashgacha Pratit – the name is a play on words, meaning both "Divine Providence" and "Private Supervision" – was founded as a totally private kosher certification agency, of the kind used by Jewish communities outside Israel and Haredi communities in Israel. It offers alternative services to those of the Chief Rabbinate, at competitive prices, and without compromising on *kashrut* standards. Simply put, the organization injected into the rabbinate's monopoly a free-market mentality: whoever trusts their certificate, can come and eat; whoever doesn't, can go eat elsewhere. But this is no mere attempt to privatize government services. It is politically, and perhaps also religiously, explosive.

Liba Yehudit, a conservative advocacy group, is an opponent of Orthodox liberalism. In late 2017 it launched a campaign against

---

display a kosher certificate from a private *kashrut* agency if they also have an official kosher certificate from the Chief Rabbinate. In practice, it is not uncommon to find Haredi businesses displaying kosher certificates issued by their own rabbis' private courts, unsupervised by the Chief Rabbinate.

Hashgacha Pratit, including a video clip promoted on social media and a report about its intentions and sources of funding. The report declared that Hashgacha Pratit's kosher certificates could not be trusted, accused it of being close to the Conservative movement, and revealed that the New Israel Fund, which is particularly reviled on the Israeli right, was among its funders, along with other liberal foundations. *BeSheva*, a religious weekly, brought these findings to a wider audience. The mud-slinging against individual members of Hashgacha Pratit's governing board marked a new stage in a war that had already been raging for several years.

The campaign was launched shortly after the Israeli Supreme Court, following a lengthy legal battle, ruled in favor of Hashgacha Pratit. It declared that while establishments that are not certified as kosher by the Chief Rabbinate are not allowed to advertise themselves as "kosher," further to the Kashrut Fraud Prevention Law, they may still publicly list the *kashrut* standards to which they adhere. The ruling was a major setback for the rabbinate, which had hoped that the expanded panel of judges would uphold an earlier ruling forbidding restaurants without a rabbinate-issued kosher certificate from advertising themselves with any words "having associations with *kashrut*."

Since its creation six months earlier as a pilot scheme involving two cafés in central Jerusalem, Hashgacha Pratit had become a nation-wide initiative providing kosher certification for some forty businesses in Jerusalem, Tel Aviv, Beersheba, Kfar Saba, Herzliya, Ashkelon, and other localities. One by one, food establishments have torn down their official rabbinate-issued kosher certificates and pinned Hashgacha Pratit's alternative ones on the wall instead.

The project began as an academic exercise, devised by Chaya Gilboa, a public policy student at the Hebrew University of Jerusalem. It was designed as a tailor-made solution for small, local businesses, opposed to some of the Rabbinate's stringencies and stipulations. Its starting point was to reject the idea of "supervision" by external actors, replacing it with trust between small business owners and their customers. The initial model was based on volunteers who visited food establishments a few times a week to help to prepare food in compliance with *kashrut* standards, such as washing lettuce greens and sieving rice to rule out the presence of bugs, and to train the cooks. As the project expanded beyond neighborhood cafés, it tweaked its business model and started using professional *kashrut* supervisors – and specifically women.

The initiative drew its halakhic authority from Rabbi Oren Duvdevani, an Orthodox rabbi and expert on the laws of *kashrut*. His decision to join this subversive organization proved, once again, how national-religious public opinion was turning on the Chief Rabbinate.

The founder and leader of the initiative was Aaron Leibowitz, an Orthodox rabbi from Jerusalem. Leibowitz took Gilboa's academic model and turned it into a practical program, which was first applied to a student café in the trendy Jerusalem neighborhood of Nachlaot. The project received additional momentum from Yerushalmim ("Jerusale-mites"), a civil society organization and local political party, and from its leader Rachel Azaria, a liberal Orthodox woman who would go on to serve as a member of Knesset for a single term for the center-right Kulanu Party.

Rabbi Leibowitz, born in the United States, was the rabbi of the Kol Rina Synagogue in Nachlaot, which became a sensation in the early 2000s. Every Shabbat, hundreds of young religious Israelis thronged to the synagogue to enjoy the rapturous melodies of the late Rabbi Shlomo Carlebach. It was one of the first so-called Carlebach *minyanim* in Israel, and probably the most vibrant and crowded. Leibowitz later founded a hippie-neo-Hasidic religious academy of Torah and headed the Yerush-almim faction in the Jerusalem municipality. In a conversation we had once, he defined himself as national-Haredi – that is, belonging to the right-wing flank of Religious Zionist society – but if so, his voice is radically different from the familiar timbre of this conservative community. He is a supporter of female religious leadership, LGBTQ tolerance, and Jewish prayer rights on the Temple Mount, and is in favor of the complete banishment of the Chief Rabbinate from the religious lives of private citizens and communities.

For the role of chief *kashrut* manager at Hashgacha Pratit, Leibowitz hired a woman by the name of Avivit Ravia, who is similarly hard to pigeonhole. When she joined the operation, she lived in the Haredi settlement of Beitar Illit. She was a graduate of a *kashrut* supervisors' course run by the women's religious organization Emunah and petitioned the courts against the Chief Rabbinate when she and her friends were barred from taking the tests for state-recognized *kashrut* supervisors. Later, when the rabbinate backed down, Ravia passed the tests with flying colors, but she did not need the rabbinate's help to find employment. Leibowitz hired her on the spot.

"I feel I'm killing two birds with one stone," she said after being recruited by Hashgacha Pratit, "both on the question of the exclusion of women and also on the matter of returning to the people the monopoly that the rabbinate had claimed for itself. As far as I'm concerned, this is my calling." Going through her daily routine, she says, "the thing that I find the most touching is the gradual return of trust. Simple people, or not simple, put their trust in one another, and all of this is based on the human element. There's trust and there's partnership between people who want to make genuine change. That's what thrills me most…. Whoever wants to eat kosher food, truly kosher food, will be able to find it with us."

What made this Jerusalem-based initiative unique was its mix of halakhic exactitude, political activism, and focus on communal engagement. It scored its first success from a small group of businesses in Jerusalem that were fed up with the Chief Rabbinate's *kashrut* supervision services and decided to chart their own course. They complained that Jerusalem's local religious council was setting arbitrary and expensive conditions for receiving *kashrut* certificates, such as requiring them to buy vegetables grown with intensive pesticides from a select number of suppliers. They also grumbled that *kashrut* supervisors were charging exorbitant fees and often barely showed up to do their work.

Jerusalem quickly proved to have a ready clientele of religious and secular residents willing to trust the new *kashrut* certification system and, perhaps more importantly, willing, if not delighted, to snub the rabbinate. Some even donated to a crowdfunding drive for Hashgacha Pratit on Headstart. The more obstacles were thrown in its way – proposed legislation to toughen regulation against *kashrut* "fraud," fines issued by rabbinate inspectors, aspersions from hardline rabbis appalled by the initiative – the quicker it branched out beyond the Jerusalem bubble. More and more Israelis, religious and secular alike, heard of the initiative, including business owners disillusioned with the rabbinate. Public awareness was given a huge boost when two business owners who held Hashgacha Pratit certification petitioned the Israeli Supreme Court with the support of the Reform-affiliated Israeli Religious Action Center. Although Hashgacha Pratit was not a party to the lawsuit and had reservations about it, the case was a do-or-die moment. A regular panel of Supreme Court justices ruled against the plaintiffs, but, as noted earlier, were overruled by an expanded panel upon appeal.

This was not the first attempt to create an alternative *kashrut* system. In the 1990s, a small initiative provided kosher certification to restaurants in Tel Aviv, including ones that opened on Shabbat, but it soon fizzled out. Hashgacha Pratit, which does not certify businesses that remain open on the day of rest, succeeded. This success is first and foremost on account of the waning legitimacy of the Chief Rabbinate, both in the eyes of ordinary Israelis and of the Supreme Court justices and the State Comptroller's office, which frequently subject the rabbinate's kashrut services to withering criticism. Stripped of its legitimacy, the only thing left for the rabbinate to do was to try to scare people away from its competitor. "You mustn't trust their *kashrut* standards, they have no value," said Rabbi Shmuel Eliyahu in a lesson in late 2017. "No wonder Reform Jews support private *kashrut* services, where everyone supervises himself. They let the cat guard the cream."

There are still legal and political question marks hanging over these alternative *kashrut* services, and the majority of owners of kosher food establishments in Israel prefer to avoid controversy and stick with the rabbinate's certification. But the religious camp has responded with exclamation points. In February 2018, the Tzohar rabbinic organization took over Hashgacha Pratit's initiative. To use the language of the free market, this was the biggest exit made by a religious initiative in the age of privatization. By adopting the initiative, this organization of mainstream rabbis, the flesh and blood of the Religious Zionist community, was buying out a start-up founded by a small group of religious-sector entrepreneurs. Tzohar's gamble paid off. It acquired a client base of around forty businesses across Israel using Hashgacha Pratit. Within less than a year, by January 2019, that number had skyrocketed to at least 110. By 2022, once the privatization of *kashrut* had been made law,

Tzohar was in direct competition with the rabbinate in Jerusalem and had a solid presence throughout the country.

Leibowitz moved on to his next start-up: halakhic Jewish weddings, sans the rabbinate. The initiative is geared toward Israeli Jews who are fed up with the rabbinate and wish to register their protest on the day of their marriage, as well as others prevented from marrying through the rabbinate, such as those placed on various blacklists for reasons that Leibowitz insists are halakhically unwarranted. He shared his intentions on Facebook, calling on his followers to turn their backs on those who wish "to turn Judaism into their private estate and force their lifestyles on us," and to join those who are "promoting change on the ground and returning Judaism to a sane pair of hands, in the fields of *kashrut*, Shabbat, ritual baths, marriage, and conversion." In honor of Tu B'Av, the Jewish festival of love, the organization reported in the summer of 2019 that it had already wed 160 couples in its first year of operations, with 126 more in the pipeline. Around twenty rabbis (male and female) joined the initiative, officiating weddings that are in compliance with Jewish law but do not expect to be recognized by the Chief Rabbinate. They are in open revolt.

The anxiety bubbling up from within the Chief Rabbinate and the organizations that support it is being hidden no more. In the summer of 2019, the rabbinate launched a self-promotion campaign to try to restore the public's trust. Earlier, as the privatization drive gained steam, it collaborated with groups on the right flank of the Religious Zionist spectrum, such as Liba Yehudit and the Chotam Forum, to host a "special conference" for Israeli rabbis. Its mission, as the official notice said, was "to preserve Jewish values and bolster the Chief Rabbinate's status and exclusive authority." It was not the first conference of its kind. It probably won't be the last.

Meir Gorodetsky, a domestic abuser, refused for eighteen years to grant his wife a divorce. Under a rabbinic court sanction, he was sentenced to a lengthy jail sentence. Imprisonment is the most serious punishment in the Israeli penal code for recalcitrant husbands, but Gorodetsky refused to back down. For nearly two decades, his wife Tzvia fought to win her freedom. Buffeted between endless deliberations in Israel's official rabbinic courts, she went on hunger strike and lobbied for legal reform in the Knesset.

Tzvia remained "chained" to this defunct marriage until, in June 2018, someone opened a small and unexpected trap door to freedom. A private rabbinic court, as noted earlier, headed by Rabbi Daniel Sperber annulled her marriage, obviating the need for a *get* – a writ of divorce – from her violent husband. The judges invoked two halakhic hermeneutics that allowed them to reinterpret the couple's status based on the miserable consequences of their failed union. They also took into account the fact that Tzvia Gorodetsky's wedding ring was purchased with her money and not her husband's, as he falsely testified under the canopy – a loophole that allowed the judges to invalidate the marriage. Just like that, Tzvia Gorodetsky walked free, as if she had never been married in the first place.

Israel's state-run rabbinic courts had failed to provide this woman a solution, but a private and voluntary tribunal – neither certified nor recognized by the State of Israel, but fully compliant with halakha – found a workaround. Even if authorities refuse to recognize it, as far as Tzvia Gorodetsky and a large section of Israeli society are concerned, she is no longer a married woman. Until a few years ago, private rabbinic courts only ever convened in secret. But now, they are openly and ever more boldly proceeding with their subterfuge against the Chief Rabbinate's legal monopoly over all matters of marriage and divorce, riding waves of protest and discontent with the religious establishment.

Private Orthodox weddings in Israel are often a statement made by those who could marry through the rabbinate but opt not to. In contrast, private tribunals to release "chained" women from broken marriages are a humanitarian endeavor. Some women, and men, find themselves stuck in halakhic dead ends; if the rules of halakha matter to them, they try to find a legal loophole, with rabbinic approval. What are they to do when the Chief Rabbinate gives them no way out?

Rabbi Sperber and his fellow rabbinic judges, along with their colleagues at Center for Women's Justice, not only set up a way to bypass the official system but used halakhic tools that the state-run rabbinic courts had declined to use, at least openly. They were willing, as noted, to invalidate marriages on halakhic grounds, even if the husband refused to grant a divorce. The court reconvened after the Gorodetsky case to "unchain" more women from the bonds of marriage, citing other halakhic loopholes, and it is not the only outfit to do so. Several more private courts in Israel and the United States were set up specifically to alleviate the plight of women trapped in marriages their husbands refuse to end.

Rabbi Sperber takes pride in his ad hoc rabbinic court. "We don't consider ourselves any wiser than the honorable judges at the [state] rabbinic courts," he wrote. "We are both citing the same *Shulḥan Arukh*... and the writings and responsa of the same great rabbis. We have not hidden the reasoning behind our rulings, and they are open for public inspection and criticism.... The failure of the [state] rabbinic courts to deliver justice and unchain these women, thereby causing immense grief and damage for extended periods, is in my view a violation of a basic obligation toward one's fellow human beings. It is a grave crime to steal these women's freedom and damage their mental health – one for which there can be no atonement on Yom Kippur. But these rabbis hold the keys to opening the gates of freedom, redemption, and salvation."[7]

---

7. "Let Us Immerse in Peace" was another Jerusalem-based initiative. A group of religious women demanded the right to fulfill the commandment of monthly immersions in a *mikve* (ritual bath) without the oversight of the attendants employed by the local religious council. The dispute was underpinned by halakhic issues (specifically whether the monthly dip must be supervised by another woman to ensure that the water completely covers her body, including her hair), but this was secondary to the public and legal question: to whom do Israel's roughly seven hundred public *mikvaot* administered by local religious councils belong, and may a woman use them in accordance with her own custom even if doing so violates the rabbinate's policy? After lengthy negotiations with the rabbinate and the Religious Services Ministry, the women decided in 2015, with the support of ITIM, to petition the Supreme Court. In late 2016, the Israeli government announced that it would permit women to immerse in *mikvaot* by themselves, and this announcement was ratified by a court ruling. Chief Rabbi Yitzhak Yosef, whose position toward the women had softened during the dialogue with them, was furious about the Supreme Court's intervention. A few days after the ruling, he said of the judges: "Why were they chosen? To be rabbis or to be judges? They should stick to their own business. If someone runs a red light, let them deal with that. Why are they dealing with matters of halakha, with matters of immersion and *mikve*?" Even today, the new protocol is still not fully enforced.

What is the meaning of all this? The power of the religious establishment has been eroded, and new halakhic alternatives are popping open, often to popular acclaim. Sometimes the revolt focuses on matters of power and authority, as in the case of the alternative *kashrut* services and similar initiatives;[8] other times, it touches on fundamental matters of Jewish law, such as the private courts terminating broken marriages on the basis of tools that the rabbinate justices are ill-inclined to use vis-à-vis *agunot*, or as pertains to conversion. The Orthodox Giyur K'Halakha courts were founded, as noted, in 2015 by Religious Zionist rabbis as a means of conducting halakhic conversions outside the realm of the

---

8. The matter of whether converts must commit to full religious observance is a fundamental dispute in matters of conversion. As a rule, Haredi rabbis consider it a precondition for converts to commit to living full religious lives and demand that their pledges be followed up on in practice (there have been cases in which Haredi rabbinic judges retroactively annulled conversions because they discovered that several years later, the converts had stopped being observant; see also the case of the annulment of Rabbi Druckman's conversions). But a large share of Israelis seeking to convert are not religiously observant and have no intention of being religiously observant. Israel's official state rabbinic courts convert most of them and turn a blind eye to the fact that many neither observe nor intend to observe religious law, in violation of an unequivocal statement that they are required to make to the court.

In 2015, I learned of a third Orthodox approach: at a court headed by Rabbi Riskin, one of the founders of the Giyur K'Halakha network, converts were asked to make a long but more general declaration than the standard wording: "I undertake to enter into the covenant with the Holy One, blessed be He, together with the historic Assembly of Israel, to come under the wings of the Divine Presence, and to accept the Jewish Torah which requires a system of commandments and to continue to grow in this system, which is leading toward *tikkun olam* – repairing the world."

Rabbi Riskin told me then, for a report I published in *Haaretz*, that his declaration was based on Maimonides and other experts in Jewish law, who had stated that "if the convert, at the stage of acceptance of the commandments, knows in his heart he will not be able to observe them because he is too weak, it does not harm the acceptance of the commandments. That is how I interpret the acceptance of the mitzvot. I, the convert, am within the system of the mitzvot and I want to be part of the system and to observe [the laws] and to grow." Riskin posits that the demand that converts declare their commitment to observe Jewish law in its entirety "cannot be real, and I do not believe in things that are not real. I couldn't take it upon myself to perform all of the commandments according to that interpretation. I am still learning, too."

rabbinate. Besides breaking the Chief Rabbinate's monopoly over conversions, the rabbis involved also have staked out a different stance on how intensively converts should be expected to observe Jewish law, and they also have taken upon themselves to deal with one major practical issue that the official conversion courts totally neglect – the conversion, with parental consent, of minors under the age of thirteen.

These organizations are openly subverting Israel's rabbinic establishment. But it isn't just that. They are using halakha to solve personal and social problems that were "created" by halakha. These activists are taking halakha into their own hands and using it – for those who care about it – as the solution to situations that were considered insoluble.

"The Collaborators of the Reform Movement in the Supreme Court – Religious Organizations!" So blared one headline on *Srugim* in 2016. The article cited a report by the Chotam Forum, which found that several Orthodox organizations, including Kolech and Ne'emanei Torah Va'Avodah, had joined lawsuits filed by the Reform movement.

Indeed, over the past few years, non-Orthodox and Orthodox organizations in Israel have collaborated to petition the Supreme Court and coordinate other activities connected to religion and state. Chotam's gloss on this collaboration, as quoted by *Srugim*, was that the Reform movement wanted to work with Religious Zionist organizations "in order to gain legitimacy."

This interpretation ignores how the estrangement from the rabbinate has spurred on this sort of cooperation. But it also provides a springboard for discussion on the Reform and Conservative movements in Israel, which have been waging public campaigns and petitioning the Supreme Court long before Orthodox groups jumped on the bandwagon, as far back as Israel's seminal debates over "Who is a Jew?" What do Reform and Orthodox activists challenging the Chief Rabbinate have in common?

In February 2016, dozens of rabbis of Reform congregations in North America arrived in Jerusalem for a conference. The atmosphere was festive; a sense of history was in the air. They held a celebratory prayer service at what is known as the "Southern *Kotel*." Arms linked, they stood by the ancient stones, at a separate section of the prayer plaza, and chanted the *Sheheheyanu* blessing, thanking God for keeping them alive and delivering them to the occasion. The year started on an optimistic note for non-Orthodox denominations in Israel, but the situation soon took a turn for the worse; by 2017, a major crisis was brewing.

The Reform movement, at the time, had two reasons to rejoice. In late January, the Israeli government had approved a compromise plan to turn the southern portion of the Western Wall, within an archaeological park, into an egalitarian prayer plaza for men and women to pray together. There already existed a spot for non-Orthodox prayer at the site, but now the Israeli government intended to transfer the management of the plaza to a new committee including representatives of the Reform and Conservative movements. The plan would have given unprecedented recognition to the non-Orthodox denominations in Israel, while strengthening the Western Wall rabbi's powers to bar non-Orthodox prayer in the traditional plaza. The historic compromise was supposed to end the legal and political battle that had been dragging on since 1988 when Women of the Wall, a cross-denominational coalition that included Orthodox women, first demanded the right to a monthly women-led prayer service at the holy site, wearing prayer shawls and tefillin and reading from a Torah scroll. The resolution had huge practical and symbolic value for the progressive movements.

Another reason for cheer was a Supreme Court ruling that ordered local religious councils to provide access for non-Orthodox converts to their *mikvaot* (ritual baths), for the climactic immersion ritual of the conversion process.

But the tide quickly turned. The Haredi factions in Israel's governing coalition, under attack from both the Haredi press and hardline voices in the Religious Zionist community, pressured Prime Minister Benjamin Netanyahu to cancel the Western Wall compromise plan. The pressure paid off, and the government officially announced the suspension of the plan, triggering a sense of historic crisis in progressive Jewish congregations in the United States. The Supreme Court ruling about the ritual baths was rendered moot when the Knesset passed special legislation to bypass the courts, stipulating that Reform and Conservative converts were not eligible to use public *mikvaot* (although the government also allocated money to build new ritual baths especially for Reform and Conservative converts).

The cancelation of the Western Wall compromise, even more than its initial acceptance, worked like a litmus test on Orthodox Jewish society. On one end were several national-Haredi organizations and leading figures from within the Religious Zionist camp, who actively rallied, among Haredi groups and elsewhere, for the revocation,[9] and on the other end were liberal figures from within Orthodox society, including Aliza Lavie and Elazar Stern of the centrist Yesh Atid Party, who were among the loudest voices against the about-face. Even though many liberal Orthodox organizations and rabbis and members of Knesset had not originally supported the Western Wall compromise, or lent it their passive support, they understood that the revocation represented a serious blow to Israel's ties with American Jewry.

The polemic over the Western Wall included a third perspective, which is also worthy of our attention. In 2014, several mainly Orthodox women broke away from Women of the Wall, claiming that the allocation of one plaza for Orthodox prayer and another for non-Orthodox prayer would leave them in the lurch. As liberal Orthodox women, who did not identify with the Reform or Conservative denominations, they wanted to pray in the women's section of the main plaza, but to do so in their own way and read from the Torah scroll, as is already customary in women-only services in certain Orthodox congregations. Being banished to a non-Orthodox plaza, without gender segregation, was not, for them, a viable solution.

Kolech, an Orthodox feminist organization that supported this breakaway group, wrote in a letter to the Attorney General, Avichai Mandelblit, that "over the past twelve years, there has been a shift in Israel toward establishing Orthodox partnership and egalitarian services, in which women wear *tallitot*, lead the services, read from the Torah,

---

9. Among the most vociferous Religious Zionist opponents of the Western Wall compromise were Matti Dan, head of the right-wing Ateret Cohanim organization, who lobbied the leaders of the Haredi parties; Agriculture Minister Uri Ariel, from the Jewish Home Party; and Liba Yehudit, which petitioned the Israeli Supreme Court against the plan.

recite Kaddish, and don tefillin – all in compliance with halakha and the halakhic rulings of various Orthodox rabbis. Many members of our organization follow this practice. Hundreds of Orthodox girls celebrate their bat mitzvas by reading from the Torah. Thousands of Orthodox women across different congregations recite Kaddish after their loved ones pass away. As such, the compromise that is being cooked up in your meetings with representatives of the Women of the Wall, which would force women's services to leave the women's section [of the main plaza] and relocate to Ezrat Yisrael [the egalitarian plaza in the archaeological park] would seriously prejudice us as Orthodox women, and we cannot agree to it. We see ourselves as part of Orthodoxy and our prayers have already become the custom of the place."

This letter, even if it represented only a small group of women, highlighted something about the nature of the Western Wall compromise: it empowered religious institutions at the cost of religious independents. It assumed that only two forms of Jewish life exist: Orthodox (including Haredi) and non-Orthodox (namely, Reform and Conservative). It also gave the Chief Rabbinate, controlled by the Haredim, the power to define the first option, and left it to US-based progressive religious institutions to define the second. The Israeli government fell back on the same dichotomy in the case of conversions. After a legal battle, Israel was forced to recognize Reform and Conservative conversions conducted abroad but left Orthodox Judaism in Israel completely in the hands of the Chief Rabbinate.

Indeed, it is interesting to keep a close eye on other battles over religion and state and to note the differences of approach between the non-Orthodox and the liberal elements of the Orthodox camp. The latter often avoid associating with the Reform and Conservative movements, apparently out of fear of giving their detractors ammunition. But the Reform and Conservative movements have not always been in a rush to collaborate, either. Consider the campaign by national-religious activists to compel the state to recognize private Orthodox conversions. While the Reform and Conservative movements spent years fighting for full recognition of their conversions in Israel and abroad, the question arose of whether to combine the petitions of Reform and Conservative converts with those filed by Orthodox converts who used private conversion courts and similarly wanted state recognition. Both sets of converts had an interest in weakening the Chief Rabbinate's grip on matters of conversion. But then it became clear that the two groups had slightly different visions. The Israeli Religious Action Center, the public arm of the Reform movement in Israel, announced that it opposed merging the petitions because these were "two completely different issues."

One of the reasons, as the Reform movement's attorneys explained, was that converts who went through private Orthodox courts "could have converted through the system of state-run conversion courts." In contrast, "the whole point of the non-Orthodox courts is to enable freedom of religion and to allow people to join the Jewish people in accordance with a non-Orthodox worldview, as behooves a Jewish state that recognizes different streams in Judaism."

The liberal Orthodox and non-Orthodox also fell out over the question of public ritual baths. The Conservative movement fought for its converts to be allowed to immerse in rabbinate-run ritual baths as part of their conversion process. It wanted both *de jure* but also symbolic recognition of Conservative conversions. After the issue reached the Knesset from the Supreme Court, a compromise was reached that suited Conservative Jews and, in hindsight, also the Chief Rabbinate and the Haredi parties: the Israeli government promised to build separate publicly funded ritual baths for the Conservative movement, which gladly saw this as a statement of equality and recognition. In contrast, the Orthodox women who petitioned the Supreme Court for the right to use ritual baths without being supervised by a rabbinate-employed attendant insisted on doing so in the regular, "Orthodox" ritual baths and were not prepared to settle for separate but equal facilities.

Non-Orthodox Jews in Israel are demanding public recognition of their particular denominations, but Orthodox Jews who want greater autonomy do not identify as a distinct "denomination." They do not form a coherent or homogeneous movement. They are a loose assortment of groups fighting for freedom from the oversight of the rabbinate as an institution. The key difference is this: the non-Orthodox denominations want equality between organizations, but the halakhic activists are a radical movement; their goal is to liberate the Jewish religion from the authority of organizations altogether.

Conclusion

The Fraying Generation

This is the privatization generation in the Religious Zionist world. It is stronger, more diverse, more extreme, more moderate, more divided, more sectarian, and more non-sectarian all at once. It is no longer united around a common focal point, but neither is it split into two coherent camps with their own centralized leaderships. It spans the vast space between conservatism and innovation.

The Religious Zionists include national-Haredi and liberal Orthodox communities and a multiplicity of religious subgroups in the middle. It is difficult, and in fact quite unnecessary, to categorize them all. Individuals might identify with rival groups on different issues, sometimes at different points in their lives, and sometimes at the very same point in time. As such, the conflict described in this book is less of a struggle between rival factions and more of a battle of ideas – between conservatism and progressivism and at times a fusion of the two.

In its essence, the Religious Zionist argument is about two rival conceptions of religiosity. One conception rigidly differentiates between the sacred and the profane and defines the sacred solely in terms of antiquity and tradition. It views halakha, custom, and prayer as existing outside of time, fixed and immutable. The second conception, also conservative by its very nature, is nonetheless increasingly open to change not just in matters secular, but also sacred. Sometimes it makes microscopic changes to marginal halakhic matters and sometimes it grabs the halakhic bull by the horns. This form of Orthodox Judaism aspires to minimize gender differences and reconcile the different parts of its religious, Israeli, and modern identities – without breaking the framework of halakha.

This is a high-risk clash between two types of conservatism. The open kind of conservatism, which hopes to reconcile an ancient religion with a changing world, operates out of an aspiration for integrity, but this aspiration is always blocked sooner or later by the fortress wall of halakha, with absolute injunctions that will dash certain expectations. Such is the Torah; it's constant. On the other hand, the more conservative type of conservatism, which by definition is not looking to break new ground, increasingly finds itself tied up in knots and trying to escape a changing reality such as in the case of cultural questions about the status of women or LGBTQ individuals or non-Jews or people with disabilities.

The awakening of this conflict has many causes, but first among them is the twenty-first century itself. The feminist movement's achievements and the broad shift toward equality, freedom of choice, and self-determination are the backdrop on which this feud has developed. For many Orthodox Jewish men and women, religious practice is part of the natural flow of life, not something that sets them apart from Western civilization. Young Orthodox Jews, like their non-Jewish peers around the world, prefer authenticity to stale convention. Crises of leadership and authority, the blurring of borders, and the erasure of hierarchies are not challenges that were set before Orthodox Judaism alone.

From grand ideas to a granular reality. Over the past several years the prevailing sentiment within the community has swung like a pendulum – with conservatives at times setting the tone, and liberals, like Bennett, at times in charge. The English edition of this book is being sent to press with the conservatives clearly on the march: the only remaining sectarian party from amid the Religious Zionist community – a party called Religious Zionism – is promoting a religiously conservative and nationalistically hawkish agenda. It has taken under its wing the Otzma Yehudit Party, which was founded by the disciples of Rabbi Meir Kahane, and together the two factions most recently won fourteen seats in Knesset. The once-fringe figure of Itamar Ben-Gvir, the chairman of Otzma Yehudit, is today a leading politician in Israel. At the same time, although they managed to field a prime minister from within their ranks, the liberal wing of the community has seen its representation diminish; Bennett has retired from politics, and his party, a joint religious-secular endeavor, has disintegrated. The news, in Israel and abroad, has shown further evidence of a decline in the influence of change-minded rabbis and activists, and yet it remains clear—the forces of change are not a passing phase.

Liberal Orthodoxy, an organic part of Religious Zionist and Modern Orthodox Judaism, is a grassroots movement within Israel's national-religious society and is creating communities with tremendous clout, even if they take shelter in societal bubbles. Coming as they often do from strong socioeconomic backgrounds, these agents of change are challenging the existing order, the rabbinic establishment, and the politicians on the other side of the religious barricade.

It is quite possible that the current ferment will push both camps in divergent directions. The liberals might stretch halakha closer to the spirit of Masorti or Conservative Judaism; the reactionaries might keep adding ever more halakhic restrictions. The liberals might continue to integrate into Israeli society; the reactionaries might close ranks in isolationist communities. In this respect, some argue that we are now witness to the breakdown of the "modern-religious" construct: that one can thrive with one foot in the new world and one in the ancient. But in fact, many Orthodox Jews feel quite comfortable with this tension, and some, in the face of these changes, are being spurred to refresh their hybrid identity.

As for the fringes, the unavoidable question looms – will ideological tension lead toward a full schism within the Religious Zionist community? Nobody knows where the many divergent streams of Religious

Zionism will lead. The fraying of national-religious society is not a past event but an ongoing drama, which is currently entering a new denouement. But it is reasonable to assume that privatization, meaning the enfeeblement of institutional leadership and the devolution of power to the rank and file of the community – a process that cannot be disengaged from the Gaza Disengagement of 2005 – will be the force that charts the paths that Orthodox Jews pave for themselves in the coming years.

In the meanwhile, the ground is shaking. New ideas are being weighed and new questions are being asked: Who is religious, who is secular, and who gets to decide? Is Israeli society as a whole becoming more closed or more open? Will rifts over Israel's national character widen and where will the various Religious Zionist groups place themselves in this argument? So many tantalizing questions are waiting to be answered in so many future books, and as always with Jews – the answers hinge on the education the community provides for the next generation and on what, halakhically speaking, they will choose to do in practice.

Acknowledgments

This book, which took several years to write, could not have come into existence without the help of so many people and I wish to thank them all.

Thank you to the editor of the original Hebrew edition, Shmuel Rosner, who believed in this project and bombarded me with the questions and clarifications needed to turn the first manuscript and drafts into a book. The manuscript was continually enriched by the eagle-eyed observations and devoted work of the editor Yael Neemani.

I worked at *Haaretz* for many years and it gave me an opportunity to observe events and transformations, large and small, in the Orthodox and Haredi communities from up close and to write about them for readers in Israel and abroad. Thank you very much to my editor, Noa Landau. It was during a regular editorial meeting with her that the idea came up of writing a series of reports about tensions in the Modern Orthodox and national-religious worlds. The series, published in *Haaretz*'s weekend supplement in 2015, became the first stage in a fascinating voyage through the many currents in this community. Thank you to the publisher of *Haaretz*, Amos Schocken, for the permission to incorporate sections that I originally wrote for the newspaper into this book. I owe an enormous debt to the late David Landau, the former editor of *Haaretz*, who passed away as this book was just beginning to come together, for encouraging me to drop other items I was covering and to focus on the Haredi community and questions of religion and state. This decision was hugely consequential for me, not just in terms of the professional pivot.

I wish to thank from the bottom of my heart the friends and colleagues who devoted time and expertise to reading the manuscript or sections of it – Vered Kellner, Akiva Novick, Yair Cherki, Dr. Hila Zaban, and Dr. Yehuda Yifrach. Some of them argued with me and helped me fix and hone certain ideas, and all spotted mistakes, sparing the readers (and me) from inaccuracy, and contributed wise advice that I incorporated. A special thanks to my mother, Esther Ettinger, as well as to Dr. Micah Goodman and Prof. Aviad Hacohen for diving into sections of this book and generously sharing their insights and guidance. I also borrowed some creative ideas from my sister, Avigail Ettinger-Ben Simhon, and from my friends Haim Rivlin, Elad Benbaji, and Prof. Nissim Leon.

Thank you to Dr. Dror Yinon, a great scholar and a dear friend, who was involved at every stage of this book and made an unparalleled contribution.

Most of the research was conducted in Israel; most of the writing was done in the United States. I was privileged to have two organizations that gave me the time and space needed to write this book – the Brookings Institution in Washington, DC, and the Shalom Hartman Institute of North America. I am grateful to Dr. Natan Sachs and Dr. Tamara Cofman Wittes for the opportunity of being a guest scholar at the Brookings Institution, and to the team at the Hartman Institute – and chiefly Rabbi Dr. Donniel Hartman, Dr. Ariel Picard, Dr. Yehuda Kurtzer, and Rachel Jacoby Rosenfield – for inviting me into the institute's Beit Midrash program.

I'd like to thank several of the good people who were my partners in creating the English edition, which is meant to be more than a mere translation. It includes many of the significant developments that occurred after the 2019 release of the Hebrew version. I was fortunate to find Mitch Ginsburg, who is not only an excellent editor but also a native speaker of many languages – Hebrew and English, Israeli and American, religious and secular. This helped open the door to readers outside of Israel. I'd also like to extend my gratitude to translator Eylon Levy for his wonderful work.

My thanks to the people of The Toby Press, a division of Koren Jerusalem, for their patience and faith in the project: Matthew Miller, Reuven Ziegler, Aryeh Grossman, Caryn Meltz, David Silverstein, Tani Bayer, Tomi Mager, Nechama Unterman, and Carolyn Budow Ben David.

Finally, a special thanks to David Roth of the Yoreinu Foundation. David believed that *Frayed* offers an important in-depth look into the many facets of the national religious sector and strongly felt that even those who have never lived in this country and do not speak Hebrew could benefit from reading it. I am grateful to him for his insight, assistance, and pivotal role in producing this translation.

Thank you to Sivan, who was invested in this book as a full partner, both as a source of optimism and encouragement and as a perspicacious editor who saw this project through from beginning to end. This book is dedicated with love to Sivan and our daughters Talia, Naomi, and Zohar. I wish to also express my appreciation and love to my parents and teachers, Aharon and Esther Ettinger, who are always the first readers I have in mind when I write.

Name Index

239

Subject Index